# Also by WILLARD GAYLIN

*In the Service of Their Country:*
War Resisters in Prison

*Meaning of Despair:* Psychoanalytic Contributions
to the Understanding of Depression

# PARTIAL JUSTICE

# PARTIAL JUSTICE

A Study of Bias in Sentencing

## WILLARD GAYLIN, M.D.

ALFRED A. KNOPF
New York     1974

THIS IS A BORZOI BOOK
PUBLISHED BY ALFRED A. KNOPF, INC.


Copyright © 1974 by Willard Gaylin

Library of Congress Cataloging in Publication Data

Gaylin, Willard.    Partial justice.
Includes bibliographical references.
1. Sentences (Criminal procedure)—United States.
2. Judicial discretion—United States.  I. Title.
KF9685.G38      345'.73'077      74-7758
ISBN 0-394-48593-9

Manufactured in the United States of America

FIRST EDITION

# TO LESLIE DUNBAR,

that retiring and untiring toiler
in the fields of justice

# CONTENTS

| | | |
|---|---|---:|
| | Acknowledgments | ix |
| | Introduction | xi |
| CHAPTER I: | Disparity | 3 |
| CHAPTER II: | The Sentencing Process | 15 |
| CHAPTER III: | The Intrusion of Bias | 28 |
| CHAPTER IV: | Judge Justin C. Ravitz | 44 |
| CHAPTER V: | Judge Garfield | 68 |
| CHAPTER VI: | Judge Stone | 103 |
| CHAPTER VII: | Judge Nicholson | 130 |
| CHAPTER VIII: | Other Judges, Other Views | 162 |
| CHAPTER IX: | The Discretion Problem | 182 |
| CHAPTER X: | Conclusions | 195 |
| APPENDIX: | Categories of Offenses | 235 |
| | Notes | 238 |
| | Index | follows page 244 |

# ACKNOWLEDGMENTS

I am grateful: to the more than forty judges who so generously gave of their time, and all of whom, save one, permitted recording of their remarks, and to the Field Foundation and its staff whose support and understanding made possible the research from which this book is drawn.

Two other groups require acknowledgment: to my colleagues at the Institute of Society, Ethics and the Life Sciences, my thanks for the informal day-to-day consultation and guidance that such an organization uniquely offers, and to my colleagues on the Committee for the Study of Incarceration*, my apologies. After two years of discussing similar issues concurrently with the writing of this book, I have not the vaguest notion where their ideas end and mine begin. I am comforted by the fact that other members of the committee admit to the same dilemma.

My debt to my wife requires acknowledgment but, like my love for her, is beyond public expression.

WILLARD GAYLIN, M.D.
Institute of Society, Ethics and the Life Sciences
Hastings-on-Hudson, New York

* Chairman: former U.S. Senator Charles E. Goodell; Executive Director: Andrew von Hirsch; Members: Marshall Cohen, Samuel duBois Cook, Alan Dershowitz, Willard Gaylin, Erving Goffman, Joseph Goldstein, Harry Kalven, Jr., Jorge Lara-Braud, Victor Marrero, Eleanor Holmes Norton, David J. Rothman, Simon Rottenberg, Herman Schwartz, Stanton Wheeler and Leslie Wilkins; Staff: David Greenberg and Susan Steward.

# INTRODUCTION

Over twenty-five years ago, Harold Lasswell recommended making use of the methods and understanding
of psychoanalysis, psychology, and social psychiatry to examine judicial attitudes and judicial behavior. Yet in 1968,
according to Glendon Schubert, and to my knowledge since
then: "No studies have been published that have employed
any of the other methods—such as direct observation—
recommended by Lasswell."[1] This, despite a growing concern about the impact of bias on our judicial system.

Professor Lasswell was something of a psychoanalytic
evangelist—one of a shrinking breed. There are certain
limitations imposed by the psychoanalytic method which
he does not acknowledge. The most ambitious psychoanalytic approach is the so-called psychobiography, seen at
its best in Erik Erikson's study of Luther and Gandhi and
at its worst in too many examples since then. Psychohistory
is an authentic supplementary mechanism for the recon-
struction of the past. Most great biographers and historians
who strive to recreate the personality and tempo of a period
are to a certain extent writers of fiction. They synthesize a
reality which, while never provable as true, by lending the
greatest amount of understanding to all of the known facts
about the time, creates the illusion of truth. The psychoanalytic frame of reference can be an ingenious and rewarding adjunct to traditional tools in this effort.

When psychobiography turns to living figures, however, it is questionable both scientifically and ethically. There is no way adequately to make a sound psychological diagnosis on most individuals (except in the most extreme cases) without using that very method which ethically precludes publication—the direct examination and treatment of the individual. At that time, of course, he becomes a patient and is entitled to the protective courtesies of the physician-patient relationship. If public psychological diagnoses are morally permissible, they probably are so when done by someone other than a psychiatrist. They do not then carry the weight of medical authority or the imprimatur of the physician. At any rate, it is not the technique which I personally feel free to use.

Yet statistics are not enough. They can demonstrate disparity and even document sentencing profiles, but they offer no evidence of the meanings of the disparity. Is it caused by ignorance, bias, legal philosophy? The early researches were primarily tabulations. Admittedly, with time the use of statistics will become more sophisticated, and Edward Green[2] is capable of defining "attitudes" which seem characteristic of sentencing procedure—but the attitudes seem separated from the human process. Nowhere is the person of the judge evident.

John Hogarth, in his excellent book *Sentencing as a Human Process*,[3] attempts to stretch the statistical and scientific method by a more subjective approach. His study is based on self-administered questionnaires of an attitude-assessing type, and decision-making form, which purport to "reveal the mental processes involved in reaching sentencing decision." Yet even in his book, despite its title, there is not the semblance of a human being; not an expression, not an emotion, not an articulated idea, not a description of appearance of behavior, and certainly not an emotion. It is a splendid book but a bloodless one.

It is my bias that nothing reveals mental processes as

clearly as the detailed examination of the process. Questionnaires are of great value in illuminating differences among people. It is less clear that they are capable of demonstrating what those differences are. This is particularly true when examining emotionally charged or psychological areas. Few are prepared to believe that what a person tells a questioner he feels is any accurate indication of how he truly feels. When you question people as to their personal feelings, the answers you get are most likely to be what they think they should feel, what they would like to feel, or what they think is prestigious to feel. And only accidentally what they really feel. Even professional pollsters, who have refined their techniques for predicting election results so thoroughly, have had their embarrassing moments. When subjectivity and emotion play significant roles in elections, disastrous errors in prediction occur.

In dealing with bias, you are dealing for sure with the subjective side of man. How accurate the answers are will depend on complicated variables. Among the most important are: the subject of the question; the degree of actual insight of the individual (i.e., how much of the answer is known to himself); and the relationship between the questioner and the answerer. At the extreme end of reliability one would assume are certain questions which are strictly factual in nature, which carry no emotional charge, and whose exposure to either the individual or the public could in no way threaten the individual—in other words, simple factual questions ("How old are you?" "Where were you born?" "What did you eat for breakfast?"). But even these can lead to distortions. "What did you eat for breakfast?" can produce a staggering amount of lying, forgetting, self-deceit, blocking, anxiety, when asked of an obese individual.

As you move away from the simple and factual area into the area of opinion, feeling, and belief, distortion becomes compounded by two pressing needs operating in every individual. The need to protect his public image, and the even more important need to protect his private image. In the latter, the individual himself is unaware of the truth, let alone capable of or willing to communicate it. The man who says he hates his mother does not necessarily hate her any more than the man who says he loves his mother. More intriguing though, and just as important in determining future behavior, is that the man who *feels* or *thinks* he hates his mother does not necessarily hate his mother more than the man who feels or thinks he doesn't hate her.

When physicians in training have been asked what they feel are their liabilities and assets, they will often expose damaging personal defects. However, almost to a man, they list as an asset their "patient rapport"—their capacity to relate emotionally. Ironically, this is one of the more common defects of the aspiring physician. These students differ in the degree of their honesty, their need to ingratiate themselves with the questioner, and their degree of insight. In other words, some of them will be lying to the questioner, some will be lying to themselves.

Why should anyone expose his fear to a stranger and injure his pride for someone else's purpose? Even in the very sheltered, protected situation of psychoanalytic therapy, where the doctor's loyalty has been proved over the years; where the patient knows that the information given will be used only in the service of his own well-being; where the truth is the one tested instrument for helping him overcome painful symptoms; even under these conditions, the patient will continue to the very end of his analysis trying to deceive the analyst and himself. What then about questions asked by a total stranger, with no protection of privacy, with no vested interest in the truth, and with all the vanities and best-foot-forwardness that public confrontation invites?

Direct questioning, therefore, often proves to be a less than totally accurate means to the truth, and depending on the kind of information can suffer gross distortion. For that reason, it is essential that some possible corroborative methods be used.

The best of statistical studies can only establish the presence of a problem and define its extent. This they can do well, and it may indeed be the primary need. To go beyond this point, however, to demonstrate the nature of such a problem, it is necessary to demonstrate the process of reasoning; it would seem that only direct observation or interviewing could adequately elicit these facts.

Interviewing is something which I as an analyst respect and cherish. While the interviews recorded in this book in no sense should be considered psychoanalytic interviews, they do utilize (often intentionally, but just as often unintentionally) the techniques of the psychoanalyst who is doing the interviewing. Some of these are: the assumption that the truth emerges best when one keeps quiet; that a nondirective interview is better than a directive interview; that questions are important not so much just for the answers they elicit, which may be the truth, but also for what they indicate about the individual's honesty and insight; that a certain amount of stress provides a different kind of information and is a valuable asset at certain points of an interview; that the stance of the interviewer should not represent his personal point of view so much as it does a useful position to be taken to elicit information at that time.

Being a psychoanalyst, my interviewing style is by fact of habit and belief essentially "nondirective"—which is already a misnomer. What it really means is that the direction of the interview is primarily dictated by the person interviewed rather than by the interviewer, thus, the very direction chosen is the first step in self-exposure. This may seem a discursive and uneconomic approach. Questions and answers always appear so much more direct, so much more informational. Yet a questionnaire not only defines that which is included, but also that which will be excluded. To think that one knows the appropriate questions to ask presumes too much in a psychological survey.

Halfway between questionnaires and direct interviewing is another form of direct observation. One of the advantages of research with judges is that while they may seem austere, remote, guarded, and intimidating figures, they are, nonetheless, public performers and for the most part on public record. The records of trials, therefore, permit one to see the judges in action; and while not nearly as productive as direct observation (the judge, after all, is in control of the situation and well aware of the fact that he is on public display), they nonetheless are more personal than questionnaires. If in control, he is never in total control, any more than any other individual.

Another advantage is that hundreds, even thousands, of records can be examined in the time necessary to set up and do dozens of interviews. And, beyond that vast scope of general court proceedings, there is the more limited literature of cases that have been appealed precisely because of alleged inequities or improprieties on the part of the judge. These cases, whether reversed or not on appeal, are still a part of the public record, which will often include the judgment of the appellate court on the presiding judge.

The review of actual cases from the judicial files of various courts cited in Chapters II and III demonstrates the processes of prejudice and discrimination involving such categories as race, sex, personal attitudes, regional differences, and so on. It also at times demonstrates the arrogance of the bigoted judge who, unlike the rest of mankind, is secure in the knowledge that flagrant bias must be tolerated in the law, because of inadequacies in our procedures.

When I turn in Chapters IV–VII to the presentation of some direct interviewing with judges, I do not attempt to reconstruct, as I have in the past, psychological profiles

of these judges, nor to probe for the "psychological meanings" of their statements or attitudes. That is a research
that could and perhaps should be done, but it is not this
one. Nor am I trying to indict anyone, or to expose villains.
Indeed, I have tended to select for detailed presentation
only the most superior of judges. The blatant cases of
bigotry can be easily demonstrated by mere quotes and
statistics. What to my mind was the more important
purpose here was to demonstrate how, in even the most
fair-minded of individuals, their values, their life-styles,
their background, their current life experiences, in other
words, their biases, are necessary and inevitable intrusions
into the processes of discretion. I have attempted to demonstrate, most often without comment, some of the factors,
conscious and unconscious, rational and irrational, which
go into decision making; to document the diversity of
sentencing; to illuminate the patterns of reasoning of a
few specific judges; and to suggest thereby the degree to
which the sentence is determined not by the nature of the
offender, or the offense, but by the nature of the sentencing
judge. The latter becomes crucial, because the character
and personality of the judge is an irrelevant and chance
event. Arbitrary factors can seriously damage respect for
the courts, and trust in their commitment to justice.

In writing interviews of this sort certain distortions are
inevitable, the most important of which is the obvious
one of condensation. When many hours are condensed
down, an unavoidable indirect distortion will occur. Such
condensation will tend to dramatize the nature of the
statements and perhaps reduce subtlety. It may open the
way for an unconscious selectivity, serving the biases of the
author. The latter may be diminished somewhat by my
intention to select only those judges who, despite disagreement, I could respect and sympathize with—men whom
I feel honor their office. I had no desire to knock down
straw men.

Added to this, however, are certain specific and intended distortions. I had told the judges in advance that none of them would be cited, that is, named in relation to their quotations. Therefore, when judges are named and cited it obviously means that this came from the literature. When there is no citation and the quotation is anonymous or, if more convenient for the reader, supplied with a pseudonym, the quotation came either from direct interviews or from tapings of sentencing seminars, where because the judges are encouraged to talk informally, citation seemed unfair.

Of the four judges to whom I devote chapters, Judge Ravitz is treated differently from the others. With his express permission, and because of the unique nature of his position, I have identified him, and all is as it was. With the other three judges I have felt certain obligations to anonymity. I have therefore taken the liberty of altering names, details of physical description, family, ages, locales, which I hope will present only a minimum of distortion. It is, at any rate, a distortion that permits a greater frankness of content. I have changed the style only where necessary for clarity, and never altered the content of ideas.

# PARTIAL JUSTICE

# CHAPTER I

# Disparity

One of the most glaring and provocative of inequities in a world not known for fairness is a disparity in punishment: when like individuals, committing like offenses, are treated differently. For most of us, righteous indignation and moral outrage are first sensed in that frustrating and ubiquitous experience of early childhood when some damnable manipulative sibling gets off whistle-clean for the same infraction for which we were "always" made to pay the full measure. "It's not fair!" vibrates with a moral fervor and conviction that "I'm sorry" rarely does. Even within the confines of the benevolent and loving family situation it is a humiliating and alienating experience, and if indeed true, and repeated sufficiently, can destroy that sense of identity necessary for our reasonable relationships with other people. If we violate a sense of fairness, we undermine that concept of order necessary for communal living. What is true in the family is equally true in the less benevolent structures of authority. The capacity for destructive rage is only compounded when released from an environment of care.

Nowhere is inequity likely to be more evident, more costly to the victim, and more infuriating to that group which identifies with him than when there is disparity in sentencing for committing a crime. It suggests a division into privileged and persecuted that is contrary to the fundamental definitions of our democracy, which (before Watergate at least) have always held that the President was no more immune from punishments of law than the commonest citizen.

My introduction to those punishments of law began with a research on the imprisoned war resisters;[1] and my introduction to disparity began with Hank. I saw Hank on the twenty-sixth day of his imprisonment for violation of the Selective Service Law. He was a tall, painfully thin, almost fragile-looking twenty-one-year-old, wearing the heavy thick-lensed glasses that one associates with the near-blind. Soft-spoken, almost inarticulate, he was trying to tell me why, despite his having available a student deferment, despite his having visual difficulties which would have guaranteed him medical deferment, he chose to come to prison. It was the usual combination of political, moral, idealistic, and emotional factors that characterized this small band of peace prisoners. Offended by injustice, repelled by violence, he notified his draft board he could not in conscience cooperate with the draft, and that he was prepared to receive his punishment. His punishment was five years in the federal penitentiary. I was shocked. I had just completed interviewing seventeen Jehovah's Witnesses, all of whom had uniformly received, from different judges, two-year sentences. Hank's was the first five-year sentence I had encountered. He was also the first black man. Inevitably, I equated the two.

"How was your hair then?" I asked.

"Afro."

"And what were you wearing?"

"A dashiki."

"Don't you think that might have affected your sentence?"

"Of course."

"Was it worth a year or two of your life?" I asked.

"That's all of my life," he said, looking at me with a

combination of dismay and confusion. "Man, don't you know! That's what it's all about! Am I free to have my style, am I free to have my hair, am I free to have my skin?"

"Of course," I said. "You're right."

Whether this disparate sentence was due to his being black (in this case the evidence seemed conclusive), it would certainly serve to create that reasonable doubt that undermines our sense of justice. But even were he not black, even were he in a society where blackness was not a socially significant separator of human beings, were he merely the eighteenth in a row of equal offenders against the same law, the disparity in sentencing would have stirred that primitive sense of outrage and evoked that early call to justice: "It's not fair!"

When serious criminals go unpunished, when minor offenses are excessively punished, when a chosen group receives lesser punishment or a despised group more punishment, it threatens all of us in that society, even the law-abiders. It corrodes the basic structural prop of equity that supports our sense of justice. An excessive disparity in sentencing threatens that kind of a breakdown.

Laws are essentially established to maintain and preserve the social structure. In that sense at least, the purpose of law is order. But it is not merely law *for* order. The orderly society is not necessarily the most desirable. A concentration camp or a police state is usually more orderly than a democracy. Law must not only preserve the society; it must, in addition, serve its ideals and values. And in so doing, it must balance its desire for stability and order against its system of values. One overriding value to which almost every society will subscribe is justice. It is easier for all societies to claim to serve justice, than, for example, liberty, because justice is so difficult to define. Whatever the definition, an essential ingredient will be a sense of fairness and equity. But beyond that will go a whole range of ethical considerations, never completely defined, which will be weighed, measured, and traded off. It is in the interests of justice that punishments are prescribed with wide latitudes to allow the judge some discretion. The expectation is that the Protean nature of individual justice can never be caged by written words, but is best interpreted in the context of its variables, by the judge in the case.

In addition, the state, in establishing the limits to punishment for each crime, implicitly places a value on the behavior violated. Punishment, to be morally acceptable, should be consistent with some fair evaluation of the seriousness of the crime. The convicted criminal, at least by the time he is ready to be sentenced, should be in a position to be aware of the punishment for which he is eligible.

In fact, according to Judge Marvin E. Frankel,[2] "A defendant who comes up for sentencing has no way of knowing or reliably predicting whether he will walk out of the courtroom on probation, or be locked up for a term of years that may consume the rest of his life, or something in between." The situation as it currently exists "is a wild array of sentencing judgments without any semblance of the consistency demanded by the ideal of equal justice." The judge concludes: "The almost wholly unchecked and sweeping powers we give to judges in the fashioning of sentences are terrifying and intolerable to the rule of law."

When I pursued the question of sentencing with the war resisters, the disparity seemed appalling and unbelievable. The cruelty of chance (in these cases, geography was a primary factor) created inequities that should be unthinkable in a reasonable society. In Oregon, of thirty-three convicted Selective Service violators, eighteen were put on probation; in southern Texas, of sixteen violators, *none* was put on probation. In Oregon, not a single man was given a sentence of over three years; in southern Texas, fifteen out of sixteen were given over three-year sentences—fourteen were given the five-year maximum allowable by law. In southern Mississippi, every defendant was convicted, and everyone was given the maximum of five years.

This is a federal crime, presumably to be judged by national standards. It has always been assumed that a judge in his values reflects those of the society he represents. The fact that the subgroup of the society he comes from is rarely the same as those he is judging is another question that requires examination. At any rate, it would be expected that where his personal values differ from those defined by law, he would, as a judge, serve the interests of the law over his personal interests—although the history of the civil rights movement demonstrates there is no guarantee of this. He is expected to reflect the defined (whether objectively true or "right" is not important) values of his society. He is not, however, expected to reflect the prejudice and bias of that society. These are the emotional components of functioning, which fair men may recognize within themselves but which, out of fairness, they intellectually reject—such rejection being enforced by law. A judge, like all of us, is expected to act above and beyond his prejudices; and while I respect the attempt of judges to overcome their bias, the expectation can, alas, be realized no more fully by them than by any other group.

Geographical differences in sentencing within the United States seem particularly offensive when involving federal crimes, since by definition the crime is seen to be one against the nation as a whole. These differences, it turns out, have been well documented. In 1944, the Federal Bureau of Prisons first began to publish in its annual report a table showing average sentences imposed by the various federal district courts. Shortly thereafter, Henry Lanpher[3] began to analyze the differences and found a marked disparity in average sentences among the judicial courts: "For all offenses combined, the shortest average sentence was imposed in the First Circuit, eleven months, and the longest in the Sixth, seventy-eight months." It is somewhat difficult to know what lumping all crimes together and producing an average proves, if anything. However, it does seem odd to find a seven-fold difference in averages!

When Lanpher broke down the sentencing, it took on a special significance. One example will suffice. Taking violations of liquor laws, he found: "In Nevada the average liquor-law sentence was two months . . . and in northern Alabama, twenty-five months."

Geographical variations of this sort are particularly galling even to professional observers. McGuire and Holtzoff state:[4]

> Some vital element must be deemed lacking in any system of criminology under which the punishment inflicted upon the criminal is dependent on the geographical location in which the crime was committed, or on the personality of the particular judge before whom the case is tried.

The judges themselves are well aware of the ironies of geographical differences. The rationalization is often given that what is seen as judicial bias is only a reflection of the feelings and norms of the community. In the Judicial Sentencing Institute of the Federal Government, Judge Edward Lombard[5] may have made the definitive comment on "community standards" when he told the story of:

> A visitor to a Texas court who was amazed to hear the judge impose a suspended sentence where a man had pleaded guilty to manslaughter. A few minutes later the same judge sentenced a man who pleaded guilty to stealing a horse and gave him life imprisonment. When the judge was asked by the visitor about the disparity of the two sentences, he replied, "Well, down here there is some men that need killin', but there ain't no horses that need stealin'."

Geographical disparity is only one example. Obviously, there are as many variables as there are personal experiences or personal prejudices, and there is a literature which adequately documents the amazing disgrace of the disparate sentence. If one reviews the mass of neglected material buried away in committee reports, archives, journals, textbooks, proceedings, deliberations, annals, and annuals, the evidence is abundant. In 1919, George Everson[6] reported on the sentencing records of New York City's 42 magistrates, covering 155,000 cases and sitting in rotation in 28 courts. Perhaps the most intriguing was the varying dispositions of cases of public intoxication. While I hesitate to start this review with a "Cohen and Kelly" joke, it is almost unavoidable. Everson reported that of 566 persons arraigned before Judge Naumer, only *one* was discharged as not guilty. Judge Corrigan, on the other hand, discharged 531 of the 673 persons (nearly 79 per cent) brought before him, suggesting a different attitude toward alcohol.

A steady stream of statistical studies utilizing every conceivable kind of variable has demonstrated disparities of an insupportable measure. So much so that cautious statisticians reveal their dismay at their own findings. One said:

> Judges do not make punishment fit the crime; neither do they make it fit the criminal, for as we have seen, in most cases they do not have sufficient information about him. It is possible, though we think not probable, that these variations have a rational basis. . . . On the other hand, the variations may be entirely due to personal idiocyncrasies of the judges.[7]

Another researcher[8] who, to his dismay, found on statistical evaluation that, "the shortest possible sentences were imposed upon the dangerous habitual, professional offenders while much longer sentences were frequently imposed upon the relatively harmless, situational and occasional offenders," concluded that, "at least twenty per cent of all received sentences which, in the light of careful social prognosis based upon verified facts of their social case histories . . . , are wholly indefensible."

Variations even in a homogenous state like Iowa can be

startling. One study[9] showed that one judge gave ten times as many suspended sentences as his colleague.

Perhaps the saddest cases of all are those where there is no demonstrable evidence of animosity; no demonstrable evidence of bias; no technicalities on which appeal could be based; and, yet, the sense of the unfairness of things is evident because of the disproportionate, extreme, unusual, and excessive sentence. There are literally dozens of cases in which seemingly like men tried for like offenses are given cruelly different sentences. Indeed, there are cases where two men convicted before the same court for the same crime with distressingly similar backgrounds are treated for reasons that again lay buried within the emotionality and judgment of the court in cruel and disparate ways. In one particular case involving a group of counterfeiters, all of the other defendants, including the ringleaders, were tried and convicted in a different district court. All of them received the same sentence, a one- to six-and-a-half-year sentence, meaning that they would be eligible for parole in less than one year. All, except for one man. Despite a guilty plea, he was sentenced to fifteen years. The appeals court in rejecting his appeal stated:[10]

> Every year numerous appeals come before this court which accentuate a seriously urgent problem—the disparity of sentences in federal criminal cases. The present appeal is illustrative. Justice is measured in many ways, but to a convicted criminal its surest measure lies in the fairness of the sentence he receives. Whether a sentence is fair cannot, of course, be gauged simply by comparing it with the punishment imposed upon others for similar offenses. But that test, though imperfect, is hardly irrelevant. It is an anomaly that a judicial system which has developed so scrupulous a concern for the protection of a criminal defendant throughout every other stage of the proceedings against him should have so neglected this most important dimension of fundamental justice.

The evidence is there, documented and overdocumented, and yet it is ignored. But what can we expect of the general citizenry when even the judges themselves seem unaware of their own performances?

What are we to make of the following statement from this distinguished federal judge, Walter E. Hoffman,[11] which he presented in a teaching seminar on sentencing for other federal judges?

> We sought information from the Director of the Bureau of Prisons as to the existence of disparate sentences recently imposed. To our gratification the reply was as follows: "In our opinion, the issue of disparity in sentencing is no longer a significant problem. While this was a serious issue some six to eight years ago, the Sentencing Institutes and the implementation of eighteen U.S.C., Sections 4208 (a) (2) and (b), have done much to correct the gross inequities we saw earlier."
>
> The foregoing statement, in our view, fully justifies the expense of sentencing institutes, and the value of varying sentencing alternatives provided by Congress in 1958. To the credit of the three branches of our Government, the problem of disparity has been attacked with vigor and substantial success.

This was stated in 1969 and repeated again in 1971. During that period, disparity in sentencing was not only reported in numbers of technical journals in criminology and law, but had also become front-page news. The prison reform movement was given impetus in large part because of the infusion of middle-class people (drug offenders and Selective Service violators) into the prison system. A front-page article in the *Wall Street Journal*[12] was headlined: "UNEQUAL JUSTICE: A GROWING DISPARITY IN CRIMINAL SENTENCES TROUBLES LEGAL EXPERTS." The article quotes such people as Federal Court Judge Theodore Levin, and James V. Bennett, former director of the Federal Bureau of Prisons (both from the same federal system to which Judge

Hoffman was addressing himself), who were almost in despair about the inequality of sentences. Among the numerous examples the article cites in the year 1968:

> Violators of the federal forgery laws received an average jail term of twenty-two months in New York seven district. But in Central California the same offense drew an average sentence of forty-five months, and in Kansas the average was seventy months. For narcotic offenses, a federal court in Connecticut handed down sentences that averaged forty-four months; in Southern Texas the average term was ninety months.

All of the judges I interviewed felt there was disparity of sentencing. Most of them felt it was a serious problem. Occasionally, however, some of them defended the disparity:

> If we're dealing with punishment alone, then the approach is one thing. If the demands are for a social approach to the problem—rehabilitation distinguished from punishment—then one's approach as a judge must be different. He should see what he could do to make the offender a useful member of society by utilizing the services which our enlightened penal system gives us to work with—that is, the probation office. They are authorized by the courts, and by penologists who motivate our courts now to make an investigation concerning the individual who is appearing before us for sentence, to delve into his background and his motivations. After this investigation by persons who are supposedly tutored and experienced in social welfare, social work, the judge is prepared to make some sort of recommendation. If rehabilitation is the purpose, then you sentence the individual—not the crime he committed. You are concerned for what is best for him and for society. And that's why you have a disparity of sentences—one judge will interpret a social worker's report one way, while another judge will evaluate it differently.

This is characteristic of those who feel disparity is defensible. It is a sign to them that they are judging the criminal, not the crime, and, as such, is taken as an essential aspect of the individualization of justice. This judge also points out the enormous dependence on the probation officer and the pre-sentence report which is his product. In many courts, the probation officer rather than the judge is the sentencer. Judge Harold R. Tyler,[13] one of the leading experts in the judiciary on sentencing, says:

> The vast majority of district judges have had little or no experience in the field of criminal law and procedure prior to their appointment. . . . Suddenly, and without training or advice, the newly created jurist is faced with that borderline decision as to what to do with a particular offender. Fortunately, the probation officer is always willing to render the necessary assistance and recommendation if the judge is equally willing to realize that the probation officer is a highly competent person in his field with vastly greater opportunities to know the defendant, his background, and what sentence is appropriate. If any word of advice as to sentencing should be given to a new federal judge, it would be to "lean upon your probation officer."

But the probation officers vary in quality and are subject to the same potentials for bias as the judges. Worse, they are not open to the public scrutiny of the actual decision maker, and they are protected by the false assumption of the objectivity of the social scientist, reinforced by the paternalistic jargon and attitudes of modern-day social workers. Whatever their intention, whatever their purposes, disparity exists at an incredible rate and is documented anew with each new researcher in each new decade.

Inequities in the processes of justice always warrant concern. They take on particular urgency, however, in a time of crisis. These are such times. The intermittent attacks on the courts from the radical left, combined with the continued disparagement of the courts by "law and order" conservatives, who see soft judges as the source of all mugging, rape, and street mayhem, suggest the kind of unholy alliance that often rules in times of fear and frustration.

The purposes of this book are to demonstrate that judicial bias exists, and is operative in the sentencing procedure throughout the courts; to demonstrate how it operates by the inevitable intrusion of subjective values into that complex human process of decision making; and to demonstrate it in such a way as to disturb the complacency, offend the decency, and outrage the sense of fairness of that vast majority of people protected from contact with the courts, but whose support is essential in the struggle for justice.

# CHAPTER II

# The Sentencing Process

In theater and movies the inevitable climax of the process of justice is visualized in that tense moment when the foreman of the jury arises to announce the verdict. "Guilty or innocent?" is the dramatic question by which suspense is stretched to titillation at least once a week on prime-time television. But real life, alas (or hurrah), barely bears any recognizable relationship to popular entertainment versions of it.

In real-life courtrooms, guilt or innocence is not the critical question. That, in the majority of cases, is decided in advance by mutual agreement in a haggling, coercing, often sordid, and always wearisome game called plea bargaining. The vast majority of criminals brought to trial plead guilty to accommodate the court, which in turn has accommodated them by agreeing to lesser charges and lesser ranges of sentences. It is the sentence which is the real pivot around which the emotions, tensions, pressures, hopes, and fears revolve. Sentencing is the province of the judge. It is he who decides whether the convicted man will be allowed to return to his everyday life, relatively free of punishment, whether he will be fined an insignificant or a crippling amount, whether he will go to jail and the amount of time that he will spend there.

Of course, the limits within which a judge must operate are set by the various legislatures. Each law which may be violated contains within the statute that establishes it as an act of law the legitimate punishments that may be imposed for its violation. By implication, I suppose, these collective and varying punishments identify a moral profile of the culture. At least they give a clue as to our relative sense of priorities. All laws are intended to be obeyed; but there are laws and laws, and the violation of some, for various reasons, demands more or less punishment than others. Historians and comparative anthropologists may find the nature of prescribed punishments key indices of the value systems of various societies. It is not just the range and limits of punishment for any specific crime that are important, but the relative punishments assigned to different crimes that are indicators of the social morality. In a primitive society, the penalty of death for stealing food or a source of income (hanging the horse thief on the Western frontier) may seem barbaric to us if we patronizingly apply our own standards, but to a culture where the deprivation of food may indeed be the deprivation of life, capital punishment may seem as reasonable as it does to us for some of the reasons we impose it.

The state, in establishing the limits to punishment for each crime, implicitly places a value on the behavior violated. The punishment, to be morally acceptable, should be consistent with some fair evaluation of the seriousness of the crime. Because of the awareness of a multitude of individual differences and in the desire to secure justice, the prescribed penalties cover a considerable range to allow for the discretionary assessment of the judge. He is at the scene and presumed most capable of evaluating the crime in terms of his understanding of the purposes of punishment.

To understand the subjective factors that sneak uninvited and unauthorized into decision making, it is necessary to have some sense of the objective and authentic factors that are presumed to be the stuff of which decisions are made.

There is general agreement, in theory at least, on what some of the purposes of sentencing are. The list is monotonously the same and was recited to me almost by rote by each judge in turn when I asked him what his considerations in sentencing were. While the emphasis and even the meaning of the words differ from judge to judge, they uniformly subscribe to the following code of principles:[1]

> Generally speaking, in western society, criminologists and penologists have commonly adopted five broad categories to distinguish the main purpose of the penal system. These are: (a) retribution, (b) protection of society, (c) individual deterrence, (i.e., deterrence of an offender), (d) general deterrence (i.e., deterrence of potential offenders), (e) reformation or rehabilitation.

To understand the thinking and indeed the language of the judges, it is important to have a more specific grasp of these principles, which I shall analyze in order of complexity.

# 1. Protection of Society

This is perhaps the simplest to understand. It is often referred to as "confinement," "prevention," or "incapacitation." In the course of the following discussions, when referred to, it simply means that at least while a man is confined he is unable to commit any crimes. He is incapacitated and, presuming he's a chronic criminal, to the degree that he is unable to commit any crimes the incidence of crime will go down. We have therefore prevented a certain amount of crime from taking place.

In many ways it is the least debatable and most irrefutable proposition. This does not mean that in the interest of "protection of society" we can lock up a man indefinitely. Obviously, we must protect not only society but the values of our society, and to do that we must make sure that the quality of punishment is somehow commensurate with the quality of crime. It seems unlikely that our values could tolerate locking a chronic pickpocket up for life. This would be an offensive concept; it seems excessive and inappropriate punishment; and it does not allow for potential change in the individual over time, which ultimately may be testable only by releasing him periodically.

Another argument against the principle of prevention is that such a small percentage of criminals are apprehended and sent to prison that a purely preventive model would affect the level of crime very little.

This is open to some debate. While it is true that only a small percentage of crimes are punished, it is *not* necessarily true that only a small percentage of criminals are apprehended. The 1 in 10 burglars (or 1 in 100) who is unfortunate enough to be caught may himself be responsible for many of the unsolved burglaries.

Another major flaw in the incapacitation theory is that it is not readily predictable who will be the recidivist (repeater). The fact that a man has committed a crime once— or more—does not indicate that he will repeat. Prediction, even by experts, is not all that good, as has been readily admitted by one acknowledged expert, Sigmund Freud,[2] and ignored by too many of his followers: "It is always possible by analysis to recognize the causation (of a piece of behavior) with certainty, whereas a prediction of it by synthesis is impossible."

# 2. General Deterrence

This is the concept that if one man is punished with a degree of severity for committing a crime, his publicized example will deter other would-be criminals from the same offense. It is the frightening example, the dramatization of the consequences.

General deterrence is another principle that has currently gained wide acceptance, and I suspect for two very good reasons. First of all, it is the great unknowable. There is simply no way to test out its hypothesis. The variables are so enormous, the controlled experiments so unmanageable, that there is absolutely no creditable way for us to measure its effectiveness, or to know if it is effective at all. Yet it is generally assumed to be effective, and that may relate to a second reason for its acceptance. If general deterrence really does not work, our present system would be bankrupt and indefensible, since all other justifications for incarceration barely warrant the expense and effort.

Certainly in some societies, much different from our own, one can find examples where general deterrence seems to work. The success of the Scandinavians in controlling drunken driving by a comparatively harsh and inviolate treatment of all offenders is one example. There, even distinguished figures—cabinet ministers, movie idols, sports stars—will go to jail for drunken driving, and the blood test is the arbitrary definition. In a complex heterogeneous society like our own, it is always disastrous to draw conclusions from societies so different. Moreover, general deterrence probably does work best for white-collar crimes committed by white-collar people.

# 3. Individual Deterrence

This is the principle that if you punish a man for a crime, *he* will not be likely to repeat it. If general deterrence is the great unknown, specific deterrence is probably the great known and it is a bust. There are very few people who believe any more that by sending someone to jail you keep him from committing that crime again. If nothing else, the recidivist rate is so large, with the repeat crime often progressively more serious than the original one, that for some imprisonment seems an encouraging rather than a deterring factor.

# 4. Rehabilitation

David Rothman[3] has traced the impact of the rehabilitative ideal in this country back to the 1820's. Certainly during the last forty or fifty years, penal philosophy here has been dominated by this concept. It is part of that humanistic tradition which in pressing for ever more individualization of justice has demanded that we regard the criminal, not the crime. It uses the medical and educative model. It sees the criminal as, if not sick, at least not completely evil, somehow less "responsible" than he had previously been regarded. As a kind of social malfunctioner the criminal needs to be treated or to be re-educated, reformed, or rehabilitated. Rehabilitation is the opposite of punishment in many ways. It pleads for a nonmoral approach.

Unwittingly, it has borrowed more heavily from the model of medicine than that of education. The ultimate exponent of this point of view is Dr. Karl Menninger, and it is not just coincidence that he is a psychiatrist. The very title of his last book, *The Crime of Punishment*,[4] indicates his feeling that a psychiatric model is the only appropriate one for criminal offenders. It is a compassionate and decent book from a compassionate and decent man, and perhaps takes us as close to the brave new world of Aldous Huxley (where the announcement that someone has committed a crime elicits the surprised response, "I did not know he was ill") as we are likely to get. The rehabilitative model may already be at its apex and ready for decline. It is now under attack, not only from the conservative community, to which it has always been a molly-coddling, bleeding-heart outrage, but from the liberal community which created and defended it. The rehabilitative model abounds with internal inconsistencies which inevitably offered opportunities for exploitation that were as inevitably accepted. It produced unexpected, aberrant consequences and numerous unpredicted side effects that were less humane or liberal than its proponents had anticipated.

When you switch from a frame of reference that is essentially judgmental and punitive to one that is medical, a whole range of corollaries is brought into play. Part of the inherent definition of a sick person is a presumption of nonculpability. We separate the patient from responsibility for his disease. When we say, "It's not his fault, he is sick," we are defining the patient as the victim, not the victimizer.

This was an especially attractive premise for humane legal philosophers, particularly during the current heyday of psychiatry when disease has been extended to include all kinds of aberrant behavior beyond the limited and all-involving nineteenth-century concept of insanity. Since the turn of the century, we have progressively reduced the requirements for a diagnosis of mental illness (no longer need you be "crazy"; simply "obsessive," "phobic," "psychosomatic," etc.) and thereby enlarged the population of the mentally ill. Psychiatry became the link between the medical and the legal models and the problems were latent at the outset.

Dynamic psychiatry is dominated by two concepts: First, every individual act of behavior is seen as the result of a multitude of emotional forces and counterforces; this is the "psychodynamic" principle; and second, these forces and counterforces are considered to be shaped and predetermined by past experience. This is the principle of "psychic causality." The only large opposing force to the dynamic view in modern theory of human behavior comes from the field of behavioral psychology; and while the behavioral psychologist finds the first principle (the dynamic unconscious) anathema, it is only because it detracts from the second principle, which is his one true religion. Both the dynamic psychiatrist and the behavioral psychologist are as one in supporting the Gospel of Psychic Determinism. This concept dictates a way of viewing any piece of behavior.

Supposing three men are threatened by a man with a gun. One flees; one stands paralyzed with fear; one attacks. The stimulus for all three is the same. But the stimulus is only one factor in determining the resultant behavior. Acting on the complex machinery of the human being, it triggers associations, perceptions, and response patterns already "programmed in" by previous experience. This view of behavior rejects the possibility of an isolated or chance act, and whether we like it or not, places psychiatry in the camp of determinism. All acts—healthy, sick, or not-sure-which—share one property: they are predetermined.

Many psychiatrists in fact do *not* like it, and are personally unhappy with determinism; they "believe in" free will. But they have not been able to incorporate chance as a relevant phenomenon into the theory of psychiatry. Deterministic it remains, and antithetical to the social concept underlying criminal law, which must assume free will, or choice in action. It really is not important which concept is "true"—or if either is true. For certain purposes, either assumption may be useful, or necessary; but to assume both at the same time is logically impossible.

This logical impasse has a further unfortunate consequence for the relationship of psychiatry and the law. The social view of behavior is in essence moralistic; an action is approved or disapproved, right or wrong, acceptable or nonacceptable. A person is guilty or innocent as more or less clearly defined in advance by law. But psychiatrically speaking nothing is wrong, only sick. If an act is not a choice, but merely the inevitable product of series of past experiences, a man can no more be guilty of a crime than he is guilty of an abscess.

I do not mean that psychiatrists are amoral or that they preach amorality. On the contrary, it is the psychiatrist's job to help a person adjust to his environment—and our social environment operates under ethical and moral systems. (The degree to which values and judgments enter treatment is an entirely different problem which equally requires attention.) What I do mean is that "guilt" and "innocence," as used in criminal law, are not functional concepts in psychiatry. To the typical psychiatrist, guilt is an emotion—and innocence an age.

Greater understanding of the implications of psychology, however, is now beginning to reveal the futility of using psychology to leaven the law. In the psychiatrist's view, if guilt is based on free choice, then no man is guilty, for behavior is predetermined. If guilt is based on intention, then every man is guilty, for every action is intended—if not consciously, then unconsciously, and the borders between the two are amorphous. The criminal law as it now stands is often using false and, perhaps worse for legal purposes, indefinable psychological concepts.

The therapeutic model is a complicated one; but worse, the therapeutic experiment has not worked out. Prisons are not more effective, not more rehabilitative. We are sending more and more of our citizens to prison for longer and longer sentences—and the crime rates keep rising. With the frustration over law and order, we have become a prison-happy society. The average sentence length for all court commitments to federal prisons has risen steadily in the last fifteen years, until now it is almost double the twenty-eight months it was in 1957.

The net result: Prison sentences have been growing steadily longer in this country—in direct contrast to what's happening in almost every other country in the world. From 1967 to 1968, for example, federally imposed jail terms climbed from an average of 39 months to 45 months. During one recent year in the U.S. no fewer than 15,000 offenders were sentenced to five years or more; in England the number was 150.[5]

The supporters of rehabilitation will say, and rightly so, that it was never really given a chance, that it was only accepted *in theory* while in practice the prison system has insisted on maintaining a punitive attitude. On the other hand, the question remains whether one can reasonably continue to expect anything different, given the extended time that reformism has had. Besides, there are some theoreticians, Erving Goffman[6] being the outstanding example, who raise the question whether incarceration in a total institution, regardless of intent and good will, can ever be other than a punitive detainment.

There are other dangers in the therapeutic model. Medicine is allowed to be bitter. Inflicted pain is not cruelty if it is treatment rather than punishment. We tolerate humiliation when it is sugared with the rationalization of treatment.

# 5. Retribution

This has recently been such an unfashionable concept that few have dared publicly to champion its claims, although it is unlikely that it is ever absent from the private considerations of those confronting crime. In a discussion of criminal responsibility, Professor Leon Radzinowicz[7] has said: "The importance of the whole issue has declined since the needs of the offender have been accepted as one of the factors to be taken into account and retribution has receded as a primary objective."

Punishment when presented as an independent category includes such concepts as vengeance, retribution, and desserts. It is not meant to include the concept of punishment as a rehabilitative or educative measure, although that is something that perhaps also should be re-examined. Nor does the use of the word "punishment" here concern itself with its deterrent aspects. We are not now talking of punishment for an end; not punishment as an educative adjunct to make the individual a better person (the behavior modifiers would insist that reward at any rate is a better modifier for behavior).

Punishment in this sense is to serve the needs or purposes of the punisher, independent of its effects on the punished. If we could cure a perpetual armed robber by giving him a life income of $50,000 a year, we would be unlikely to adopt the principle, not merely because it might then encourage armed robbery, but because it would offend some moral sense of the rightness of things. When the word "vengeance" is used, it has a punitive connotation of a most un-Christian sort and as such has been rejected. "Retribution" seems more refined. One argument for retribution on the part of the state has indeed been that it may forestall the uncharitable and dangerous desires for vengeance on the part of the individual. If retribution is repayment, it may assuage a sense of having been wronged.

When punishment is expressed in terms of just desserts, it is stripped of all utilitarian purposes. Here punishment is not to soothe anyone's conscience, nor because it is more effective for this or that. It is because it is right; because it ought to be. There is the feeling of a Kantian imperative behind the word "desserts." Certain things are simply wrong and ought to be punished. If we took the case of a well-known criminal of our time, Adolf Hitler, and we examined all of the previous reasons for incarceration independent of desserts, an argument could be presented for allowing Hitler to live out his life in peace. At his age, rehabilitation was unlikely and probably unnecessary. Stripped of his power, what was there that he could do—return to his painting? There would have probably been little to reform. He seemed capable of living out a life of luxury on an Argentinian estate without running afoul of the law. Protection of society was unnecessary; he could never have regained the kind of power he had held—we were amply warned about him. Individual deterrence is meaningless; there was no chance for him to be a recidivist. General deterrence? Unlikely. Hitler was not deterred by his knowledge of what happened to Napoleon. And, indeed, what happened to Napoleon or Hitler represents a minority example; most abusers of power survive the abused. Yet I, for one, would have been unhappy to have simply allowed Hitler to retire. The nature of his crime required punishment, and of a severe form, independent of any useful purpose it may or may not have served.

The concept of desserts is being re-examined. In the deliberations of the Committee for the Study of Incarceration, it was remarkable to see the emergence of this concept, almost unpredictably, to the forefront of considerations as a justification for incarceration, despite early objections that approached aversion in some people.

The concept of desserts is intellectual and moralistic. In its devotion to principle, it turns its back on such compromising considerations as generosity, charity, compassion, and love. It emphasizes justice, not mercy, and while it need not rule out tempering justice with mercy—by shifting the emphasis from concern for the individual to devotion to the moral right—it may lead to an abandonment of the former altogether. It is not a happy principle to embrace.

On the other hand, the rehabilitative model, with its emphasis on understanding and concern, has dominated our modus operandi so far; under it we have abused our charges, the prisoners, without disabusing our conscience. It is beneath this cloak of benevolence that hypocrisy has flourished, where each new exploitation inevitably has been introduced as an act of grace.

The problems, as already can be seen, are not easy. This brief survey is introduced with no claim to being a definitive, or even adequate, discussion of the issues. Its purpose here is simply to assist in appreciating the reasoning of the judges, and to supply an aid in understanding the complexities of their dilemmas, the forces at work, the very language of their deliberations as they attempt to determine an effective and just sentence.

# CHAPTER III

# The Intrusion of Bias

The principles discussed in the preceding chapter frame a set of purposes; the ill-defined and vague intentions of a society unclear and conflicted in its attitudes about crime and punishment. But sentencing is done by judges, and judges are human beings with purposes of their own, equally vague, equally ill-defined, and not necessarily governed by the same motives, nor motivated by the same needs as the society. Man is a hero-hungry animal, and we want to believe that these shrouded figures are the detached descendants of Solomon. But they are not. The austere black robes, the elevated positions, the exalted title, the formalized deference may extend and magnify the office without in any way enlarging the human being residing in that setting. As Justice Black reminds us: "Like all the rest of mankind, they may be affected from time to time by pride and passion, by pettiness and bruised feelings, by improper understanding or by excessive zeal."[1]

A mass of studies exists which, by implication at least, attempt to prove that personal bias and motive are introduced into the sentencing process. The traditional method of these researches is to demonstrate a statistically significant disparity. This has been done by a variety of ingenious methods: geographical differences;[2] differences among various judges in a single state system;[3] studies that focus both on the sentenced[4] and the sentencer.[5] Some have dealt with the obvious problems of bias.[6] Others have used less dramatic but equally important criteria. Stewart Nagel, for example, demonstrated that bipartisan Supreme Court judges carried their original partisan political orientation right into their courtrooms. He found that he could very readily deduce the political affiliation of the judge from his sentencing behavior, even in a state system where the bipartisan selection was presumed to have eliminated the political orientation of judges. His study of the California Supreme Court indicated that the Democrats averaged 85 per cent pro-defense, while the Republicans averaged 18 per cent for the defense.[7]

Another intriguing study was one done by Leon Stern which demonstrated the effect of the Great Depression of the 1930's on the sentencing behavior of specific judges. He found that during the course of the Depression, the number of convictions and commitments became higher and higher. In addition, the tendency to greater severity was indicated by "an increasing preference which the judges showed during the Depression for using penitentiary for commitments in which serious property crimes were involved."[8]

As can be expected, where racial biases are concerned, there are veritable encyclopedias of research proving varying things, depending on the crime studied and the location.[9] We must not be too glib, however, in our assumption of the direction in which bias will work. When most of us think of bias it could be characterized by the statistics compiled by Partington in Virginia, who found that "since the installation of the electric chair in 1908, forty-one executions for rape, thirteen for attempted rape, one for robbery and rape, and one for attempted robbery and rape have been carried out. Every single executed convict was black."[10] But another study showed that juries gave blacks guilty of murder shorter terms than white. The author postulated that the white juries gave blacks guilty of murder shorter terms because the victims were generally black (murder being largely an intraracial crime) and white juries are not as concerned if one black kills another; whereas, in largely interracial crimes, such as a burglary, white juries impose larger sentences on black burglars than white burglars, expressing, according to this author, the white juries' concern about potential black burglary of their homes. Indeed, in support of this is one of the most respected studies in the field, by Edward Green. He demonstrated, at least with crimes he was studying in his area,

> that Negro offenders against Negro victim crimes resulted in the mildest penalties with half as many penitentiary sentences, and four times the number of probations as either Negro-white or white-white offenders, who get approximately the same degree of punishment for the different possible penalties.[11]

Throughout all of these studies it is the disparity of sentencing which is used to imply specific biases and even different attitudes. They indicate the extent to which individual differences in the judges influence the distribution of justice. They imply that a different set of standards is being imposed on what is usually assumed to be a common concept of law within the community. They strongly suggest that biases are introduced, they even demonstrate the extent to which they may be; but they tell us nothing about the nature of the bias or the purposes behind the judges' varying decisions. While it is intriguing to note the disparity, the "why" is missing. Where is the bias? What is the bias? What is to be corrected? What is the direction of change indicated? None of these questions is answered; only the disparity is evident.

While no direct evidence is offered, the indirect evidence can be most persuasive. Still, it can be rationalized away in any area in which the variables are as overwhelming as they are in human conduct. As Hogarth has said:

> In previous studies, students of sentencing have been restricted to an examination of sentencing as revealed in the official record. . . . The frequently replicated finding is that observed variation in sentencing behavior cannot be totally or even largely explained by either variation in the types of cases dealt with, or the official reasons for judgment given. It is then often suggested that sentencing is an irrational process.

Hogarth attempted to rectify this by extending the procedure to include questionnaires, and on the basis of this he found that "while magistrates were inconsistent with each other, they were consistent within themselves." He concluded that "age, religion, education, social class, background, and previous employment experience, all were shown to have a relationship to a magistrate's behavior on the bench."[12] But even this kind of study avoids the most dramatic and truest expression of attitude—the articulated ideas of a human being involved.

If you want to meet the judges as people you can, of course, as with any other group, consult the people around them. Everson[13] spiced his report with all sorts of "courthouse gossip." Unscientific though it may seem, this kind of information generally represents such a consistent picture and such a degree of concurrence that, while not itself scientifically acceptable, it is an invaluable background and guide to more authentic methods.

A vast resource of information lies in the quasi-scientific, reportorial, gossipy, "everybody knows" world of the criminal court. This became apparent when I interviewed district attorneys, defense attorneys, court clerks, judges' secretaries and clerks, and newspaper writers who cover the court beat. Off the record there is a delight in spilling the beans. "Everybody knows that Judge White is a 'softy'—except in cases of violation of public trust. Time and again an official who takes a bribe will be given a whopping sentence, yet a man on an assault charge might well 'walk out.' "

"Judge Grey is great at handling drug cases expeditiously. Never mind how he handles them, we make sure to send the bulk of these cases to him."

"Judge Brown is a patient man. He doesn't seem to mind long trials and therefore he sits in court almost continuously and handles most of our longer trials, including most of the homicides. Some of our other judges refuse to handle trials at all, hearing only guilty pleas." Of eleven criminal judges in New York County, for example, only three or four regularly sit in trial.

"Judge Black has become absolute hell on car thieves since his car was stolen some six months ago."

"Commonly, new judges tend to be harsher than old judges. They need to prove themselves and they take a little time to mellow. Therefore, I [a defense attorney] am always more likely to plead not guilty and take a case to trial with them. At least until I learn what can be expected from them. Sometimes you win in another way. You can delay a case until a judge you can count on is sitting."

From a clerk of court: "Of course, most of the judges give stiffer sentences in cases convicted following a trial. After all, those that are settled by a pre-trial guilty plea helped us with the work and deserve some reward."

While not directly usable as any "proof," this material tended to prove out more often than not. But we all tend to distrust the secondhand report, and the secondhand motives. Fortunately, even without direct interviewing we can approach the judges directly. They do speak both off and on the record, and those words are often available.

When we think of bias in the courts, we are conditioned to thinking in terms of racial bias. In part, I suppose, because racial bias was for so long a period of time not only accepted but flaunted. So much so that judges who are usually extremely discreet when off the bench (to prevent disqualification for bias in future cases) have with equanimity announced their feelings in this area to the public. For example, *Time*[14] magazine quoted two Southern judges in 1964, during the height and heat of a voter registration drive. Georgia's judge, J. Robert Elliott, saying:

"I don't want those pinks, radicals, and black voters to outvote those who are trying to preserve our segregation laws and traditions"; while Mississippi's Judge Cox referred to two hundred black applicants for voter registration as "a bunch of niggers" and "chimpanzees," who "ought to be in the movies rather than being registered to vote."

Repeatedly, judges in their official role have referred to defendants as "niggers";[15] addressed them directly as "nigger";[16] patronized them with insulting references such as "three black cats in a white Buick";[17] and even gone so far as to direct the sheriff to get the right kind of young men for jurors because "we want to break this nigger's neck."[18]

Sometimes the dignity of the defendant stands as a dramatic indictment of the cruelty and humiliation of the official representatives of our society, as in the following case. Mary Hamilton, a black woman, was cited for contempt. She was given five days in jail and a fifty-dollar fine. The official reason given was that the defendant refused to answer the third question proposed to her by the prosecutor. During the cross-examination the prosecution was as follows:

Q: What is your name please?
A: Miss Mary Hamilton.
Q: Mary, I believe you were arrested—who were you arrested by?
A: My name is Miss Hamilton. Please address me correctly.
Q: Who were you arrested by, Mary?
A: I will not answer a question—(at that point Miss Hamilton's attorney interrupted and said, "The witness's name is Miss Hamilton.")

*Simultaneously, Miss Hamilton answered:* "I will not answer a question until I am addressed correctly."
*The judge then directed:* "Answer the question."
*The witness:* "I will not answer them unless I am addressed correctly."
*The judge:* "You are in contempt of court."

The citation was appealed to the Supreme Court of Alabama. The court said in the instant appeal: "The record conclusively shows that the petitioner's name is Mary Hamilton, not Miss Mary Hamilton." And on this elliptical reasoning the court affirmed the conviction.[19] Anyone who has lived any length of time in Alabama cannot be unaware of the implication of first-name forms of address. It has been a traditional distinction between races and a means of humiliation to the black community. Certainly, the Supreme Court judges of Alabama were aware of the implications of this kind of address. If Miss Mary Hamilton is *more* than her official name, Mary is *less* than her official name. The word "Supreme" before Court, whether state or national, tends to intimidate the average layman with its otherworldly connotations. But Supreme Courts are not occupied by Supreme Beings, and there is no reason to assume that the Supreme Court of a state is any more immune to blatant prejudice than any other court, including the Supreme Court of the United States.

I start with examples of racial discrimination because in many ways they are the most flagrant and because racial discrimination in general has been one of the most offensive moral crimes of our particular culture. There is, however, a danger in always seeing bias in terms of a racial, or even for that matter, a religious minority. Abuse of the disenfranchised has little effect on the political processes and receives relatively little of that kind of attention from the public media which is necessary to shake the frail and somnolent conscience of the powerful but complacent majority.

It is the majority which wields the power necessary to influence legislators and to institute reform, and that majority will not do so when apparently it is always the other man's ox that has been gored.

One way or another, however, we all find ourselves members of some minority, whether it be in terms of party affiliations, sexual practices, geographical location, aesthetic considerations, temperament, personality, gender, or whatever. This has been observed most flagrantly via some recent convictions that roused the American middle class. The anti-hippy and anti-youth hysteria, encouraged by public pronouncements of an often manipulative government in need of a scapegoat, has resulted in the application of unbelievably high sentences for first offenders for marijuana conviction. The state laws which lump marijuana possession with that of heroin facilitate this. Numerous cases of twenty, thirty, forty, and fifty years have been reported. If this occurs in a state with an appellate review of sentencing, some remedy may be available; if not, we get a situation like the following. A man was convicted on fourteen counts of a violation of the Federal Narcotics Statute. This was based on one sale of marijuana and two sales of heroin and possession of these drugs. However, the defendant was a first offender and according to the appellate court there was absolutely nothing in the record to indicate that "the case was an aggravated one." Nonetheless, despite the fact that he was a first offender, he received fifty-two years of consecutive sentence and a $3,000 fine. The appellate court said with no uncertainty that this was "greater than should be imposed," but the court also said that under the federal practice the appellate courts are without power to modify sentences within the fixed statute.[20]

The shameful treatment of the young war resisters who openly chose prison as an alternative to service in a war they either felt to be immoral or a violation of their basic religious beliefs became progressively worse until near the end.[21] As the frustration with the unwinnable Vietnam War began to affect the attitudes of the judges, and before the national revulsion caught up with the premature judgments of these young men, they were given progressively higher sentences. Punitive judges often gave them maximum five-year sentences despite the fact that they were young men, first offenders, made no attempt to evade their responsibilities, presented themselves before the court, pleaded guilty, and had led exemplary lives. Vindictive parole boards, contrary to general practice for first offenders, routinely refused them parole when first eligible and enforced their serving a minimum of two years. Despite the fact that a man's religious conviction is theoretically not to be a factor in his treatment by the institutions of this government, the Jehovah's Witnesses—in every way identical to the other young men who refused serving except by the nature of their religion—were given a preferential treatment, both at the level of sentencing and the level of parole, over those who refused induction for political reasons or for reasons of individual moral conscience independent of church affiliation. Of course, the fact that the Jehovah's Witnesses were in jail at all seems clearly a violation of *their* religious rights. The Quakers routinely were allowed probationary treatment because they agreed to do alternative service to the government, but to the Jehovah's Witnesses any service to a secular government was against their religion. They were then not free to do alternative service and were forced to go to prison.

Almost anything can become a matter of evangelical fury, if it stirs the passions of a particular judge. The persecution of young drug offenders merely mirrors repeated persecutions for alcohol offenses by evangelical dries. Morality leads into sexuality, and here, too, the ignorant are always prepared to confuse their propensities with God's mandate. Judges have continuously foisted on the public their own often distorted sexual taste by endowing their peculiar and personal conduct with the force of law. The sexual style of a particular judge is always equated by him with the natural order of things. Judges have railed against that "abominable and detestable crime against nature,"[22] referring to fellatio; yet *Deep Throat* has become a household title across the nation, if not yet a totally accepted household activity. One judge insists that "the natural functions of the organs for the reproduction of the species are entirely different from those of the nutritive system," with which it would seem contentious to debate, but then continues, "It is self-evident the use of either opening of the alimentary canal for the purpose of sexual copulation is against the natural design of the human body. . . . The moral filthiness and inequity . . . is the same in both cases."[23]

Unfailing in their determination to preserve the moral good, judges, in that paternalistic way that seems to be the curse of all professions in authority, reassure us that it is our own good about which they are concerned, so that one judge will in the smugness of ignorance state that "all unnatural forms and methods of coitus have proven themselves detrimental to both health and morals."[24] How grateful I, as a student of sexual behavior and a practicing psychoanalyst, would be to have that judge's secure definition of what is natural and what unnatural in form or method of intercourse. Morality is the one area most capable of revealing the fears and confusion of even the best of our judiciary, as anyone can affirm who has examined the pathetic, illogical, inconsistent shilly-shallying of the Supreme Court on the questions of pornography. Here the nadir may have been reached in the following statement by a judge to a defendant: "How was it, or why was it that you were out on the streets at three o'clock in the morning? You ought to have been in bed. Honest people are in bed at three o'clock in the morning."[25] This was in 1962.

There is no limit to the area in which bias can be introduced. Judges can be biased against ex-convicts,[26] against the eccentric and emotionally unstable,[27] against the disabled. In a particularly poignant case, a trial court denied a petition for the adoption of a deaf child by deaf-mute parents who had raised another such child, despite the fact that all the evidence was in favor of the parents and there was not one word of testimony presented in opposition.[28] There are examples where judges have tried cases in which they were personally involved,[29] where the prosecutor was the judge's son,[30] where the judge's salary was dependent on the profits from convictions,[31] where the defendant was a political opponent of the judge in an upcoming election.[32]

But the bias that cuts most to the heart of our democratic system is political bias. It is the concept of political freedom that ultimately supports all other freedoms. If this is to remain a government of free ideas it is essential that the courts be antagonists to, rather than instruments of, political coercion. In addition, political issues more than most others seem to corrupt even the good people involved and to embroil not just the defendants but the lawyers and the courts in acrimony and emotion. In major national cases, any example of political bias will usually be well monitored by the press. The degree to which political prejudice can influence, unattended, the smaller cases can never be measured, but in all probability may be even more destructive. One of the most famous and most examined cases where political passion, and perhaps political bias, was most evident was in the trial of Communist Party leaders, the case of *Dennis v. U.S.* After that trial, Judge Medina held the counsel for the defense in contempt for their behavior during the trial and sentenced them to up to six months in jail. The major issue that was presented on appeal[33] was whether a different judge should have tried the contempt proceeding rather than Medina. In Judge Medina's contempt charge, he claimed that the defense counsel had conspired against him to "impair my health." The Supreme Court in support found that the attorneys' behavior had not only offended the presiding judge but had also affected the trial order and dignity. What is most interesting, for the purposes of this book, however, were some of the statements in the dissents.

In his dissent, Justice Black wrote:

> The presiding Judge was convinced that the lawyers had deliberately and calculatingly badgered and insulted him throughout the long months of trial. Among these insults, so the Judge believed and declared, were insolent, sarcastic, impudent and disrespectful charges that he angled for news-paper headlines; connived with the United States Attorney; entertained racial prejudice; judicially acted with "bias, prejudice, corruption, and partiality." . . . As the trial pro-gressed, the record shows that the Judge expressed stronger and stronger fears that the alleged conspiracy to destroy his health was about to succeed . . . but the record shows a constantly growing resentment of the Judge against the lawyers. The Judge repeatedly called Sacher [attorney] a liar in open court.

Black feels that Judge Medina imputed the character of the defendants to their attorneys:

> It is difficult to escape the impression that his inferences against the lawyers were colored, however unconsciously, by his natural abhorrence for the unpatriotic and treason-able designs attributed to their Communist leader clients.

Justice Frankfurter, in his dissent, stated:

> The Judge acted as the prosecuting witness; he thought of himself as such. His self-concern pervades the record; it could not humanly have been excluded from his judgment of contempt. Judges are human, and it is not suggested that any other judge could have been impervious to the abuse had he been subjected to it.

Justice Douglas's dissent:

> I agree with Mr. Justice Frankfurter that one who reads this record will have difficulty in determining whether members

of the bar conspired to drive a judge from the bench or whether the judge used the authority of the bench to whipsaw the lawyers, to taint and tempt them, and to create for himself the role of the persecuted.

A judge is, even on the bench, a human being, and therefore subject to the same lack of controls and disciplines as are we all. If the conditions of his life outside the court can introduce factors that will influence his decisions, so can his exposure to the defendants in the court produce emotions which modify judgment. This can generate compassion, identification, sympathy, but also antagonisms. More often than not these can be buried and hidden from view but, buried or no, they will be reflected in his decisions on sentences. Consciously or unconsciously, the animosity that may develop during this period can find the satisfaction of retribution to a degree beyond what most of us are allowed in satisfying our personal hostilities. What is interesting is how many cases there are where even with the knowledge of this awesome power to strike his offender down, the judge simply cannot control his own passions. In one such case, a judge found an attorney to be in contempt twelve times and sentenced him to ten days in jail. A court of appeals reduced this to forty-eight hours of confinement, but the persistent attorney fought it all the way to the Supreme Court, where it was reversed on the basis of the judge's behavior. In reversing the conviction, the Supreme Court wrote:

> But judges also are human and may in a human way quite unwittingly identify offense to self with obstruction to law. Accordingly this court has deemed it important that district judges guard against this easy confusion by not sitting themselves in judgment upon misconduct of counsel where the contempt charge is tangled with the judge's personal feeling against the lawyer. Plainly . . . there was an infusion of personal animosity.[34]

The files are filled with such transgressions. In one case in which one man indicted testified at the defense of another, after only a few questions the judge ordered the jury out and said:

> "In view of this witness's testimony I don't see why this case should go along any further. . . . I am punishing him for telling a lie. The whole bunch of them. I think he is a liar from the word go. Bring back the jury. I'll stop this case. . . ."

Then to the jury the judge said:

> "Now you may think this fellow is the biggest liar in the world. I'll go along with you. I think so too."[35]

Or another judge who simply said:

> "Why don't you plead this man guilty? I'm going to find him guilty anyway."[36]

This, of course, before the trial.

Perhaps my favorite case of demonstrable fury on the part of the judge, evoked for reasons that are regrettably lost in history, is illustrated by the following transcript from a divorce action.

> Q: Did you support your wife while you were there together?
> A: Support my wife? I am on disability for twelve years. I have a letter from my doctor . . .
> *The judge:* "She didn't ask you that . . ."
> *The witness:* "Excuse me . . ."
> *The judge:* "Pay attention to what is asked you. I don't blame your wife for leaving you if you talk like that."
> *The witness* (the husband): "At that time she hit me on the head . . ."
> *The judge:* "Don't go talking so much!"
> *Husband's counsel:* "Don't say a thing . . ."

*The judge:* "That is probably the reason she hit you on the head, you talk too much!"

Q: Well, for how long a period of time have you been under disability?

*The judge:* "What is your disability, mental or physical?"

*The witness:* "I got hurt on the job, I fell down."

*The judge:* "Did you fall on your head?"

*The judge:* "Did you try to get in touch with her?"

*The witness:* "No use trying because she didn't care for me. . . ."

*The judge:* "Well, I don't blame her for that."[37]

Whatever pettiness, whatever malice, bigotry, fear, paranoia, resentment, vengefulness, and spite are generated in the hearts of men can be demonstrated in the sentencing decisions of judges. It is not the purpose of this study merely to show that meanness in human character does not respect the boundaries of profession, title, or authority. To protect against the bias in the worst of us is of course essential. But to serve the purposes of equity, it is equally important to protect against the bias in the best of us. The paranoid bigot is a comfort. He permits us to seal off self-examination with a wall of self-righteousness. But it is imperative to admit the bias beyond bigotry; to recognize the individualized and personal values that intrude on the deliberations of any human being; to understand that there is no judgment of human behavior that is not subjective; and to appreciate that objective sentencing is a myth that will never be achieved even if we were capable of elevating to judgeship solely the purest in heart.

These subtle forms of bias can only be appreciated in a detailed examination of the reasoning processes of the individual judges. It was tempting to select for dramatic purposes the few monsters that I did uncover in the sequence of judges interviewed. These straw men are deceptive cases;

while they serve to titillate, they also obfuscate. Rather, I thought it essential to examine the biases of the highest quality of men: the men respected in the field and dedicated to its service. The four judges presented here in detail to my mind represent the best we have.

These four judges—of different temperament, different background, different age, different courts—all share a dedication to their work, an integrity, and an intelligence. They are men of principles and their dedication to their principles is self-evident. Because they are principled, they are believers, and they will support and defend their beliefs. I have selected judges from a wide spectrum politically to demonstrate the unbelievable variation in treating an offender that the legitimate exercise of discretion allows. It is precisely the dedication of these judges to principles of justice *as they see it* which demonstrates the awful inequity inherent in our current sentencing system.

# CHAPTER IV

# Judge
# Justin C. Ravitz

In November 1972, a thirty-two-year-old, jean-clad, boot-shod Marxist lawyer, Justin C. Ravitz, was elected to a ten-year term as judge of the Detroit Recorder's (Criminal) Court in what may have been a confusion of identity with a popular but unrelated councilman, Mel Ravitz. No confusion now exists in anyone's mind.

Within one month of taking office he was challenged by a Wayne County government committee as to his "moral and ethical fitness"; called a "Jewish Communist Anti-American" by a prominent right-wing defendant; attacked by the American Legion for not honoring the flag; threatened with having his salary cut by a county commissioner; and accused by the newspapers of "making an ass of himself."

Judge Ravitz is not an ass. He is long-haired, young, and radical—all atypical for a county judge. But he is, in addition, concerned, intellectual, questioning, sensitive, hardworking, and dedicated—also atypical of county judges. He is a political judge. But no more, I suspect, than his Westchester County Republican counterparts. Political values and political bias, however, are rarely evident as such when they conform to those of the viewer. The value system of the majority is so much a part of the automatic thinking processes that it rarely is even identified as present. "The last thing a fish is likely to discover is water."* The deviant political position, right or left, when introduced is always seen as an intrusion, a new and unfair addition, rather than a substitute for the values and biases normally introduced. Justice Ravitz turns us upside down. Like those curious and twisted fictional "mirrors" of Jonathan Swift, Samuel Butler, and Lewis Carroll, whose distorted caricatures often better reflect the truth about ourselves than our own familiar self-image, Justice Ravitz, by offering us an alternative system, may help us the better to see the system under which we now operate.

I started the interview by asking him, vaguely and generally, what "goes into" his sentencing considerations.

It's a very tough subject. Why don't I just flow for a moment, just to give you my general perspective, and then you can hone in on areas where you want greater explicity? I start with the following premises: one, the penal system in this country is one of daily, systematic, government criminality. I say that because the supreme law of the land is, theoretically, the United States Constitution, which contains, among many things, an Eighth and Fourteenth Amendment.† Anyone who applies standards of civility, which ought to exist in any sane and mature society in the year 1973, to the factual situation that I suspect exists in nearly all penal institutions in this country would be objec-

---

* Robert Morison at a Hastings Center meeting recalled this quotation from Oliver Lodge.

† Amendment 8: Excessive bail shall not be required, nor excessive fines imposed, nor cruel and unusual punishments inflicted.

Amendment 14: No State shall make or enforce any law which shall abridge the privileges or immunities of citizens of the U.S.; nor shall any State deprive any person of life, liberty, or property, without due process of law; nor deny to any person within its jurisdiction the equal protection of the laws.

tively forced to conclude that in terms of what they do to human beings, it's probably all unconstitutional.

As a person who doesn't want to be part of government criminality, institutionalized criminality, I obviously have very strong reluctance to send anyone to prison. That's my view. By the same token, I recognize one can't be puristic sitting over here; the reality is that there are certain people in this society who really do pose an ongoing daily threat to the well-being of other human beings. Since there is no avenue for meaningful, constructive rehabilitation available, one has to make the hard choice—either they're going to be out there ripping off other little people or *they're* going to be ripped off, by being subjected to the cruel, barbaric treatment that is imposed on prisoners. When I must, I am capable of enforcing prison sentences.

The prisons, on the one hand, are correctly criticized in that they don't even make an effort to "rehabilitate." Ninety-five per cent of the budget and 95 per cent of the personnel is consigned to nothing other than custodial tasks. On the other hand, I don't believe they have the capability of really rehabilitating because of the conditions in society. Even with a more humane prison system there would, nonetheless, be a relatively high rate of recidivism for obvious reasons. People go to prison, and most get out. They return to a society, (1) often separated permanently from their families; (2) without any increased skills, capacities to function in a job; (3) penniless after having worked for the state as slaves making license plates, you know, for a quarter a day. You can't very well go to a local factory in your jurisdiction and say, "I want to get a job." "What can you do?" "I can make license plates." "Where did you make them?" "I made them in Jackson Prison"; (4) they come out with the stigma of being cons and into a society that already has an unemployment rate of about 190,000 to 200,000—just in the city of Detroit—and somewhere between five and six million nationally.

As long as those conditions exist, there is going to be crime. If, for example, people received better job training in prison, then maybe they wouldn't be recidivists—at least in the wholesale statistical numbers they are now. Yet, by the same token, someone else would be unemployed; someone else would be committing the crimes and being sent up so that it would be erroneous to focus upon the prisons. The illness in this society is not in individuals. The illness is in the economic arrangement governing this society. It is created to serve a special class and to enhance its profit capabilities, rather than serving the people by enhancing their prospect of a decent life.—An overview—O.K.?

*Given this society, is there nothing that can be done that would make prisons rehabilitative?*

They can't. Nothing in what I call "the criminal injustice system" can cure the basic conditions that breed crime in this country. Once we see the *system* as criminogenic, we can no longer point to the police and say they ought to be able to solve the crime problem; or point to the courts and say they ought to be able to solve the crime problem; or point to the so-called corrupt "Corrections Departments" in this country. That doesn't mean for a damn second that we shouldn't point to the police and the courts and the penal system and clean out corruption and institutional racism. They all exacerbate the problem greatly.

It's plain to me that insofar as a part of the rehabilitative process is the assumption of individual responsibility (although I personally don't accept individual responsibility in a criminogenic system), individuals should have a shot at purging themselves. In order (and I'm just speaking within this framework) to be able to think "rehabilitated," a person must not always blame the other person. But so long as we have, as we do in Detroit, 90 per cent of all people being convicted by guilty pleas—coming out of the assembly line as guilty—as long as people who go to prison are justifiably able to blame their presence there upon America's only working railroad, the criminal justice system, they will deny personal responsibility. They will say, "It was the lousy judge's fault." And it often is. "It was my lousy hack lawyer's fault." And it often is. "It was the racist cop's fault" . . . "It was the vicious prosecutor's fault" . . . On and on.

Even by bourgeois standards, in order to be rehabilitated one has to look in the mirror and say, "What did *I* do, what can *I* do about it?" And once they get to prison, folks have daily legitimate grievances against the institution that they're housed, or chained, in. They sit around day after day talking about the goon squad, about the vicious corrupted warden, etc.

So, even if one accepted for ten seconds their framework, you can see at each institutional stage, from the police on the street to the cop in the court, to the hack lawyer who doesn't visit you in jail, where the bondsman can't write a bond because you can't afford the price of bail (though presumed innocent), all the way through the assembly line and up to the disposition sent by the state corrections' department, folks will always be able to use all their time and energy *correctly* in rapping the system that sent them there. All this limitless potentiality for people to focus on the many gross defects in this system precludes rehabilitation even in the terms of this system—which I don't accept. Is that clear?

*Yes.*

I can tell you read me. That's cool. So you see, by my political analysis rehabilitation is not possible in this system.

*Let me see if I understand to what extent you would carry this argument. Should you not similarly say that the advan-*

taged, white-collar, Watergate criminal *is* also the victim of the very same system, and therefore no more responsible?

O.K. It really varies, and I guess one could put forward that criterion, I think it would be accurate. I've not thought that through before. Let me think. The cops who engage in police brutality, no less than lower-level soldiers, must be held responsible for their misconduct. On the other hand, I do indeed regard them, on a certain level, as victims. I guess I would have to say cops are victims. They happen to be such damn oppressive victims that one rarely has a chance empathizing with their plight, but the cops are simply tools. When you get up to Watergate you're reaching the folks who either directly are the problem, or very consciously represent that class that is the problem. And they're not victims for ten seconds.

*Why not? Isn't everyone raised in a society, according to your view, shaped by that society, and if you're going to follow that line of reasoning, equally victims?*

There's a point there. O.K. Assume that Richard Nixon is on trial and I'm his judge. Which would be just fine—I could trip on that for days. He'd get a fair trial here. There won't be a change of venue. I won't disqualify myself. By and large, I don't focus principally upon individual responsibility. While I might be able to understand how people can be socialized to victimize people, when it gets to that level it wouldn't decriminalize their conduct. Surely, one does draw the line at certain points? I think I can enumerate those.

Notwithstanding the fact that we're all conditioned to conduct ourselves in certain ways—is the person doing so motivated by his own profit, his own greed, his desire to maintain the inequities that exist by engaging in this type of criminality? When we talk about genocide; when you talk about corruption at the level of price fixing; when you talk about corruption at the level of maintaining plants and factories that, partly because of greed, kill people at a rate much greater than homicide in this country (if we were to provide for safe modes of protection, we would cut into profits); when people profit from crime that's institution-alized—then they are a *source* of the problem, they're not just *symptomatic* of it.

*Let me press you on this to make sure I understand your philosophy. Let's take a case of two men who are involved in highly organized, massive destructiveness—like active drug circulators, nonaddicts themselves—one coming from a white middle-class background with its advantages, and one com-ing from a poor black with its disadvantages—would you, in judging between personal responsibility and societal respon-sibility, say one warrants a greater or different sentence from the other?*

I might draw distinctions, given racism in the so-cialization process, but it would not be distinctions of any great moment. I'd burn both of their asses.

*So that when it comes to certain types of crime, you're will-ing to put aside your criterion of how much a person is a victim and how much a victimizer. Is that fair?*

Absolutely.

*So even though you were saying a while back that you don't fix responsibility on individuals as much as on systems, but recognizing that by your theoretical constructs almost every individual, including Richard Nixon, could be viewed as a victim, you resolve the dilemma by weighing the degree to which that individual is also the victimizer?*

Right. Maybe this clarifies it a little, although I'm not sure. When I send someone to prison who's a down-and-out person, who persistently engages in violent assaults on other little people, I regard that person to be both a victim and victimizer. I have sympathy for the defendant, and yet, I can't see any alternative. Even though the victims of this person's assaultive crimes are limited in number as compared with the number of victims of the criminals responsible for the Vietnam War, nonetheless, I feel obliged to send that person up. I'm doing so in order to protect society.

If it's the Ford Motor Company, than I add other elements to it. On the one hand, I ain't got a whole lot of sympathy, like while I can understand sociologically and psychologically how one comes to be this kind of exploiter, nonetheless they profit from it and engage in it on a wholesale basis. Then, I punish them to protect society and for exemplary purposes, thinking that the deterrent principle might mean more at that level than locking up someone who is raging mad.

*What if, in the previous example, the "little man" who is a criminal takes it out, not on other little men, but on big corporations?*

My framework operates this way. When I do imprison, my major concern is protecting people from assaultive crimes, rather than protecting property. Protecting people who are essentially defenseless. All right? I've gotten into situations where perhaps I've given some minimal time to a junky who's not assaultive, but he's got four or five previous arrests; he's been on probation; he's violated probation. Obviously, if he has been proven unresponsive to more sensible programs, then I might give some little sentence. I'll try to jolt him to be a little more receptive. Probably give him house time as opposed to prison time (in your terminology, jail time instead of prison time). Less than a year. Then I'd put him on probation and add some probationary conditions, hoping to jolt him so he'll be more receptive toward treatment. But that's the persistent violator of property. The persistent violator of people, the person of violence, and so on, I put away. To protect society I'd put that person away.

This is interesting, and I'm glad you've raised it—I haven't seen anyone who is persistently engaged in criminality directed against the wealthy. There are certain people that see themselves as political whose agenda is ripping off the wealthy. And I guess we see examples of that in different ways—if the Rap Brown defense was legitimate, that might be an example. There's a case out at Boston a couple of years ago that got a lot of headlines: a political left doing bank jobs, and one was from Brandeis University. It would be interesting if I got one of those cases. I'm not happy . . .

*You're not sure where you'd come down?*

I'd have to see. I sure wouldn't feel—it's hard to say. I'd have to see.

*Don't you have any absolute sense that when the law says "Thou shalt not steal," it is independent of from whom?*

No, I do look at from whom. The law also licenses a whole bunch of people, who have been dominating influences on what the law is and how it's enforced, to steal every day in this country. There's more than $2,500,000 stolen in oil depletion allowances every year in this country. When people talk about welfare bums, we know who the welfare bums are!

*Your position sounds like the opposite of what I've heard from some other judges, that is, "My jurisdiction is the law, not justice." Are you telling me that you see your responsibility is to justice and not to the law? [I asked this question knowing that this was not the case. Previous inquiries had* elicited, often grudgingly, respect for Judge Ravitz from many who hated and feared him. *He has proved to be enormously hardworking, dedicated, knowledgeable, and respectful of requirements of both the law and his office in ways not always anticipated.*]

No, I would say I'm obliged to function within certain limitations imposed upon me; by definition of the job I hold; the oath I took; and whatever value I ascribe to maintaining my position as a judge. Further, when I make decisions I'm willing to talk about them openly and not hide them. It means I can't cheat and go beyond certain bounds. The day might come when I'll think those boundaries are so constricting that I'll want to split, tell the public why I'm leaving, and walk out. But a whole part of what makes us radical judges effective today is that we *can* be open and honest, 'cause we don't have anything to hide— 'cause *we* ain't fixing stuff!

*Within legal bounds, then,* I'm concerned with exercising my discretion in such a way that I can lessen systematized oppression on certain classes of people by using the power of this office against the oppressors, should they ever find themselves coming through these portals.

*And that discretion based on personal values is ethical, legal, acceptable, and valid, within the contract of a judge's position?*

Right. Here's a contract. I took it openly; they wrote their own laws and I can abide by it better than they can. We're at this stage in an evolutionary process where, hell, if they just followed their own laws, that would be enormous progress. "You wrote it—we didn't. We might not subscribe to your system even, but all we want at this stage is, Follow your law!" We're following their law better than they are.

*If I understand what you have said so far, your value system is essentially this: for property crimes, almost any alternative to prison might be sensible; with crimes against the person, you will consider prison. This implies that you not only do not believe in rehabilitation, but do not accept the concept of deterrence, or for that matter desserts or punishment. Could you tell me a little of how you feel on these?*

When you're functioning on a day-to-day basis within a system that's in itself criminogenic, the concept of deterrence doesn't mean anything. It's almost nonexistent. Most folks don't decide that they're going to become criminals because they think that's hip! Most people who engage in criminality do so out of desperation. So I don't regard deterrence as any major factor. I can think of occasional cases when I think this might mean something. I guess it can only mean something in the most conspicuous cases that get attention. There was a right-winger who recently came into my court—a zealot patriot of the right, who has an ongoing feud with everything left of Mussolini, and with the Catholic Church in particular. He's disrupted services, things of that nature. Finally, he was charged with assault and battery on a priest who was holding a peace service after the escalation of the bombing by King Richard Nixon. I *did* think in terms of deterrence when I sentenced him to forty-five days. It was a case that had a lot of attention. I was saying to folks of his ilk that, if they violate the law in the name of super patriotism when they obviously don't have much allegiance to the First Amendment or the Constitution, they're going to get their asses locked up if they come through this court. I was not speaking alone but for a number of members of this bench. I used an advisory council before sentencing; maybe that would deter a few people who engage in misconduct on the side, rather than on a regular basis. But other than such special circumstances I don't regard deterrence as too important.

*Were you suggesting that maybe jail is only effective as a deterrent with middle-class "law-abiding" types?*

It's certainly true, to the extent that conditions of life either do or don't impel or force criminality. When you're dealing with poor people, conditions of life *force* criminality. There can't be deterrence when the crimes are impelled through desperation, or something like that. On the other hand, when it's an act of pure greed, it's absolutely unnecessary because the person already has two cars, swimming pool, etc. If the price fixers, and those engaged in white-collar crime, were burned in a fairly uniform way whenever we found these cases coming through the courts, and if they would come through with greater frequency proportionate to their high level of criminality, then, yeah, I think there the concept of deterrence would be operative.

*What about punishment as a reason?*

That's a good question to ask me in a year, not next week. I've got two manslaughter cases awaiting me. In one of them there is a history of assaultiveness but no prior record and my guess is if I sentence him to do some time, there would be a measure of punishment in it, coupled with protection. When I think of people taking life in ridiculous situations (both cases are totally ridiculous—really needless, almost motiveless), then you think, what can you do? Doesn't the person deserve some time? And that's thinking and talking punishment. What about the family of the deceased; how could they tolerate probation?

The other case is tougher. I'm really faced squarely with the question you asked, and I don't have an answer yet. Some of the criteria I'm examining now—for what it's worth to you—the guy is thirty-two, no prior criminal record; got drunk as a skunk with his roommate, his buddy; they worked together, drank together, lived together, got into a fight, and this guy killed him. His buddy was fairly assaultively oriented, but he didn't need to kill him in any way. It was in a sense an aberrational act. And yet it happens a lot. Now, I don't think he's likely to do it again; I don't think society needs protection from him; I don't think there's much rehabilitation needed. And yet he doesn't seem a whole lot remorseful—that's an interesting side note almost. I'm faced with the question of whether a person convicted by a jury of manslaughter in a senseless killing ought to be punished. Can he be placed on probation or not? The question is there and I don't know what I'm going to do with that one. Over a period of time it will, I suspect, come up with some degree of repetition. So the answer isn't in on that one. I don't have a very fixed spot on it, one way or the other. In this case I'm asking the probation department to look very carefully into his background, look carefully into his present situation. It's true that he's supporting his wife, five kids, and has been steadily employed. And if he had remorse—he might get probation.

That raises the questions of remorse. We're looking at very subjective factors here. It could mean only that he doesn't *show* remorse, phony or otherwise. And what does it mean that I'm looking for it—if, in fact, I am? I'm wondering about it, I'm not sure, I'm curious at this point. It's a couple of weeks off. People can feign remorse.

It's a commentary on this society that you see people who can senselessly kill, without a motive, people they know and don't hate and really not show remorse. Very interesting phenomenon. The ultimate was in a case that just amazes me. I've kept psychiatric reports on it although I wasn't directly involved. My old law firm represented a Chrysler worker who killed two foremen and another worker and the defense was one of insanity. The cause of the crime, I think we demonstrated very clearly, was American racism and conditions at the plant that drove him to the breaking point where he took three lives. But Chrysler Corporation and white racism took those lives, not John Doe. We had a very good case and we won it. Sometime thereafter, another worker in another plant killed a foreman after the foreman had fired him and there were some similarities, racially and otherwise. We were called in. When I interviewed the man in Wayne County Jail, he knew about the John Doe case, and he knew whom he was talking to; and he knew that if he even feigned a certain political posture, that would enhance his likelihood of having very, very capable counsel, at a minimal price. He had the flattest personality imaginable—it was just amazing to me. His position was "Look, I admit I needed my job. And I wanted it. And I killed him. And I thought it out first. And I knew the difference between right and wrong. And I didn't feel compelled to do it. I just did it. And I knew that I could have just kicked his ass because I'm a whole lot tougher than he. But if I kicked his ass, I'd have to always keep my head turned in case he was coming back to escalate it. So the only real way to solve the problem was to kill him. And I did."

He wasn't uptight, in any way. I was sure that any conventional psychiatrist would find him loonier than a bat and say it's a perfect insanity case. We didn't get in the case but I referred his family—they have some money—to hire a good psychiatrist, more than a lawyer because that's what they needed as step one. The psychiatrist—we're very limited in choices here—came back and said no insanity exists. I think he is probably wrong, but on the other hand it's perfectly right. This man was a product of society. He was the perfect product shaped by propaganda and everything else. He coldly analyzed it. Not an ounce of remorse. It was very bizarre. I don't think I've characterized it very well but there are the facts. It was the ultimate to which society really drives people and that is killing another person and not having an ounce of remorse and being able to justify it in many ways.

*Let me pin you on a hard one. You obviously give great weight and credence to sociological and economic mitigating, or even exculpating factors. What about psychological*

*excusing factors? Couldn't everything you said about socio-
logical conditions and the nature of the society forcing certain behavior be true of psychological factors? Supposing it
isn't the broad impact of society in general that victimized
him, but the narrow impact of one aspect of society, his
family, for example, his mother was bad to him, he was deprived; just the way society treats the black as a second-class
citizen, certain families may treat a child. In the same way
you introduce sociological factors, why not psychological excusing factors? Do you credit them? Do you use the same
reasoning and rationale?*

O.K., I don't, and I'll explain why. I share in, or
agree essentially with, your statement that you can always
take back the chain in causality deep enough to say that it
was predictable or darn near inevitable that this person
would do that action—we could offer some rational explanation to any act. But that is really taking free will out, damn
near, and then it really isn't leading to anything that might
approximate a solution. O.K. You can look at the political
and sociological and economic factors and you can say,
"Look, damn it, I'm on one side or the other." Being crude
and simplistic, for the purposes of establishing a point, you're
either on the side of the people or you're on the side of
profits. Whenever you rule, and act, you exercise your power
in a manner that's consistent with what side you're on.
For me that is people.

When you simply look at the psychological history, it
leads to really individualizing each case. In reality there usually is some rational explanation, but things aren't done in a
vacuum. Let's try to take it into a framework. Let's say that
a child of some member of the ruling class comes through—
a young adult engaged in a crime outside the spectrum of
what Daddy does—wasn't price fixing or anything like that.
Maybe he was selling some drugs, or merely using some
drugs, and I were to look at that person. I really *would* indi-

vidualize, I think. If the person wasn't an oppressor who victimized people on a wholesale basis, if it was an individual act of criminality, I would be sympathetic. I would take it into account even if he wasn't oppressed, in the political sense, but only in the home. I would at the same time try to make clear *what* I was doing and *why* I was doing it to try to raise the consciousness of that individual.

*You rightly worry that if you take the psychological route back, no one is responsible for anything. Isn't that also true when you take the sociological route? Also, 90 per cent of the poor blacks don't commit crimes, yet they're exposed to the same oppression. Aren't you still dealing with an aberrant minority? If it were only the system, why wouldn't you expect all the poor, all the blacks to commit crimes?*

Well, there are a lot of answers. I'm talking along class, not race lines. Only a minority of poor people do commit crimes, but it's a larger minority than statistics would have us believe. Only 20 per cent of the most serious crimes that are recorded are apprehended. So long as the system continues with the current divisions in society—economically, racially, and otherwise—there will remain predictably this substantial amount of crime. A *large* percentage (albeit a minority) of the deprived will persistently engage in crime and the only things that will change are the identities of the particular individuals, who because of breaks, heightened consciousness, or any number of fortuitous circumstances that cross individual lives and paths are apprehended. Is that clear?

[It was not clear. Judge Ravitz was caught in the same dilemma of causality that confounds psychiatrists in the law. It does not matter whether one ascribes behavior to emotional forces within the individuals or social pressures outside. To exempt broad classes of behavior from criminal

responsibility is to risk exempting all. At this point I felt I
had pressed sufficiently to mark the illogicality and was prepared to go on.]

*There is a whole movement these days against discretion in
the law. Both of us understand why discretion is in disfavor.
How do you feel about it?*

A caveat before I begin. There are two separate
considerations, local and national. First let me answer as it
presses upon the local milieu. They want to abolish discretion here in Detroit and I've got a very clear analysis of why
they want to do it here. Let me consider that first.

For decades, here as elsewhere, the "law and order" mentality has governed. The extreme disparities only exaggerate
the usual cruel and unusual punishments inflicted by a
whole rash of lousy law and order judges, who are invariably oppressive and racist. When extreme enough, it in-
vokes the liberals' response. But the lower end of those disparities, the common and accepted sentence, is itself excessive. Overriding that, you have a smaller number who are
serving triply harsh sentences. These are ones that are seen
to be cruel and unusual for sure. Now they want to level it
out this way: the *fewer* in number, who are getting doubly
and triply screwed, will get screwed a little less. The consequence will be that the bulk of the people will still get
screwed, except it won't show so blatantly. That's one level
of analysis that I think is probably true on a national level.

Bringing it home more locally, what's happened is that
the people in the city of Detroit have finally gotten it together and elected some progressive judges. I'm here, O.K.
Judge Gardner* is upstairs. Judge del Rio* is down the hall.
Judge Crockett* is upstairs. There are a number of people
in this institution who are not only refusing to impose the
double and triply bad sentences, but are also avoiding the

_____
* A group of radical or minority judges recently elected in Detroit.

traditional and still repressive sentences. They are imposing
sentences that more closely approximate justice.

In response to this is a whole movement in Detroit and
throughout Michigan. First, they now want to standardize
sentencing—to take away our discretionary power because at
long last there are a few individuals who are using it on the
side of the *people*, and in conformance with the Eighth
Amendment. They want to dilute our power. Coinciden-
tally with that, they want to take away the right of franchise.
Let's not vote in judges any more, let's have the élitist Bar
Association decide who is going to be our judges. Democracy at work? It doesn't work—we can never win! O.K.? So
they want to take that away.

The whole movement in this jurisdiction as elsewhere is
to disband the jury system. "Get rid of civil juries." Warren
Burger travels around this country calling for the abolition
of civil juries; civil juries are already down to six. The first
precedent for no longer requiring unanimity was in civil
juries, and last term, the Supreme Court said the same in
respect to criminal cases. And in the city of Detroit, they
want to destroy the local court and make it county-wide to
dilute the impact of minority jurors. We cleaned up the
jury system in a famous, historical case with respect to how
juries got picked in Detroit in 1970. Washed it out completely. Exposed it to be what it was. It was a gross example
of institutional racism.

Whenever there is any incursion into the system of persons who represent the people and are willing to follow their
laws, they somehow dilute it! I regard the standardization of
sentencing, as they want to apply it here, as enforced, institutionalized oppression. And so it's very dangerous.

Now when I think about it nationally the best example
is the California indeterminate sentences (which are pending in Lansing as well). What this really does is put vast
power in the hands of the select few, who have the mandate
to perpetuate the dominant law and order mentality which

controls all these institutions, but to do so in a way that won't be too transparent. And, so long as there aren't *too* many George Jacksons or Ruchelle Magees, it'll look O.K. But while less glaring, it is still consistent, across-the-board repression and oppression.

Now, what's the answer and alternative to all that? In my judgment it's what is happening here in Detroit, but in few, if any, other places. That is, the formation of an independent, mass political movement in this country. It's a race to see whether they will allow us enough latitude to continue to be able to use the electoral arena to put in people like myself who can change the institutions so they serve the people's interests, without having us stripped of power first.

That race is going on here—there are lots of crosscurrents. A case upstairs that was decided today—I don't know if you've heard anything?—the major political trial in the city of Detroit was just concluded. A jury of ten blacks and two whites just found Hayward Brown not guilty of anything on four counts of assault with intent to murder four Stress Officers in Detroit. The history of that case is too long to detail but the short of it is: Sam Gardner, who was elected along with me and is a progressive person, drew the case through their blind draw. He reduced, in total, the bonds from $72,000 to $8,000. In a cast that might be unprecedented in the annals of American jurisprudence, the prosecutor appealed his bond! Now the Constitution guarantees the right to a reasonable and not excessive bond. It doesn't in any way guarantee to the prosecution the right to an excessive, unreasonable, pre-trial bond when one is presumed innocent. And try as one might, one can't find a case anywhere where an appellate court raised a bond. The appellate court raised the bond back to $72,000 without having the trial record before them; without knowing anything about the individual before the court. They couldn't say how old he was, how long he'd lived in Detroit, does he have a prior record, does he have a family, is he employed?—they didn't know any of that shit which is standard criteria for a bond. They *summarily* raised the bond back up to $72,000 and disqualified Judge Gardner! This was an appellate disrobing and disenfranchising of Gardner, and the electorate of the city of Detroit at the same time. It was just incredible. The case went to his alternate who was, ironically, Crockett.* But they still have overriding power to dilute enforcement of the law in an unfair way.

*You, unlike most judges I've interviewed, admit that your politics, values, and feelings are a part of your sentencing?*

Sure.

*I assume that what is true for you is true for other judges. And since the biases of most judges would be, by your standards, opposed to the interests of the people, aren't you concerned that discretion will be abused?*

Yeah, there's no way . . . it's bound to be abused. I believe the solution to abusive discretion has been a part of the law for almost two hundred years. That's the Eighth Amendment of the American Constitution, which has been applied by the United States Supreme Court only three times; has been applied by the Michigan Supreme Court only twice (once they didn't even say it, but that's what they were doing—that was in 1880). You can shear excessively harsh sentences by using the Eighth Amendment. An amendment, however, which none of the appellate courts in the country have ever been willing to uphold. There might be some interesting reasons why they're unwilling to uphold it. One is that they'd have to touch too many sentences; two is they would have to touch the penal institutions as well, which also impose cruel and unusual punishment. So the answer isn't to homogenize or standardize, and to keep it all

---

* A liberal black judge.

bad. The answer is to enforce the damn law that has been in the books all the time.

*Do you think that things like appellate review of sentencing and sentencing by tribunals are hopeful or helpful?*

Yeah, I worked very hard on a case just today before coming here. I think it's fundamentally important, particularly in Michigan where you've got comparatively speaking a good Supreme Court. Probably one of the better Supreme Courts in the country now. I'm entirely in favor of appellate review but only in one way, that is, you may reduce excessive sentences—but you can't raise sentences any more than you can raise bonds. I'm very much for that.

In any state that has an automatic right to appeal, as Michigan does, you can go to the intermediary appellate court and see that the great majority of the appeals are really for sentences. That's because most of the convictions are on guilty pleas. A person sitting up there on the rock sees his rock partner got half-time, "You're here with the same background I have—yet you got half the time." All that should be handled by way of appeal and would incidentally reduce the expenses of litigation. I'm all for that.

Sentencing by panels—it's a little hard to say. It's good and it's bad. In this court we may use a sentence by panels; it's not mandatory and is left to the judge as an individual responsibility. I, for example, sought the advice of a sentencing panel before sentencing the right-winger referred to earlier. I did so in order to benefit from other judges' thinking, so as to make sure I wasn't being excessively subjective.

*What, by your standards, do you consider a tough sentence?*

It's too general. I mean, anyone who understands the nature of prisons knows it's a tough sentence to go to prison for a year. That's a tough sentence, and any person who thinks it's not should spend a year. If they're right and it's not so tough, it won't have cost them much! If they're wrong, the point will have been well proved and they won't doubt it again. So that's a tough sentence. But obviously people who are into asking those questions are doing so in another context, that of the individual case. Obviously, I can see where a one-year sentence, albeit tough in the terms of what it subjects human life to, still can be called a lenient sentence.

*Do you have any feelings about capital punishment? Is it ever justifiable?*

No. I suspect that I am in all candor a lot less hung up in terms of taking human life than a whole bunch of liberals. I recognize how people die in the world and have died historically. I'm not reduced to a fit of tears, as many bleeding hearts are, over the concept of capital punishment. Nor am I moved by certain religious feelings that other people have, not meaning disrespect for those principles. I'm just not motivated by those sorts of conventional, moralistic views that make some people zealous, anti-capital-punishment figures. Though I'm against it.

I'm against it in this country, at this time, because I know two things. I know, for one, it won't work. The state of Illinois from 1931 to 1965 had capital punishment; the state of Michigan did not. Those are fairly comparable states, and Illinois's rate of homicides year in and year out should have been less than Michigan's. It wasn't. The national statistics consistently show that states with capital punishment always had two to three times as many homicides as without. So I know it doesn't work and I know, which is more important, it is a tool of the repressive régime. It is a tool that's trying to exploit the hysteria of crime on the street—a very good political topic for rightist opportunists and it's trying to exploit it in a manner that offers no solution to people's real problems and in a manner that simply heightens the repressive apparatus of the state.

Its purpose is to promote an atmosphere conducive to creation of a police state, which they want and which they're actively working for. You can see it in all sorts of ways. The local prosecutor here who wants to run for governor has come forth with the proposition that we wouldn't have the problem of crime in Wayne County if only we would just abandon completely parole and probation. All persons convicted of felonies would get time. That's vicious, political propaganda on the part of a vicious reactionary who's politically ambitious. It doesn't offer a solution because all one need look at is reality in this country where 60 to 80 per cent (most figures are around 75%) of those who go to prison come back—recidivism. So what would we accomplish? You'd only give people the only thing the penal system is noted for, and that is an advanced degree in criminality. It's a nonsolution. Richard Nixon calling for capital punishment—a nonsolution. The local police commissioner running for mayor calling for Stress (you know, licensing police to kill citizens)—a nonsolution. All those folks have controlled these institutions for decades and they don't have any damn answers. All they have is dividing the people along race lines; along different layers of economic lines; all geared toward essentially following the pattern of movement toward fascism. There's a fantastic quote I'd be delighted to read to you from Adolf Hitler—are you hip to Hitler's quote? In 1932, he said:

> The streets of our country are in turmoil. The Universities are full of students rebelling and rioting. Communists are seeking to destroy our country. Russia is threatening us with her might and the Republic is in danger.
>
> Yes, danger from within and from without. We need law and order. Without law and order our nation cannot survive.
>
> Elect us and we shall restore law and order. We will be

respected by the nations of the world for law and order. Without law and order, our Republic will fail.*

Like him or not (I like him), agree with him or not, it is crucial to appreciate that what Judge Ravitz is doing when he utilizes his political evaluation to determine his sentence is what the law *requires* of him—and what every judge does, although rarely admitting it. Discretion is built into the sentencing procedure to allow each judge to exploit *his* perception of crime, criminal and circumstance, to plumb his mind and heart, to serve, within limits set by law, that elusive concept of justice which the law in its wisdom refuses to define. That is precisely what Judge Ravitz does.

* This quote is widely attributed to Hitler, but to my knowledge, has never been confirmed.

# CHAPTER V

# Judge Garfield

Judge Garfield received me in his home rather than the office, and the symbolic implication of that gesture foretold the openness, candor, and warmth that characterizes the interview and the man. Handsome, intense, and idealistic, he cooperatively started right in when, after a few formalities, I simply said: "Tell me about yourself."

I was born in X̲. The only boy—the first son and first grandson—psychologically I presume that is important. Lower-middle-class parents, father was a salesman. Neither mother or father graduated high school. Father was an immigrant, mother was first-generation. I grew up in a large family—my father had nine brothers and sisters, my mother seven brothers and sisters; my maternal grandparents lived nearby, my mother was the oldest, so I always had lots of younger aunts and uncles around me and lots of younger cousins. It was a very warm family atmosphere in growing up. Never impoverished in a very hard, gritty, no food on the table, no clothes on the back, sense. I'm forty-two. My father had had some money before I was born which he had lost in the Depression—I mean a few thousand dollars. He worked as a salesman, would travel a lot. He was a middle child. He had had a lot of trouble with his parents and difficulty with some of his siblings—had been forced to work at an early age—he never got to high school. He worked as a traveling salesman—not as the term is generally understood with long trips, he was home every night; but he would travel by car and peddle things by catalogue. Very warm father—mother was more the head of the family— fairly good relationship between them. Arguments and so on, but a solid relationship.

*Who were you closer to?*

It's hard to say. My father was very warm, less pushing, less ambitious. He accepted me more for who I was. My mother was more ambitious, more driving. But in a different way she was accepting too. I always had a bent for getting myself involved with controversy. On occasion this isolated me from others, made me unpopular, caused adverse comment and all that. Through all that, my mother was always supportive—as long as she felt I was doing right.

I was always outspoken. Went to public schools. Worked summers from my seventeenth birthday on—busboy, waiter, soda jerk, that kind of thing. I moved out of the house at, I think, about eighteen or nineteen when I was going to state college. I've been away ever since. My father died when I was twenty-six. My parents didn't support me after my eighteenth birthday. I was fortunately able to go to college where it didn't cost much money. I went to law school on the G.I. Bill, married once before when I was twenty-four in the army. Got separated while I was in law school. Got re-married when I was thirty-three.

My identification, for reasons not entirely clear to me, has always been—at least until I was a judge—with the underdog. Never had any doubts that I wanted to be a defense attorney for indigent people. I was a very aggressive and outspoken lawyer, and if I have to look for interpretations (I haven't been analyzed) I'd look to my mother. She was very strong and, in a way, I had to fight against her a lot over all the typical small things. She was very orderly and I was very sloppy, that kind of stuff. I cannot accept authority easily—I always fight authority. Had to be independent, had to be always pretty much my own boss. I did not take direction well or easily. I had some troubles when I was in the army—always fighting. But despite that, working pretty well within it; maybe that's something that related to the judgeship too. In our society it's a little ironic that I should be in a position of such authority—more power than any individual ought to have.

I was drafted in the army out of the law school in '52 and discharged in '55. Had trouble as an enlisted man, but went to OCS. While at OCS had trouble (graduated at the bottom of the OCS class, but graduated). In a way I think I was inconsistently thinking that I could combat the system, and yet live within it, without sacrifice of principle. The judgeship is very compatible with that—it may be the same dilemma.

[Unlike almost every other judge, Judge Garfield started, not with his opinions, but with himself. This could have been a psychotherapeutic session. Judge Garfield knew he was talking to an analyst and therefore he gave the analyst what he wanted. But it reveals more about Judge Garfield than his capacity to size up a situation and to do that which must be done. Certainly, it implies the devotion to duty of the latter, but also the sophistication to recognize the nature of psychoanalytic data; the openness and willingness to expose himself; and finally, it indicates that he is part of that liberal, intellectual, urban tradition that respects psychoanalytic premises. In many ways he epitomizes the best of that tradition and offers us a superb example of the strengths and limitations of the prevailing intellectual, liberal philosophy afield in the thickets of courtroom reality.

More specifically, Judge Garfield implies, and then directly states, the sources of his "identification." He is prepared to recognize that that which he "is" may be a greater determinant in his intellectual process than most judges are ready to concede.

After some discussion about the nature of judicial power and authority, I asked him how he would relate that to sentencing discretion.]

Sure. Do you want me to talk about the general problems, or my own approach to them?

*Either way—whatever you want.*

In effect, any defense attorney who is any good, and that automatically limits the number of lawyers it applies to, tries to control the sentencing process. Before becoming a judge, I was a defense attorney and my first concern was "Who am I going to appear before?" Could I get it before the right judge and could I get a commitment from him. *Certainty* is what the defense attorney wants. Given the nature of plea bargaining in our system, I would say that in 50 per cent of the pleas I accept, I have indicated on the record that my sentence will not exceed a certain amount. So the defendant knows at the time he enters the plea, generally, what his sentence will be. My own feeling is that that number could even be greater if we had in our court what they have in some—the device of pre-pleading investigations. A pre-pleading investigation would tell the judge everything that he would know anyhow after the pleading, but tell it to him before the pleading so that he could indicate to the defendant at that time what the sentence would be. Many cases go to trial primarily because the defendant is uncertain what the final result is going to be. If he knew, he would often plead guilty. A man might say he's innocent. He might or might not be, I wouldn't know. But the evidence against him might be substantial and the likelihood of his conviction might be great. If that were the case, as a defense attorney, I would say, "Do you want me to see if I can get a lesser plea in this matter? Is that something you're interested in?", and he'd say, "If I don't have to go to jail, I might be willing to plead guilty"—or, "If I wouldn't have to do more than six months," and so on. Then I would see what I could get for him. Obviously, that still goes on.

*You mention that when you were an attorney you were concerned with which judge you would go to . . . tell me a little about that.*

Well, there is no question that judges differ. Any defense attorney who has practiced for any period of time knows there are harsh judges and easy, reasonable judges, and so forth.

*Could you be more specific?*

Sure. We knew, for example, Judge Doe. He is widely renowned for his dispositional capacity—he was able to grant a great many pleas. He was excellent in terms of leniency on all kinds of cases, except those involving physical violence. Even with crimes against the person, such as a purse snatch, he'd be all right, as long as there was no accompanying physical injury. In that kind of case—white-collar crime, etc.—I'd try to get the case before him. Very often, by the way, the prosecutor is complicit in this. His interest is almost never in what happens to the criminal. His concern is with the conviction. It's an absurd dichotomy he draws. Having his conviction, he loses interest in the process for the most part. Very often, for purposes of expediency, he would cooperate in getting a case away from a judge before whom you were unwilling to plead, and getting it to a judge to whom you were willing to plead.

In addition, the administrative judges of our courts are very mindful of the capacity of individual judges in obtaining disposition. There are some judges who are excellent;

others are unable to engage in the process at all. Obviously, in a system that is overwhelmed with volume, it's important to know those judges who can dispose of cases and those who cannot. Good administration means assigning those judges who can obtain dispositions to those parts that have the most heavy calendars.

*What makes a judge good at disposition?*

It's hard to say. I'm viewed as one of those judges who is good at that. Perhaps since I'm one of them, I'll dress it up so it will sound somewhat favorable. But I think there are many fine judges who are not able to do that. First off, there must be neither a personal nor a philosophical revulsion against the process of plea bargaining. He must acknowledge the necessity of it, even while acknowledging the defects of the process. In a system inundated with cases, many of us feel we must do it—and are prepared to do it. Many judges are totally turned off by the concept of plea bargaining. If you want to get into that we can.

*I would like to get into that.*

Well, my own roommate right now is a judge who will not engage in plea bargaining. He feels it denigrates the dignity of the court. He feels it cannot be done in a principled way, because often the judge is compelled to enter into bargains when the motivating factor is the number of cases in court; or there are cases where a defendant cannot bargain voluntarily if, for example, he is locked up already. He feels it is a system that does not work fairly, and he will not participate in it. That's one level of it.

At another level is a person who may feel the same way but acknowledges the inevitability and the necessity of doing so in our system because our volume is so great. Nonetheless, for personal characteristics, he may not be very good at it. He may not relate well to people; he may be too rigid, or, if flexible, his determinations may be unrealistic in terms of what a case is worth, that is, evaluating the strength or weakness of a case. So that may be a judge who is prepared to engage in it but doesn't do it well.

I think the judges who *are* good at plea bargaining would not dispute the concerns of the other judges, but they begin with the necessity of it. There simply is no way out of our system, as presently constituted, but to plea bargain. We must do it. To do it well you must be relatively flexible. By flexible, I don't mean unprincipled—I mean familiar with the wide range of sentencing options, the techniques involved, and with a realistic orientation as to what a case is worth.

A case is dependent on the seriousness of the offense; the quality of evidence against the defendant; and often most important, the calendar condition of the court. You'll find disparity of sentences will always be higher in those counties where the plea-bargaining pressure is least. Plea bargaining brings down a sentence, never up. Of the neighboring counties, Purple County has much less volume. The sentences are correspondingly higher there. The D.A. will insist on higher pleas for the same kind of offense, same kind of defendant, same kind of prior record, same quality of evidence, since he can try more cases. Given the fact that he can reach more, he is prepared to do so. In our county, the volume is so overwhelming that these accommodations—however extraneous to the purposes of general justice they may be— are dominant. It simply can't be avoided.

*Are you saying that plea bargaining is a necessary evil—or that it is necessary, and it may not be such an evil?*

Well, I would put it this way. I wouldn't accept either formulation. Plea bargaining is ethically neutral. It can be done well, or badly. It is done well when extraneous factors are not present. It is done badly when they are. For example, a judge in the federal court told me his calendars are so light that on a given day he will have only one case scheduled for trial. Therefore, it's been his practice to call the parties in to his chambers to exchange all the information on which a good evaluation should be made. All parties would then indicate what they think the disposition might be. If all can agree on a fair and reasonable compromise, fine. If not, they can then go outside, pick a jury, and litigate the issue.

It seems to me that's plea bargaining in its ideal state. The case is discussed on its merits; the offered plea is one that appears to be fair, without any concern for the condition of the calendar; it is individualized and relates to the individual defendant, his background, etc.; he's under no pressure, he doesn't feel he may be rotting in jail another few months before trial, so he's under no pressure to plea for that reason. Under such conditions, it seems an entirely healthy process.

Now that is *not* the condition that prevails in our courts —it simply cannot. We have now thousands of cases pouring into our courts daily, most of which are entitled to a jury trial. We're confronted with the fact that until last month we had only one operational jury trial part; this month we have three operational jury trial parts. If you figure that a jury, working at maximum efficiency, can try one, two, or maybe even three cases a week, you get maybe ten cases a week disposed of. What about the other thousand that have entered that week? We have to find a way of disposing of them. If not, the jails will burst or the defendants will rot for a very long period of time.

*Does that mean that only calendar considerations are now operative?*

No, not only, but calendar considerations so distort the ideal that we're not even close to it. One of the unlooked-for benefits of such calendar congestion is that, in effect, if not legally, we have decriminalized our system. That is, those things like marijuana possession, gambling, prostitution, drunkenness—all the things that shouldn't be in our system—have by and large been moved out because we simply cannot process them. It's a matter of necessity. Most of the things I mentioned will be disposed of on the day they come into the court, and that I think is a healthy development although it has been produced by necessity, not by choice.

Obviously, there is some system of priorities for both parties. Working on the defendant is the feeling that he would like to keep the case as a misdemeanor in the lower court. If he's charged with a felony, he would like to put a guaranteed maximum on his sentence by getting the charge reduced to a misdemeanor. The temptation would be to plead to a misdemeanor as a way of limiting his punishment, rather than taking a chance of going to a felony court where the punishment is unlimited. That's one way the system operates. Now the judge and district attorney have to evaluate whether the charge is too serious to permit it to be properly reduced to a misdemeanor. So there is some discretion there in the evaluation process that goes on.

*For all practical purposes is it the judge and the D.A. who get together?*

For my part, we all get together. A case is called and papers are handed up to me by the court officer. The first thing I do is look at the court papers. Yellow back is a felony, more than a year; blue back is a misdemeanor, a year or less; a white back is a violation with maximum of fifteen days. Well, if it's a violation or misdemeanor I will automatically call the people up to the bench and start the plea-bargaining process. If it's a felony, I'll look at the complaint to see whether or not plea bargaining is in fact possible in the situation. There are many instances where it is not—homicide is one where it is not. The man may or may not be guilty, but if he is guilty it is not the kind of crime we *want* to reduce to a misdemeanor. It is too serious. So I look at the case and see whether there is a possibility of reduction of sentence. An armed robbery, a serious physical injury precludes it—can't really do anything. The issue to me is . . .

*Precluded in your mind but not in some other judge's?*

Oh no. When it gets up to the higher court, then the plea bargaining will be concerned with that and even more.

*Is it precluded because of law or your own moral feelings about it?*

Here it's precluded by law. But obviously in terms of judgment, I'm not prepared to reduce a murder charge to a misdemeanor. It's far too serious. It's interesting, some people, whom I admire widely, have indicated that either the judge or the prosecutor or both have too much discretion. My own feeling is that neither of us has too much discretion. To a large extent we are slaves to the system. While I have the appearance of great discretion, I don't have the reality of it. I work under the constant awareness of the burden of cases in this court which demand resolution.

There are only two things that will reduce pleas in our courts. One is incarceration, the other is the prospect of immediate trial. It has gotten so that, given the calendar congestion, if a person gets out on bail or parole, there is no opportunity to bring him back to trial, so there is no need to plea bargain. We have developed a whole new concept called "bail acquittal." For example, when I was teaching at the law school I had a murder case in which a mother

was accused of killing her child and was indicted for murder. I wanted to get her out on bail if I could. I worked it in
such a way that I was able to get her out on $10,000 bail.
When I got her out the D.A. said, "You've just gotten yourself a 'bail acquittal.' " He was right. Four years have passed
and that woman has never come to trial. The murder rate is
so great in Baker County, and there are so many *jailed* prisoners awaiting trial on murder charges, that unless there is
a notorious case, the fellow who is out on bail or parole
doesn't have to plead because he may never come to trial.
He's not rotting in jail and his case can't be reached for trial,
so he has every incentive to just sit it out and wait. The disparity here between the rich and the poor is particularly
important. The rich man, unless his case receives wide publicity, is much less likely to ever reach trial than the poor
man—just in terms of the way the bail system operates.
Physically, the case cannot be reached for trial. So, in effect
then, there is a bail or parole "acquittal."

I was just speaking to an assistant in the homicide office
on Friday who told me that he is going out of his mind.
They have so many murders that have to be tried that they
are plea bargaining with murder defendants who are dictat-
ing the outcome! They say, "I'll plead and get this case off
your hands. I don't care *what* I plead to, so long as I don't
have to do time. You promise me probation and I'll plead
guilty, but short of probation, I'm not going to plead."
They're in a good position to say that because there is no
other way we can reach the cases. There's no way to process
them all.

*Are you saying that even when the charge is murder, these
"bail acquittals," as you call them, may go on forever? Will
they never be brought to trial?*

If you want to make a pain of yourself, you can get
yourself tried. But you really would have to work at it. In
other words, having gotten this woman out on bail, if I

started making motions for speedy trial or dismissal of indictment, if I made a real nuisance of myself trying to get a
trial, then I'd get one. Then you emerge from the anonymous mass as a thorn in somebody's side, and they are going
to pluck it out. But normally you come in and they adjourn
the case for six weeks and you leave, and it can keep going
on like that. If you acquiesce to the system, don't make
motions, and so on, you can go forever.

*So you think the probability is that this woman in your
example will never come to trial?*

It's a little more complicated in her case. The D.A.
doesn't like to dismiss homicide cases. It's bad for his political image. They probably would offer her a felony with a
promise of probation right now if she wanted it. But because she has other children, and such a conviction would
endanger her right to the other children, she is unwilling to
take any plea whatsoever. As a result the thing will hang
around for seven or eight years, and then they'll work out
some way of just dismissing it. It will never come to trial.

*So if this is true for a homicide, it's certainly true for lesser
cases?*

Unquestionably. The big battle for a lawyer is getting them out of jail. If you don't get them out, you have
the pressure of incarceration. It may well be that once out,
the case will never be reached. Even when they're in, very
often the fellow will be offered less time on a plea than he
would do just *waiting* for a trial.

*Then judicial discretion, in a calendar as crowded as yours, is
reduced to a minimum?*

Yes, it is. Both the D.A. and the judge have to be
very conscious of calendar projection in the court. Every day
I get what we call tickle sheets indicating the amount of

cases on my calendar, the amount of cases in the jury trial part, how that calendar builds every day on that basis. I can know how to adjourn cases; when the calendar is getting out of hand; whether cases are building up; whether dispositions are falling low. It's a very big numbers game we work in. The sentencing is in large part dictated by those practical considerations. There's a terribly large gap between the volume problem in the federal court and the state.

[Judge Garfield describes a situation not appreciated by many students and critics of judicial procedure. Whether discretion is good or bad, and it will be seen that he is a strong proponent of the discretionary system, is somewhat irrelevant. For all practical purposes, discretion is minimized in the crowded calendar of the big city courts.]

If one compares the crowded and uncrowded calendar, one sees that only time allows consideration of the individual over the docket. In the crowded court, individuals are seen more in terms of their yellow sheets than their persons, and the nature of justice, in terms of individual considerations, is vulgarized. It could be argued that this is good. It is true that it will minimize the intrusion of the judgments of the sentencer and by excluding this will exclude his sensitivities and value systems. At least at the subtle level it will. Unfortunately, there is always room for the gross bias of the bigot, who only needs the fleeting moment it requires to establish the race of the victim. It, of course, also means that in the large city, where crime is often the highest, punishment is the least. This has often been explained in terms of desensitization; that is, by the fifteenth rape, rape begins to be seen as an everyday event. While this mechanism probably operates, the mechanical aspects of docket are equally determinants. Then once, for whatever reason, one begins to treat violence lightly, it encourages a general desensitization.

*Are you left any discretion?*

Yes, we're left some discretion. We can be selective. If the fellow is in jail I have some discretion. Take a situation where I have a man who is jostling [pickpocketing]. I select that because it's a crime that has a high degree of recidivism. A jostler will generally jostle again and again. He usually has a long record of it. You know when he hits the street he's going to go back to it. It's a case that calls for time, simply as a way of keeping him off the street and keeping him from doing this.

Although the crime is not one that shocks, it's not an unserious crime. When a person's wallet is stolen from his pocket he feels violated, deprived, unsafe in that kind of city. He feels outraged. So you'll get a defendant who will come before you with eight yellow sheets—forty convictions for the same kind of thing. Now he's back for the same thing again. Now that kind of defendant would get a substantial sentence if we were in the federal court. By substantial sentence, I mean nine months to a year. There's little sense in not giving the maximum in that situation. Not that you expect him to change—although that hope dies hard—but simply because you know if he returns to the street in a few days he'll be back doing it again.

By and large we can't do that and the defendant can become quite arrogant in that situation. They'll come in and say they want thirty days, they'll sort of dictate that. They figure it's worth pleading and getting thirty days because they'll probably be lying around the jail for thirty days until they get to trial anyway. In criminal court we can get to trial with some expedition if we select out the cases properly. Those in jail are most likely there because they've got long records, and they're not wealthy people. Well, I won't give them thirty days, but a judge in arraignment will often offer them sixty or seventy days simply as a way of getting some pound of flesh and keeping them in jail for a little while. Then we turn them back on the street. Much of the increased crime wave of late, I think, is because plea bargaining has so reduced sentences that we turn rather confirmed recidivists back on the street much earlier than we used to. Then we have to catch them all over again. It's very disturbing. Not that jail is a happy solution. It's never more than a partial solution; it never does more than protect the community for a period of time.

[Judge Garfield believes in "heavier" sentences. Judge Stone,* on the other hand, wants to reduce them. No better example exists to indicate how little can be told about a man by the nature of his generalized statements of philosophy. This is not to impugn the honesty of either man. I believe Judge Garfield as I believe Judge Stone. But such statements only have validity within the context of the definition of their terms. It is by their definitions of "heavy" and "light" sentences (which vary among the men using them) that one understands the nature of judicial philosophy.

Judges, too, have self-images. None of them likes to think of himself as harsh nor, on the other hand, do they like to be believed pushovers. Almost everyone believes himself to be a moderate sentencer. Again, it is not in defense of his public image that a judge will say this. It is in defense of his personal and private image. It is what he wishes to believe about himself, not what he wishes you to believe about him.]

*Do you think if there were heavier sentences it would do more?*

Yes, I think it would. I think when the sentences are as low as they are for many of these crimes, it becomes almost a risk of the business. It's like an occupational expense. If all you do is thirty days, it's worth it once or twice

* See Chapter VI.

a year. It's not a deterrent any more. If you're away for a year, however, you think twice. It's more of an inconvenience. Thirty days these fellows can do standing on their hands, but a year I don't think they can.

*A year is a significant thing, then. How about five years?*

Well, I don't know. I've thought a lot about it. I don't think a sentence should ever *exceed* five years except in the most outrageous of circumstances. And by saying that I don't deny that a lot of the defendants we have to deal with are so confirmed, and so hardened, so unaware of the impact that they have on others' lives, so indifferent to that, that they'll be back and do it again. But we don't know! That's one of the things that occupies me and it seems to me that a five-year term even for a most serious crime takes a significant part of a man's life away—gives him too much time to live with that, and may have some adverse effect on him.

I work on rather gross criteria. My own theory is that, excepting such crimes as jostling, a man's criminal life is limited. The only two solutions we have for crime are aging and weather. The crime rate goes down in bad weather, and the crime rate goes down with aging. If I have to, I'd say a man's active criminal life is between sixteen and thirty. I suppose hormones have something to do with it. A few burglars are older than thirty, a few active robbers are older—but they are very few. The ages between eighteen and thirty, the late teens and twenties particularly, are the optimum years for criminality. After that whatever happens, happens. You slow down.

*Yet you set the limit at five years. Some people are talking about twenty years, life sentences.*

I just think it brutalizes us too much. I'm not satisfied this fellow won't go out again, but I'm satisfied five years has got to be a factor any man reckons with. It has to be something that has impact, not like thirty days. It may make him worse, although I don't believe that it necessarily does. I do believe (however psychologically poorly grounded it is) that men are generally formed by the time they come to the criminal courts. Characterologically there is precious little we can do to change that; we don't have the resources or the know-how and it may be good that we don't. I'd worry a little if we could change people at will. I am not sure it isn't better that we can't make them so malleable and responsive to our desires. I think I would worry about a society where we set out to do that—through psychosurgery, conditioning, or some other way. It's good that we can't, and yet it creates a lot of problems. When you've taken five years from a man's life, and I assume that is justifiable only for the most serious of crimes, he may go back to it again—but he may not. How do we know? It seems to me after five years, he's entitled to another chance anyway. We would at least hope that we would try to make re-entry easier—halfway houses, etc. I think we should move toward the European system where, with very few exceptions, the sentences don't exceed five years. It's certainly true in Scandinavian countries, anyway. By and large, that should be a maximum sentence. I'm not talking now about a mass murderer or anything like that. But in robbery, or that sort of thing, one or two years can often be enough.

*What is the chief purpose of the sentence?*

For me, the purpose of the time is purely incapacitation. I have no illusions about jail as presently constituted, and I don't think I have much illusion about jail even as potentially constituted. For me, jail is incapacitation. It's the knowledge that if I return this man to the street, within a half-hour he'll be back doing the same thing, and there-

fore I cannot. It may make him worse, it certainly will not
rehabilitate him. It may even complicate his life in terms of
ultimate rehabilitation. But I simply cannot return him to
the street.

Obviously, where the crime is one of jostling I can live
with ninety-day or four-month sentences; and while I think
it is not an ideal, nobody's blood is in the street because of
it. But where, especially of late, we have a lot of crimes
where young men steal and beat old men and women, I feel
differently. It is a terribly frightening crime for the aged.
You have to see what it does to the victims. My own feeling
is, that has got to be treated in terms of prison (although
even there you can't be inflexible).

I have had two young men before me for that kind of
crime last week, where I allowed them to go into a Court
Employment Project—it's a diversionary project instead of
prison. They're both nineteen, from what we know they
have no previous record. What they have done is terrible,
but before I am willing to say there is nothing to do with
these fellows I would like to see if we can utilize this program with which I have had experience and some faith. If
it doesn't work I can always send them to jail, that was my
feeling. Jail should be a last resort. But I think quite clearly
it ought to be a resort when you're satisfied nothing else will
work, and they'll go on.

[Judge Garfield is the quintessential liberal—at the end of
promise. He is, willy-nilly, psychiatrically and developmen-
tally oriented. He can no more shed this completely than
he can shed his body image. His intellectual sensitivities tell
him that there is a limit to that sociological tradition which
has been the pervasive religion of the intellectual community. He feels betrayed by its methods. He can tell us that
he does not "believe in rehabilitation"; but Judge Garfield
is a "believing" man; he is a humanist, and he must believe

in something. So while he no longer trusts his frame of reference to shape the future, he must cling to it to rationalize his past.]

*What about the argument that even when used for purely preventive purposes, jail is ineffective because you are getting such a small percentage of the criminals, maybe one out of fifty?*

I don't think so. While I cannot substantiate it, my feeling is that in the course of a year we capture almost all of the street criminals in the city. We let them go again. If a fellow is robbing an old lady of her pocketbook, I assume he is doing it fifteen times a week. That old lady has maybe three or five dollars, maybe ten—but it's very little. If he's doing it for a drug habit, or because he wants to live high, he's got to do it with some frequency—he can't stop with one. It's a rather compulsive thing. I've had some defendants before me on various hearings where the issue has been something else, who have admitted to seven or eight snatches, shoplifts, robberies, etc., a day. Why only one? These fellows aren't mastermind criminals who sit down with plans and maps and timetables; they're just stupid criminals. Our system is so structured that unless someone commits crimes in great numbers, they'll never get caught. Statistically the probabilities then turn against them. You have to trip over a police officer to get arrested. If you commit seven or eight robberies in the course of a day, you *may* manage to get arrested.

My feeling is we probably get all the purse snatchers in this huge city. But we work as though each is an isolated crime. I can't sentence them for eight robberies when they're only up for one. In my sentencing I will sometimes go into it with the defendant, whether he's committed others, or whether he's in court for only this one. It's unfair, however, to sentence him for the unsubstantiated ones. But to be immune to the fact that he probably has, is equally wrong. How much weight to give it is a difficult problem. So my feeling is we reach them all because that is the nature of the occupation. To earn a living they do it repeatedly and every day. Except for bad weather.

*Were we in a more ideal system, what would be some factors determining prison, or otherwise? What are the factors that weigh on you now in such a decision?*

Well, the dominant factor would be whether I would be satisfied that if I release them they'll go back and do it again. How do I make the judgment? Partly on past records; partly on current circumstances. If in the past he's been arrested for five robberies in the last twelve months, then most likely he'd go back. Is he employed; addicted to drugs; does he have a family; is there any evidence of any attempt to reform himself at this time; is the crime one of violence or seriousness?

I suppose it would break down into three categories: the defendant who clearly falls into the category of no jail; another clearly jail; another marginal. Sometimes there are strong arguments for incarceration, and yet you don't feel at ease with it, because the man evidences a degree of tiredness with the criminal style of life—some voluntary attempts at change, either job seeking or drug programs, or what have you. What I've done increasingly there is simply to acknowledge what has been done, and say I don't know if this fellow is a good risk or not. But then I see if I can't get him into a program, and I defer sentence. I tell the defendant that if he goes into this program and does well, he need never worry about going to jail, I won't send him. If, on the other hand, he absconds from that program, as some of them do, he must be prepared to do the maximum amount of time. I tell them honestly that I don't know them, the information I have is incomplete, but he'd indicated to me his seriousness in changing his style of life. It may be sincere or gratuitous, and I can't know which. The only way I can find out is by what he'll do in this situation.

*A lot of the things you list are factual things, like number of previous convictions, job status, and so on, that we might feed into a computer for sentencing. What about you— you're a person—could a computer replace you in determining sentence?*

My own feeling is that a computer might replace me with profit.

*Are there not things which are specifically you as a person and which go into sentencing decisions?*

Yes, I think so. It's hard to speak abstractly as to what they are. I try to indicate it through specific examples.

*In the beginning of our talk, you mentioned Judge Doe, who's pretty soft on anything except violence. Now if we were talking about Judge Garfield, what would you say about your hierarchy of crimes?*

Well, I ride my bike to work so you might think I would be harsh on bicycle thefts, but that's not so. I think my position is: except for the most serious crimes, I would generally opt for nonincarcerative sentences with a defendant who has no prior criminal record. That is, if there is a reasonable program as an alternative, and the probation officer thinks there is any reasonable chance of success, I would rather err at that time in that direction. There is always time to send a man to jail. If he quits the program and goes back to what he was doing, he most likely will fall into our net within a month, and then I can send him to jail. I can always send him to jail if he doesn't take advantage of what little we do have to offer.

[Here we see the continuation of the paradox and contradiction. Judge Garfield doesn't "believe" in rehabilitation, but he still *believes*. If incapacitation, isolation from the community, is the only remaining purpose of incarceration, as he has previously stated, why does he now "opt" for nonincarcerative sentences? It does seem a contradiction. Perhaps it is that Judge Garfield recognizes other considerations beyond rehabilitation. He is aware that while there is little good that prison can do, there is much harm. It may be that his opting for nonincarcerative sentences is his willingness to give up the incapacitative value in order to prevent the potentially greater cost of the impact of imprisonment on the offender.

For our purposes the crucial question here is not why Judge Garfield does what he does, but that he does it. Judge Garfield does not imprison offenders when he can avoid it. What does this mean for justice on a comparative basis? Obviously, while justice may represent more than equity, equity is an essential part of any definition of justice. Judge Garfield is a fair man, as fair as we are likely to find. He will treat all his charges with equity. But even had he no measure of personal bias (an impossibility), he, in his person, would introduce a depressing inequity into the legal system, because one must juxtapose his attitude about incarceration against an unknown Judge Y's. What kind of equity or justice exists in a system where the luck of location, time of event, change of docket—not nature of offense—determines which judge the offender appears before, and, therefore, at which end of the broad spectrum of potential punishments the deliberations will begin?]

Given my general bias against incarceration, I then try to grade consideration of it. We had a woman who was arrested for shoplifting. At that time we didn't exactly dismiss the case, but said don't do it again. I wasn't the judge, but I would have done that too. Here is a woman of thirty-five who has never been in trouble before but gets arrested for shoplifting. Maybe it's impulsive as opposed to professional. She's probably been frightened; you count to a certain extent on the trauma induced by the involvement with the system, and maybe the fear alone will be the deterrent. That was in January. Then she came in again—not before me. The judge gave her a fifty-dollar fine or five days in jail. *That* I think was a mistake. I would have given her a substantial fine and no jail. In effect, she walked off scot free. Now this is a different condition: she finds it's not bad, it's a good business, high profits and low overhead and it feeds whatever psychological mechanism is working here. Then last week she comes back again for shoplifting and now there is good indication she does it regularly. I sentenced her to thirty days—not because shoplifting is so terrible—she does it only in department stores, not little shops.

[This is an interesting bias which Judge Garfield shares with the general community, who might join with Abe Lincoln in walking a mile to return a dime to the local merchant but will enjoy and entertain every opportunity to cheat that apotheosis of arrogant anonymity, the Telephone Company.]

I didn't do it in rage but it seems to me that she has to know each time she comes in, she's in for substantial periods of jail. Thirty days isn't so much, but for someone who has never been in jail it will make her think about it in the future. She may or may not go back to shoplifting, I don't know. What I try to do is deal in certain increments. In this case, I could see another judge giving her a five-hundred-dollar fine, but I felt she was being encouraged by merely fining. No real time had elapsed between being brought up. I feel jailing at this point is rational in the sense that I can explain what I've done, but I don't have great confidence that it will work. For one thing, there is no guarantee that she'll come before *me* the next time.

In a way it's all absurd: we're not breaking the chain, or intervening in such a way that, apart from incarceration, we're doing anything. It is characteristic of judges like myself. We accept those defects in the system, even if we don't acquiesce to them.

*Obviously, you have certain values about various crimes, independent of the individuals. For example, beating up a helpless old person bothers you a great deal.*

I have both a mother and mother-in-law who are somewhat aged, but I really don't feel that's crucial since neither has been victimized this way. Seeing these people in court is terribly troubling, especially since the injury is gratuitous. They grab the pocketbook and the woman says, "Stop," "Don't," or "Please," and bang, they smack her on the head and down she goes. The fear these older people show! I haven't really analyzed it, but there is a disproportion between these young strong boys and those old ladies. That shouldn't by itself be enough. I suppose it's also what the crime indicates about the criminals which frightens me the most—the absence of any awareness of the impact of what they've done on other human beings. I find this most frightening. I don't think you can break through that! It's either their own bringing up or some deficit of expression, of feeling, or perceiving, of warmth. I don't know. You see a kid of nineteen or twenty. He's doing this to an older person, and there's no sense of his awareness of them as people, or even awareness of his own predicament. He simply doesn't care. In jail, outside, what difference does it make? I don't think many defendants we deal with share the abhorrence of jail I would feel, or most of my friends would feel. There is a resignation about it, a willingness to accept things as they come. Very often I think even when they're bargaining for less, it's part of the game—it's not real. It's not really something they are especially interested in, but it's the male thing to do.

*Do you think you take the crimes more seriously than some of your fellow judges?*

I tend to think most judges would view that as a serious crime. As a defense attorney I used to see all the different judges. Now as a judge, when they're sitting, I'm sitting, so I don't see other judges. I have lunch with them occasionally but I really don't know. I tend to think, from what I know about them, they would evaluate that kind of crime as more serious than most, short of murder.

*Aren't there some crimes that you take lightly, others would take quite seriously?*

Oh sure, we have our judges who are very upset by. obscenity prosecutions. I think obscenity prosecutions are a total waste, doomed to failure. They're futile. There are other judges who are very concerned with prostitution. I don't think prostitution should be *completely* decriminalized, I think it retains certain public nuisance aspects. I have no problem with the call-girl type of thing. I don't mind if they just hold themselves available on the corner or what. I have problems with women overtly soliciting, bartering.

*Why does that bother you?*

I think people should be able to walk the streets in relative freedom and without unnecessary nuisance. The idea of a man and woman sleeping together certainly doesn't bother me, even the money doesn't bother me. There are other aspects which seem sad. I think it's outrageous that we should have put the whole weight of this on the woman, allowing the man to be the hero of the prosecution. Apart from those considerations, it seems to me that if a man and a woman want it, they should be able to have it—those who don't should not have it thrust upon them. A number of people complain that they're walking the streets with their wives and someone comes up and solicits them. I don't know how true that is. A man is not going to leave his wife and go with a prostitute, so it doesn't seem like a good business tactic. It's never happened to me or anyone I know directly. While I don't think there should be this aggressive solicitation, I would like to see it legalized, so the girls can have medical examinations, they could have a union—the whole damn thing. So I'm not generally concerned with the moral issue. There are some judges who are—they tend to be the older judges.

*Do you think it generally tends to be an age or a religious difference?*

I think there is probably a religious difference in it. The more religious will be that way. I think I find both Jewish and Catholic judges who are actively involved in their religion are more moralistic and judgmental in that regard than the others.

*What about the suggestion that, on a morals charge, one is better off with a Jewish than a Catholic judge?*

As a general rule, I think that's right. Although the Orthodox Jewish judges can be hard on that. Some of the toughest judges in the obscenity area have been Jewish.

*Are there other generalities that you think are true that you could make?*

You know, I haven't been brought up in those terms—not even as a defense attorney. I was determined to know the judge I was in front of, and what he was like. If I didn't know from past experience, I would assiduously contact other defense attorneys who may have had a lot of experience to find out about the man.

*What choice does the defense attorney have?*

He *had* much more choice then than he does now. But he has choice. For example, if a defense attorney is good he should get a schedule of who is sitting in arraignment. If the case is not disposed of in arraignment, what court will it be assigned to? Who is in that all-purpose bar? Who is the back-up judge who supports the one that is sitting, and who is in the jury bar? Then you ask yourself which one is best, and where can I get the best deal?

*Is the prosecutor doing the same thing? Does he have more power or less?*

He's not interested. He's just disposing of cases— he doesn't care which judge he comes before. Occasionally, a case will arouse his interest and his ire. But by and large he's not that interested. Judge Apple [a federal judge] has been engaged in a war with John Lemon [district attorney], and I with Fred Plum [another D.A.] in trying to get their offices to take a position on sentencing. Both of us find it incredible that a prosecutor should go to all this trouble to get a conviction and then lose interest. They don't care what the officer has to say about the case, what facts might be known, what policies might apply. Why are they in this if they just don't care? They're not only totally disinterested, they're *aggressively in opposition*. It's a frightening thing. I can't even get the D.A.'s office to bring their files to court on the day of sentencing! They file their cases away once the plea has been entered. They could bring the file for me to take a look, and see what there is of interest and relevant— but they won't.

*Would you be considered a tough judge, an easy judge, a defendant's judge?*

Well, my background was always defense. As a matter of fact, in twelve years at the bar, I never represented a client for a fee. For the first six years of my legal life, I was a legal aid attorney. For the next four and a half years I was director of an O.E.O. antipoverty legal services program. For the last year and a half I was a full-time professor at the law school just representing indigent people and running a criminal law program there. During that time I had written and lectured on defense of criminal cases. I was very active in civil liberties work. So everybody would have thought I would have been defense-oriented. I think that, given the spectrum of judges and in terms of sentences, I'm still viewed favorably by defendants. The way I judge, that is, when a man takes a plea before me, I always offer him the option of either being sentenced before me, or letting the case take its course, in which case the judge who's sitting at the bar that day will do it. Obviously, if I were horrible they would rather choose the unknown on the basis of chance. I would say 95 per cent of the time they ask me to keep the sentence in front of me. They know, I think, that where I have an old lady beaten up by a defendant who has a prior criminal history, the guy's going to do time; but they may feel that, even there, I may give less time than another judge.

Obviously, there are more lenient judges. So, in fairness, if I said, "Do you want the case before me or before Judge Lenient?" they would say, "Before Judge Lenient." But that's not the choice. I would say I was somewhere in the middle.

The way I define my role is that I want to be extremely demanding of the attorneys who appear before me. I want to insist upon the best preparation I can get from them. It seems to me that's the only guarantee of integrity in the system, that both sides are well prepared, creative, aggressive, and thorough. Good counsel is what makes the adversary system work, and if I don't have it, then I'm going to make more errors than I would otherwise. A demanding attitude is the first part, fairness is the second part of it. I don't want anyone else to feel I'm their man—the prosecution or defense. So . . .

*Do you think your time on the court has moved you toward cynicism or toughness?*

Obviously, my perspective is different as a judge than a defense attorney. When I was a defense attorney, I could represent a man accused of beating an old lady and do my very best, even if I knew or had good reasons to suspect that he was guilty. While as a citizen it might give me some pause, as a defense lawyer it did not. I was aggressive, thorough, and forceful in my role. So obviously my perspective has changed in that regard. I don't think that's a change in principle. Just in perspective. I want defense attorneys to be the way I was—to fight as hard as they can for their clients—and do the very best for them. That's what I say will guarantee the integrity of the system, to the degree it can be guaranteed.

I'm fairly guarded in my judgments of people. Having worked with defense for many years, I know they can lie and be manipulative. And they can be so sweet and likable; they vary. The puzzle for the judge is, "Who is this guy standing here?" He comes out here, and there's a wall between us. He's worried about what I'll do to him. He's waiting to hear the operative words—in or out. I don't feel conversation with the defendant is especially fruitful. Often they're inarticulate, confused, fearful, simply lacking insight. Probation or pre-sentence report doesn't tell me too much about him. In many ways it's a blind thing. If it's someone who has never been arrested before, my impulse is to take a chance on him—try probation before sending him to jail. If I'm wrong, there is always time to send him to jail. If the fellow has nine yellow sheets, forty-five convictions, and now he's here again, and he just got out a week ago, then my feeling is he's a liar. I don't know.

[Judge Garfield trusts his "impulse." This is an honest response, and not an unsophisticated one. Ultimately, it is the response only the secure intellectual will offer. Most professional evaluators recognize that decisions are made within the first ten minutes of an interview; that they are made on the basis of an emotional Gestalt; and that the reasons filled in on the rating form are usually rationalizations after the fact rather than descriptions of the mechanisms of decision making. This does not mean that there are not rational factors which go into the decision, but they may be on such an automatic level that they are both unwitting and unanalyzable by the person making the decisions.]

*What good would more time for evaluation do you? Would it really help? Wouldn't you be up against the same thing?*

You're asking what I think we ought to have, to make more discriminating sentences possible. All I've got now is "in or out"—which is terribly inadequate. Since "in" is rarely good except for incapacitation, and "out" rarely good for meaningful intervention in the lives of the defendants, you get a sense of futility no matter which way. Largely, you use jail where you feel the public safety requires it. If you're saying what would I like to see, I would like a wide range of alternatives with graded emphasis: intensive, meaningful halfway houses, work-release programs, weekend incarcerations, sometimes men working in the day and coming in at night. All kinds of more comprehensive programs. The problem with the programs now is they're too singly focused on employment, without attending to the other aspects of the person and his problems which may be causing the difficulty. Unemployment may be one of them, but only one. What about his alcoholism, or addiction, or the place he has to live?

*Do you think all this is going to bother you even more when you start handling felonies, where the sentences are higher?*
[Judge Garfield was about to be elevated to a higher court.]

It seems to me if I had wider alternatives, I could put fewer people in for whatever sentence, and that it would work out better. Obviously, the issue would be, Is there a reasonable expectation of success for this program? With many programs now, after interviewing, the report invariably says they feel the person is sincerely motivated. They say that 100 per cent of the time, but they're right only 50 per cent. I don't know how to tell if they're right or wrong. I'll guess too, and I'll be wrong often. But that's the responsibility I have to take. I'll look into the defendant's past history, then decide.

One of the interesting things that comes out from the bad working of our system is exemplified in a case I had a few months ago. Another judge of my court had sentenced this defendant to a year in jail for robbery. A legal aid attorney got the defendant out on a low cash bail pending his appeal. Having got him out on that certificate, they failed to do anything—they simply forgot about the appeal. Meantime, the appeal was dismissed because it was never perfected. The defendant received a notice to come in and surrender, and serve his year in jail—this, mind you, a full year after he had received his sentence. I asked if he had been arrested during the year, and he had not.

What struck me was that this guy, out on fifty-dollars bail, gets a notice to surrender, and in he comes! That struck me as very positive, it didn't seem like he was still addicted. I

said, "Make up a new pre-sentence report, and in effect, he'll
be out on probation." Sure enough, the new report showed
he's off drugs, he's employed, he's single, etc., hasn't been
in trouble that we know of. In addition, he makes a nice
appearance, returns to court three or four times, always on
time, alert to what was going on. I placed him on probation.
From the original pre-sentence report, most judges would
have given up on him and placed him in jail. But here,
through inadvertence really, we find out it wasn't necessary
at all. It's a shock. These people have resources which because we don't know of them, we have no way of allowing
for. That to me is why I move increasingly toward deferred
sentences. When I have doubt, I feel I should put it over
for four or five months and get another probation report
then. If rearrested, in you go. That's the only way I can
attempt to reach that kind of individual.

[The difficulty of accurate predictions of behavior is here
confirmed by Judge Garfield, although he would be the first
to recognize that one exception does not altogether upset
the validity of certain statistical determinants of behavior.
Still, on an individual basis, it can be shockingly inaccurate.

More important, Judge Garfield expresses little faith in
the pre-sentence report. Generally, most of the judges interviewed approached these with great faith. In actuality, pre-
sentence reports are not very good. Those that I have in-
spected would not have been highly valued in a department
of sociology. But if not good on an absolute scale, in comparison with what else is offered to the sentencing judge
they seem spectacular. Judges with lesser intellectuality are
very impressed by these reports. But so also is an intellectual
like Judge Stone. Here, the respect for the pre-sentence report derives from a different source. It is merely one more
extension of the respect for professionalism that is traditional to the conservative. This respect for the expert is en-
hanced in Judge Stone by a training that is distant enough

from the social sciences to permit glorification. The closer one is to the field of behavior and sociology, the more familiar one is with the incredible failure of these disciplines of man in solving the problems of antisocial behavior. Repeatedly, one sees judges publicly pleading for more psychiatrists to treat, for example, drug addiction. Why? Dynamic psychotherapy has never been effective in the treatment of drug addiction and given the nature of this acting-out condition probably never will be. Why then a constant clamor for a larger budget for this conventional kind of treatment? It probably represents that massive denial that occurs with frustration. When there is no treatment for a condition except an inadequate one, rather than face the despair of a hopeless problem, we utilize the inadequate one and pretend that it is effective.]

*What percentage of the crime that comes up before you do you feel is drug-related?*

A lot of them are drug-related, but I don't really think that it is crucial. An addict has a lot of ways of satisfying his habit, and the *way* he chooses is very self-revealing, and that has very little to do with drugs. The guy who robs old ladies and is an addict is very different from the addict who shoplifts, or the addict who sells small quantities to feed his own habit. My feeling is that most drug addicts, more than half, would be criminals anyhow. Obviously, some of it is drug-related, and it manifests itself mostly with people who do nonviolent crimes.

*How do you feel about capital punishment?*
[This is a question which, because of its emotional and political implications, I asked of all the judges.]

I can't answer it briefly. In a way I'm not opposed to it. In a way I am. I'm not concerned with Manson or

Speck*—my feeling is the world is better off without them and I don't think psychiatrists will learn anything much of any benefit. My problem with capital punishment for the most part is dispositive, the way it operates in our system, not with the concept itself. I do believe that capital punishment deters in a small number of cases. Most murders, where people know each other, there the deterrence doesn't operate meaningfully; but in the small number of more calculated murders, the law does operate meaningfully, and I feel there is a deterrent impact. The argument about lack of deterrence, and sanctity of life, does not bother me. What does is the discriminatory impact of the law. Over time, it's clear that the poor and the black (although they commit most of the murders, too) will be killed most of the time. That I find intolerable. Further, I don't like what it does to our system of justice—the circus quality of the trial; the torturous quality of the endless appeals that go on and on. And I don't like what it does to the individual involved.

The spectacle; the lack of certainty; the bending of the law to avoid a particular result; the inequities. These are the reasons why ultimately I come down against capital punishment. I don't think our society really believes in the sanctity of life that much—it's interesting that often those who oppose capital punishment most believe in abortion. I don't understand that. I feel abortion shouldn't be part of the criminal system either.

*How hopeful are you there is any way out of the criminal court dilemma?*

There are ways out, but I don't know if our society is that interested, or is prepared to commit the resources and intelligence. The thing I find most discouraging is the level of rhetoric and public discussion by our political leaders about crime. What is frightening is that I think some-

* Charles Manson and Richard Speck were notorious mass murderers.

times these people really believe they are seriously discussing the issues. The Rockefeller proposal in New York State was preposterous! If a student at the law school had proposed it, I would have flunked him. The President's recent pronouncements are frightening—his wanting to do away with the insanity defense as a way of fighting the crime wave is just insane! I can only conclude these are the most cynical of men, who are trying to mold public opinion in a short-term way to be favorable to them. They're an astonishing group. In a way, though, one of the outgrowths may be larger appropriations of funds and this may result in some good programs.

*Do you see yourself staying on as a judge?*

I don't know. There are times when I've been very depressed by it. And of course there are times when I haven't found it intellectually challenging. Partly because the routine and conditions under which we work are often hard to take. There are things about it which I find very appealing. You are independent. I don't feel beholden to anyone, or need to play up to anybody. And it is a position of service. I like it better than teaching at law school. I did not like that. I will be moving up to the higher court and probably will spend the rest of my career there. That will be more challenging and it does appeal to me. I'm appointed for ten years and I come up for reappointment in 1980. It's hard to tell what the status of courts will be by then. I try not to think about it. I can see myself staying on and liking it—because, you know, to do justice under law— well, that's sort of a noble thing.

# CHAPTER VI

# Judge Stone

Judge Stone is a tall, gray-haired man in his mid-sixties, impeccably dressed in conservative and expensive clothes. He is meticulously well groomed. He greeted me with charming old-fashioned courtesy, and while he is obviously formal, he somehow manages to avoid being stuffy. "Courtly" is one word that comes to mind; "cultivated" is another; and I was not at all surprised when later I learned that he is fluent in French. To borrow a current phrase, which would be opprobriously rejected from his vocabulary, he is "together."

He apologized, with obvious distress, for having kept me waiting (five minutes); was well briefed as to the purpose of our meeting; and after inquiring as to my comfort (something to drink, a comfortable position for myself and the tape recorder) went directly to the business at hand.

I regard sentencing as one of the most difficult and responsible duties that I have to perform. I take the matter very seriously. I try to study my pre-sentence reports; I never sentence anybody on the spur of the moment. I always try to put a distance of time between the trial—if there is a trial—or the plea—if there is a plea—and the time of sentencing. This is necessitated anyway by virtue of our common practice of having a pre-sentence report which takes from four to six weeks. In nonjail cases, sometimes it takes less than jail cases. I study those reports very carefully. I generally take them home so that I can sleep on them, so to speak. I

never want to be rushed in considering them. Very often I
will reread a report. Then I will always confer with the probation officer who wrote it. I seek him out, sometimes I have
more than one conference with the probation officer. I will
also read the letter that people write in about sentencing,
although in the course of time, I've changed somewhat. I
think I was much more affected in the beginning by these
letters I'd receive from friends and family, but I now feel
they all sound much the same. Now, I turn them over to the
probation department for evaluation and then I discuss the
letters with him [the probation officer]. I feel that's a wiser
and saner course than exposing myself to them without the
help of someone who is detached, as the probation department can be.

I have on a few occasions changed a sentence after I have
imposed it for reasons that have occurred to me after the
sentence, or because I felt perhaps the sentence was too
severe. I went through quite a crisis with a man who was an
important witness in a case and who had been a tremendous
aid to the government. He cooperated with the government
and went through personal sacrifices and had to withstand
some pretty terrible strains and criticisms in order to do
what he did to help the government. But this was a case of
commercial corruption, and he had a prior conviction which
also involved a form of bribery and corruption; I felt I
couldn't give him a suspended sentence. I know I offended
the government as well as this man and his family by sending him to jail for four months—and later I relented and
gave him only two. On one or two other cases, I've also
reduced sentences. Most of the time, in fact, the vast majority of time, I have been able to sleep with my sentences.
I've been able to rest on what I did and feel it was the best
I could do and the best the man deserved.

[To the initiated it is already apparent that Judge Stone
is in all probability a member of the federal judiciary. The

kind of relaxed pace, leisure to examine and consider, is unlikely to exist in either practice or potential in the harried atmosphere of the state and local courts. This may seem only as it should be to the uninitiated, for whom the term "federal offense" implies those of the greatest magnitude. But the crimes that offend common sensibility most are not those that appear in the federal courts. Street crimes, crimes of violence, murder, rape, mugging, mass killing are local crimes. The federal courts are primarily concerned with white-collar crimes, income-tax evasions, postal crimes, and certain special aspects of the general crime picture which are designated federal to facilitate either apprehension of the criminal or clear-cut prosecutions. Therefore, automobile theft, which often includes transportation across state lines, will be part of the federal system. The federal courts, indeed, do have great influence but often in terms of their shaping of government policy outside the criminal area. They are in many ways, therefore, our most political courts, and in that sense our most powerful. It is important, however, that this confusion about "seriousness" be resolved. It extends further into the evaluation of prisons, where, quite to the contrary of public opinion, the federal prisons are generally the least dangerous and the most civilized. Corruption, brutalization, degradation, all tend to increase on the local level.]

I've always tried to reach an accommodation between what I believed to be the legitimate interests of the law-abiding community and the personal interests of the defendant and his family. With respect to the government employees who have violated their trust—and specifically, now, internal revenue agents who accept bribes (distinguished from small post office employees who steal a letter) —I have, always and invariably, sentenced them to jail even when they have pleaded guilty *and* cooperated, because I feel very strongly that the national financial condition rests

on their honesty. The tax-collection authority of the government would be seriously impaired if there were a rule which
gave them a chance to commit a crime without going to
jail. So, in those cases, perhaps, I've been severe in the sense
that they have all gone to jail, but I don't think I've been
severe in the sense that I don't give them maximum sentences. I seldom give maximum sentences. I always follow
the rule of thumb that where a man pleads guilty, and saves
the government the expense of a lengthy trial, he deserves
consideration; and my rule of thumb is to give him half of
the maximum to start with. Then I see what the other individual requirements are for sentencing. But normally if a
man is exposed to a ten- or twenty-year sentence after trial,
and he pleads guilty, I'd start with saying, five or ten is the
maximum—now what else is he entitled to?

[The clear-cut mark of a twentieth-century conservative is
already evident in what Judge Stone has said, and will influence the rest of the interview to the extent that even where
he is concerned with precisely the same issues as the one
radical and two liberal judges represented here, even when
he is accommodating his sense of justice with mercy, the
results will be very different because the very words "justice"
and "mercy" will bear different definitions, with different
indications. Judge Stone, in marked contrast to the judges
to the left of him, starts almost immediately with balancing
"legitimate interests of the law-abiding community" against
the personal interests of the defendant. This is certainly an
authentic position with a great and valued tradition, and yet
the individualistic orientation of the liberal tradition in this
century is so strong, the therapeutic and rehabilitative model
so ingrained in the liberal judges, that the law-abiding community as such—that is, as distinguished from the individual
victim—is rarely mentioned. It is not just chance that it is
mentioned first by Judge Stone.

Nor is it just chance that Judge Stone *in a discussion of leniency* speaks in terms of five- to ten-year sentences. Again, remember that Judge Stone is more likely to be dealing with the less violent crime, and by his standard the five- or ten-year sentence is an adjustment in pity. Compare this with Judge Garfield, who reserved five years as the maximum for almost any sentence short of murder. The point that must be understood here is that while a Judge Garfield or Judge Stone might both be exercising their desire for tempering justice with compassion, the value systems for each are so different that even were they to appreciate and perceive a given case in the same way (itself unlikely given their different normative codes), they would end up with monstrously different means of exercising the same desires.]

I've tried to visit jails regularly—I've felt that you have to know what a jail smells like, tastes like, prison clothes look like, to really know what a jail is like. I was confined to an army hospital for two and a half months during World War II, and I felt very keenly at that time some of the claustrophobia and heartache I think a prisoner must feel. I've always felt very strongly (and I've always urged my colleagues) that we should never go too long without visiting a jail.

In talking to prisoners I've been somewhat astounded by the intelligence and the attitudes of these prisoners. One of them complained that their library was deficient because they didn't have the books that were in the week's Sunday literary supplement. I said most people waited before they could get those books—he said, no, he felt they should have them right away. Then, another prisoner told me how they would carefully study the sentences of judges all over the country to see in which areas of the country they tended to be more lenient with respect to specific crimes. He told me, for instance, that in the state of Washington, for some reason, judges would give shorter sentences for truck hijackings; he said it is common knowledge to truck hijackers. Once you've pulled a successful job, you retired to the state of Washington because if they caught you, there you signed a rule 20, had the case disposed of. In Washington the judges don't seem to think that's such a terrible crime, whereas other states do. In different states auto thefts, narcotics, and so on, are also treated differently.

*You're suggesting that those judges in the state of Washington are encouraging crime by their light sentencing?*

Well, if what this prisoner said is true, they are in a sense underwriting it. That's a very strong reason against disparate sentences because to the extent that prisoners can figure out where they'll get leniency, they're manipulating the court processes in their favor. I don't think they should have the opportunity to do that.

*You mention that if someone pleads guilty, you start with half the maximum sentence and then take into consideration other things. What sort of other things?*

Well, for instance, if he's an incurable invalid, suffering from a serious debilitating disease requiring medical attention, and it's his first offense, and I'm fairly sure that the man is going to be an invalid and not undertake any more crime—I'll think twice about sending him to jail for a long time. Because he's going to be an expense to the government and he's going to create problems in jail for himself and others. If, to cite another example, it's a woman with young children, I'll think twice about sending her away for a long time because I'll think of the consequences of disrupting a family; or if it's a man who is sure of re-employment. If it's a man who has never worked and doesn't want to work, and we're almost sure he'll go back into crime, that's another thing.

*I was interested also in the example you first selected, the government worker in internal revenue. In your particular value system, do you see that as an especially heinous crime?*

Well, no it's not, but I think the consequences for the community at large are terrible and that's why. The deterrence factor is pretty important here. The tax-collecting functions are at the heart of our system, but we must punish to deter in other areas. My neighbor's daughter was mugged in the streets along with another girl. She and this other lovely young girl were walking one night about 8:00 P.M. This other girl wanted to take a cab but my neighbor's daughter said: "No, let's take the bus." They were pursued by a black man who beat the two of them and grabbed the purse of the friend. The man ran, and as they went bruised and bleeding to the police officer to make their complaint, along comes a black policeman with the man by the collar and the pocketbook in one hand. The case was never prosecuted! They canceled all their appointments to go down to court one day, waited all day, they were imposed upon by members of the X Institute who said to them, "You don't want to blacken this poor man's record. Just sign this paper"—They refused to sign. They wanted a hearing; but at the end of it, after a private conference between this man's lawyer, the judge, and D.A., they were told that the case was deferred indefinitely. That's the system they call "deferred prosecution"! They weren't sworn; the man was never accused of anything. He had a frightening arrest record, but no conviction record, and they were absolutely appalled—so am I. That's happening in this city all the time.

*Why is that done?*

It's done because they haven't time or facilities to deal with the mass of crime that's going on in the city. Most of the crime that goes on is neither reported nor made the subject of any prosecutions. They don't have jails, they don't have enough judges, D.A.'s. Their way of dealing with this is to engage in what they call "deferred prosecution." No conviction, fine; you want to be rehabilitated? Yeah? O.K. Tell them you want to go to college, tell them you want this or that. "This young man wants to go to college, Your Honor. He comes from an impoverished background, and I would like to help . . ." Fine—case deferred, postponed indefinitely. That's the end of it. The witnesses are there with their wounds and they don't need you any more.

*What justification is given for this?*

There is no justification. Deferred prosecution is what it is called, and in effect it means *no* prosecution. You postpone a criminal case indefinitely, you lose your witnesses —that's the end of it. I wrote a very bitter letter to the D.A., to the Legal Aid Society, to the judge, and never got the courtesy of a reply or acknowledgment. A year later, the D.A. was running for office and he dared anybody who knew anything about criminal law to criticize his office. Well, I took the dare. I wrote him a very stinging letter. This one he answered. He admitted that the facts as I stated them were correct, and he said if there was any blame, we have to accept our share of the blame. That was it. I think it's just a way of disposing of cases. Using the excuse that the man is a first offender! He's not really a first offender, he simply had no prior conviction. This man, for example, had arrests for manslaughter, narcotics, and so forth. They fudge up the rest of the case in order to get rid of him. Terrible injustices are occurring. Criminals know this. In any large city today, it is practically impossible for a guilty person to be success-fully prosecuted. It has to be some outrageously sensational crime involving murder or mayhem. Otherwise, the proba-bilities are very strong that the criminal won't be caught up.

*What seems to be the solution for this?*

Well, it goes very deeply. I don't think there's a very quick solution. One solution has got to be a sense of greater integrity on the part of our police, our law-enforcement officials, and on the part of the courts. I don't think, judging from what I know about our city, that it has the law-enforcement caliber it deserves. We have a great reservoir of administrators, lawyers, judges in this state, and yet our state court bench is a shambles. We have judges who are in many cases political hacks who have been put up by local politicians and are answerable to these politicians. We must have a state bench which is appointed for life. Until you get the kind of bench which you have in the federal courts, you're going to have judges looking over their shoulders all the time to see if they'll be reappointed or re-elected. You can't have a good strong judge under those circumstances.

*Do you think being strong is a deterrent to reappointment, re-election?*

Yes, definitely. Because you can't do favors for your friends. Political hacks come in and say, "Now look, John, you've got this little boy coming up here. You know, he's a nice boy, he didn't mean any harm, it's bad company that brought him in." What are you going to tell him? He's put you on the bench—do you tell him to go to hell? *I* can tell him to go to hell. Or a fellow judge will come in and say, "So-and-so is afraid to come to talk to you, but I'd like to say a good word for . . ."

I had a case involving one of the most vicious criminals that ever came before me. An extortionist loan case, where this man threatened (we have tapes of his threats) to come over with two 5-gallon cans of gas and burn a man alive in his house if he didn't pay up certain money by three o'clock and so forth. He was arrested when he went with an accomplice to this man's house, and they had a blackjack each and a loaded gun in the car. They approached this man's house, obviously for the purpose of beating him, and there was a policeman who posed as this man's cousin who was supposed to give them the money. He arrested them. You know, it was an open and shut case, but it was brought before a judge of the state court and, you know, he was put on probation. The judge, on the face of it, swallowed the story that this was really a dispute between two loan sharks and loan shark #1 was competing with loan shark #2, and #2 was merely going there to have a little business meeting with #1. He made a great big joke of it, and this man was allowed to go out of court. If this were my case, this never would have happened—this man would have been put in jail for ten or fifteen years, which he deserved.

*Do you have the feeling then that, in addition to not enough of the criminal element being prosecuted, when they are, they are sentenced too lightly?*

Yes, definitely. In the state courts it's generally too light. For instance, the state courts have a peculiar way of saying, "Two to fifteen," "One to ten," knowing perfectly well that he'll only serve a few months. I think it's an outrageous imposition on the law-abiding community. There ought to be a firm period of time which they serve, or we should adopt the California system, which takes it out of the hands of the judge. You sentence the person routinely to the maximum term and then the parole division decides how much of that term he serves.

*You say there ought to be a fixed time. Why ought there to be?*

I'm thinking of a community where people can go to bed at night without fearing that somebody will break in and beat them up, and rape them, and rob them. Of a community where people can ride through the streets without having their doors and windows locked. Where people in business don't have to have two guards accompany them to the bank. Where a man at night after business can go to the corner bank and put his deposits into the night depository without being shot through the chest, which happened to a neighbor of mine only a night or two ago. I'm thinking of all the joys and blessings of a law-abiding community, as opposed to a community which is in a state of siege.

Everybody I know is afraid. The other night I was walking down from my house to the corner—it was still light and while I had no hat or coat on, I think I looked like a law-abiding citizen—and this nice middle-aged lady turned around with this face of absolute terror, and asked if I was following her. I said, "No, madam, I live right here." And she said, "Thank God, thank God. I knew there was a man close behind me, and I was afraid he was going to do something to me." This woman was in fear and she didn't look like a crackpot. She looked like a perfectly nice woman. But it's frightening to me.

I was born and brought up in the city, and I remember a time when people could go to the park in the evening, enjoy it, even in the evening. Nowadays you can't be caught dead in the park in the evening, and you've got to have armed guards to go there in the day. I'm told it's worse in New York, that you can't go into Central Park at all any more. We've allowed the delinquent, the small minority, to take over the community, and I think that's wrong.

*Do you think locking up people for long periods of time is an effective mechanism for a more law-abiding community?*

It's the only solution we've found that seems to work. It certainly works to the extent that while a man is in jail, eating perfectly good surplus food, he's not breaking down my front door; he's not raping my daughter; he's not mugging; he's not committing crimes in the community.

*So as a preventive measure. But can we lock them all up?*

If we ever reach the point where there are so many we have to lock most of the community up, maybe by that point we will have collapsed as a civilized community.

[It is crucial to recognize again the distinction in Judge Stone's point of view, whereby the defense of the community is seen as the central function of the judicial system. It is easy to disparage this point of view, which has become unfashionable. But it is the essential thesis on which all legal systems are founded. There is a tendency to discredit all exponents of "law and order" because too often in recent times the term has become a euphemism for racism, bigotry, and hatred. Nonetheless, it is essential to recognize that it is a point of view which ultimately may have a greater claim to priority, a greater central legitimacy, than a philosophy which sees individual justice as the primary focus.

Of course, we would all want that perfect balance whereby the state could be adequately protected while the maximum respect for the separate needs and conditions of the individual could be maintained. But complete individual justice will never be possible in a state under law. Laws must define categories, and every category is going to be arbitrary at its borders of inclusion and exclusion. Wherever the line is drawn, the cases proximal to the line on either side will be so similar as to make the line drawing seem foolish unless, of course, the line is drawn at the absolute extreme. Yet line drawing is essential, even if it includes the injustice of the foolish and arbitrary distinction.

Because the "law and order" position has been essentially a paranoid and persecutory one in our time, one must not forget that it may be respectably presented, for honorable purposes. This position does not come easily in our particular age of liberalism. It is a peculiarity of our time that the ideal of the priority of the community seems to be shared only by the conservative and the radical-Maoist groups.]

*Do you feel locking some criminals up has a deterrent effect on the others?*

I definitely do, yes. I also think that a lack of publicity would do. I think it's a great pity that the news media and papers give so much space to crime. I remember that during the dictatorship of Mussolini, they didn't give publicity to crime. When a man committed a crime he didn't get his name in the paper. There was a very strong law-enforcement activity—he went to jail, and so on—but no man ever became a tin-horn hero by committing a big crime. There should be some control. I know here we're getting into the sensitive area of freedom of the press, expression, and all that stuff, but I am convinced that the excessive degree of publicity given to crime is a counterproductive element in our law-enforcement spectrum, and that an effort should be made to avoid excessive publicity of crime, so that it will not inspire this moron delinquent element to want to become important by hitting the front page as a criminal.

*But don't you need publicity for general deterrent purposes?*

Yes, I think it's a good idea to let news of *sentencing* go out.

*Beyond prevention, which is certainly valid and a deterrent, do you feel any rehabilitation goes on in prison?*

Very little. But I feel there are some people who can be rehabilitated. My heart goes out to them because they're often lost in the rush. I think probation officers weed out very carefully, and if there is a person who can be rehabilitated, they certainly try to do it. While some [weeding] goes on in the prisons, it is mostly among probation officers outside the prison.

*Do you feel the very little rehabilitation in prison is the fault of the way prisons are or the way prisoners are?*

The way prisoners are.

*You don't think a better system would mean more rehabilitation?*

No, I don't think so. I think the bricks, the mortar, the food, the intentions, the personnel, are all there, but unfortunately the atmosphere of the prison is dominated, not by the administrators, but the inmates, and those inmates are the ones that carry the message and leave the imprints.

[Judge Stone's response came as a distinct surprise, after an almost unbroken series of interviews in which the failure of rehabilitation has been seen as lying in the deficiencies of the institution, not the individual. The uniqueness of this conservative position will obviously dominate his consideration as to proper length of sentence, nature of parole, desirability of probation, and so on. Judge Stone says that rehabilitation doesn't work, not because we have insufficient psychiatrists, psychologists, teachers, and rehabilitative personnel, not because we do not spend sufficient money on the prison system, not because we are guided by a punitive philosophy rather than an educative one, but for the simple, old-fashioned concept that in the same way that youth is wasted on the young, the facilities that are available are wasted on the incorrigible. A better class of prisoner would be able to utilize the advantages they are given. Again, to the average reader shaped in a liberal tradition, this may seem a hopelessly patronizing and old-fashioned point of view. It is, however, a view that had its popularity in the psychiatric literature in which the concept of the criminal psychopath was developed and, indeed, has other support from members of the intellectual community who while not necessarily placing the *blame* on "the nature of the criminal" might say that, given the nature of the criminal, rehabilitation is a false hope and certainly not possible within the prison establishment.]

*Maybe we should then forget about rehabilitation as a goal? Maybe it's a false goal?*

No, I don't think it's a false goal. To the extent that it can be made to work, we should make it work. There is the typical story of the woman who finds a piece of gold that she's been missing, and is so glad she found it. It's like the lost sheep that comes into the fold. I think the effort should be made even if it only works with 5 or 10 per cent of the cases—it's a pity, a human waste that even one should be lost. Because a splendidly rehabilitated person is a great person—even greater than the one who was never rehabilitated. And I think he could come back with such a fantastic contribution to society that it should be encouraged by all means.

*But I take it you feel rehabilitation for the most part is over-stressed—it's not generally effective?*

That's true.

*So you would emphasize prevention and deterrence. I sense a third factor—something which is a little out of popularity now—I sense you feel a moral purpose; if a man has done something wrong, he ought, on an ethical basis, to be punished. Is that a fair inference?*

I think you're right. I think it's true. For instance, if there were a divine way of punishing a man instantly—the instant he committed a crime—if the minute a forger finished a signature he could be struck down and punished. Or if the man who pulls a trigger to murder his neighbor is struck down, that's perfect justice in my concept—my fantasy idea of justice—and is completely unattainable as a human concept.

*So you're a moralist in the old-fashioned sense?*

I think that's true.

*Where does that come from?*

It may come from my Catholic upbringing, for one thing.

*Are you a practicing Catholic?*

Yes, to this day.

*Is that a very important part of your life?*

It is. Very important.

*Can you tell me a little about your life?*

Well, I was born in X̲ in 1907. I've always worked hard all my life. I went to the public schools. I went to college, law school. I studied abroad during summer sessions and got credits so I was able to graduate in three and a half years. I also graduated from law school in two and a half years—went to summer schools there. I was Phi Beta Kappa, and Law Review, which means I attained the highest scholastic distinction when I graduated from college, when I was barely nineteen, and law school when I was barely twenty-one. So that I'd been all through it the hard way— I've worked hard all my life. I've always had hard jobs and challenging jobs. I've had a rich life, fascinating experiences.

I served abroad in the U.S. Army during 1943–45. I was exposed to a great many interesting cultural influences.

I've always been a practicing Catholic. I've always felt, especially during my war years when I saw boys who were maimed and frightfully injured, what it meant to them to have faith in God and pray. I realized there was one last irreversible process that prevented them from complete panic and disorientation and that was it—the religious sense. I remember how touched I was when I saw a dying boy in the hospital being helped to say his rosary by a Jewish boy who was holding it in his hand, helping him, and giving him some water before he died. I was so deeply touched by it because both of them were religious—they both had something in common. It was a great reliance, a common religious sense.

*Do you feel the decline in religion may be related, in some way, to the increase in crime?*

Oh, surely. I'm convinced that it is. I'm convinced that the dissolution of religious values has in turn brought about a loss of moral values, and in turn made people terribly pragmatic about wishes, desires, and modes of life. I think very few people have a plan of life, or an ultimate goal—they live like animals. They keep themselves clean and they have surface manners that are all right, but I think that down beneath more and more people are just attractive animals. They are attractive animals with a brain within that body, but they don't think very far ahead—what life means to them and how to live, what values they want to hold, being dear to them.

*How do you feel about the emphasis these days on sociological justifying, mitigating, or exculpating factors?*

Well, where there is extreme poverty, disease, or where there is an element of coercion by prolonged bad

examples it might be acceptable. For instance, a young boy
who had a drunken mother and a delinquent father and
who has had to forage for his food and his bedroom. I had
one example—this boy used to sleep in the room with prostitutes because they were the only people who were kind to
him; they'd give him some warm food when he needed it;
they would buy him some clothing; he would sleep on the
floor in the corner. He got some kind of maternal reaction
from being with them. During the day he'd be on the Common as a truant, but at night the prostitutes would take him
in and give him shelter. He became a very bad delinquent
at the age of nineteen, and I couldn't help feeling terribly
sorry for that boy, so I thought there were mitigating circumstances—but outside of that, I find it very hard to find
mitigating circumstances. Of course, now we're dealing with
generalities. It's the hardest thing in the world to talk about
sentences and generalities all in one breath. Every case is
special. Every case is different.

*Being a religious Catholic makes a difference in the way you
look at things. There's a great deal of generalization that
Jewish judges are tougher on "this," Catholic judges on
"that." Do you subscribe to any of that?*

To a certain extent. I think in an outright pornography—like *Deep Throat*, which everyone seems to agree
is outright pornography—there I think a Jewish judge is
capable of treating that as an exercise in entertainment, or
aesthetics, whereas a Catholic judge would be inclined to
look at it in a far different way, not only as an intolerable exhibition of people's genitalia, but also a debasing of
women and a form of immoral entertainment which
couldn't be tolerated. In those cases, they might look at it
differently. But when you get to crimes of violence or commercial fraud, the general spectrum of crime—I don't think

so. With particular individuals—particular defendants and particular judges—they might look at it differently.

*Given the fact that judges differ in background, doesn't it seem a little inequitable and unjust that a prisoner is at the mercy of the chance values of his particular judge?*

It's terrible. I know. I do feel terrible about it. One occasion when I felt particularly terrible about it was when I attended one of these seminars of judges on sentencing procedures. The most important thing we did was to break up into work groups with hypothetical cases, give the sentences we would impose, and the reasons why. I was absolutely astonished and appalled at some of the things the judges took under consideration. I said, "Thank God, I'll never have to be sentenced by anybody," but I realized then the element of human frailty and the preposterous differences in sentencing that take place because the elements of human sensibility, background, and outlook affect different judges in different ways. I don't know what the solution to that is. As long as we have one human being judging another human being, I'm afraid we're going to have that problem.

*You say you were appalled at some of the things at this seminar. What were some of them?*

I can only remember one, but I remember being in a state of shock the whole afternoon. After each judge got up and gave his reasons, I was ready to take a little stimulant. Here's one. It involved a man who committed commercial fraud. As part of the background, it emerged that his son traveled frequently to Switzerland and admitted to having a small bank account in Switzerland. His son was a salesman who worked for a company that had business abroad, and his account was merely used for the purpose of defraying his expenses there. This judge imposed a heavy sentence on the father, giving as one of his principle reasons his feelings that that account in Switzerland was a "stash box." He had "no doubt about it." It "had to be, why else would he have it?" The reason was explicit in the case! But, "No," says this judge, "I'm sure that was the stash box"—even though there was no basis for his being sure. "The sales job was part of a facade. This guy got away with murder for years, etc." It was just one fabrication built upon another upon another; he had no right to come to any such conclusion.

*What about Judge F's solution of removing discretion?*

.     I frankly disagree so violently with so many things he advocates that I probably disagree with this too. What is it?

*He feels there should be little discretion. Punishment should be rigid and defined by legislation.*

Oh, I think that's terrible. It takes no account of the nature and extent of the crime itself. It couldn't be defined that specifically. I have a husband and a wife involved in a narcotic offense. The wife was a good woman and good mother who disliked the narcotic business and didn't want her husband to be in it. She did everything she could to keep him from it. Short of going to the police and reporting her husband, she did everything. Yet, she was found guilty by a jury of aiding and abetting her husband. He did secrete a small quantity of narcotics in the house, under circumstances which would permit a jury to find her guilty, and they did find her guilty despite the eloquence of defense counsel and the great reticence of the prosecutor, who himself was appalled at the guilty verdict. She was guilty, she was found guilty. Now if you have Judge F's system, the two of them would have the same sentence, and that would have been an appalling injustice, because he intended to violate the narcotic laws and did violate them. She did not want to violate them, and did everything she could, unsuccessfully, to reconcile her obligations as a wife, mother, homemaker, and ended up by being convicted.

[Here we see the ultimate confusion of a system of public justice that seems to be coming apart: the conservative defends the humanistic tradition of individualized justice, while his liberal counterpart is determined to categorize defendants into groups. The inconsistency is characteristic of a system near bankruptcy, the bankruptcy referred to here being not of the courts, but of the concept of criminal justice. Such confusion is inevitable in a society approaching the end of one era with no vision of the one to follow. The rehabilitative model, the therapeutic model, is rejected by those who created it. It is defended finally only by the conservative, who in his faith and adherence to tradition generally has now latched onto a liberal ideal he might have rejected on first introduction, but which has gained legitimacy by its fifty years of survival.]

*What about some other solutions offered? One is that there should be a review of sentencing.*

I agree with that because I've worked with that. I was a city magistrate for three years. I worked under that system and it works, but only in one respect. Not for complete review, because the man who's got his nose in the problem, and who's got to sweat with it, and work with it, is the trial judge—and I don't think that should ever be taken away. Except for one thing, and that's undue severity of sentences. There, under the state law, the appellate court had the right to reduce the sentence, either under application, or on its own motion wherever it saw fit to do so. It didn't have the right to increase sentences. I felt it was a good system, because it kept in line those judges who like to be publicity seekers and pariahs in this business. You've read of that judge who's called Maximum John, the one in Washington who's got all of this Watergate business. He's called Maximum John because he gives out maximum sentences all of the time. We had a judge like that. He used to come on the bench and give people one or two years for things the other judges gave one or two months. He was a short fellow—he used to be sanitation commissioner at one time. Once a poor defendant was about to walk up and thank the judge—he thought he had gotten a two-month sentence. It turned out he'd gotten two years! It went up to the appellate division and they reduced it.

The only way you can be protected against excessive severity, which is a terrible thing, is by an appellate review. I agree to that extent. I don't think there should be a whole rehash. I don't think there should be a Commission of Justices. We've got all the help we need. If you have a conscientious conference with these probation officers (all of whom are wonderful men; tremendous experience!); and you read those pre-sentence reports carefully; and you make a careful, conscientious appraisal of the case, there's no reason why you can't come close to a good and optimum result. There shouldn't be disparate sentences. But there's always the possibility that some fellow will go off half-cocked and throw the book out, and I think there ought to be some remedy for that. It's just too much power for one man.

*There are some suggestions that judges ought not to do sentencing—it should be done by, maybe, a social worker, psychologist, or whoever.*

Once in jail. I don't think it should be done anywhere else.

*What about taking sentencing away from judges altogether?*

I would not agree to that, unless there was something like that California system, which grades the sentences once the man is in jail. That would be perfectly all right with me—put the man in jail, and once he's there the committee of social workers, and so on, appointed by the government decides when he's done. There was this case of a doctor who killed his wife in California—a sensational case out there—he was in love with his nurse and she helped him, although she wasn't actually there when he did it. She was let out of jail after a relatively short time. I think he served six or eight years. They allowed him to change his name and go and practice in another part of the country. Then there was this fellow Jackson, who was enamored of a black girl who was involved with the abduction and killing of a judge. That man was sent in I think for assault with intent to rape, something like that. The California authorities just kept him in jail because he absolutely was defiant and he told them, in so many words, that: "If you let me out I'm going to do it all over again." He called them a whole bunch of mother so-and-so's, so they just kept him in jail. They made a wild man out of him. That's the other side of the coin. There are some of these people who are literally honest and will tell you that when they get out of jail they're going to do it all over again. But if you keep them in jail you have a man who's going to abduct the judge, shoot up the prison, and everything else.

*What should be done with a man like that? Under that system?*

I think he's got to be kept in jail, but we've got to find a way of preventing him from becoming a wild man.

*Do you think on balance that the California system has worked?*

I'm not sufficiently familiar with it, but from what I've heard of it—from a superficial exposure to it—I would say yes. If there were going to be any change in our system,

I would be inclined to approve only two changes that I know a little bit: (a) revision of sentences downward by an appellate court, and (b) California system of gradation of sentences after confinement to jail. In other words, if the judge puts him on probation in the first place, that's the end of it; if he sends him to jail, fine, they decide how long he should stay.

*Let me ask you one tough question. You said something that intrigued me—I interviewed Judge F and you. You both are obviously well educated, very bright, and articulate, both went to Ivy League law schools. Both sincerely dedicated to justice, yet you said, "He and I differ on almost every question." How do you explain that?*

I don't know. It could be the makeup of our bodies. I don't know. Maybe we associated with different people too long. I don't know. He's made a lot of proposals that just bother me. For instance, he was upset about the fact that he'd get ready for a trial, everything would be there, the jurymen would be there, all the witnesses would be there, all at great expense, and the defendant would then say: "I plead guilty." So, he wanted a rule passed that anyone who wanted to plead guilty had to serve notice a week in advance, so that the court could take proper cognizance of its program and not waste the money and work that was caused by these last-minute pleas. It was constitutionally objectionable! Because there is no way you can make a man advise you in advance that he's going to plead guilty. Pleading guilty is a very important, irreversible step if it's done right. I don't know why, I just end up on the other side of the argument every time he's come up with a proposal. I've met him, you know. I find him charming. I find him personally very agreeable, and he's got a wonderful sense of humor, a terrific capacity of making fun with understatement and I like him for it. Personally, he's a very agreeable person—*sympathique*. But we come out on different ends of the same proposition. I can't explain why.

*Do you think of yourself as a conservative?*

Everybody says I am. I never think in those terms in classifying a judge. I don't think a judge has a right to be conservative, liberal, or anything else. We're not in a political forum here. We're not advocating legislative policy. We're trying to make the law as written, and the decisions as handed down to us, viable in a community that needs orderliness and needs peace.

*But everyone says you are a conservative judge?*

Well, not everyone, but my impression is that my friends think of me as conservative.

*Why is that?*

Well, it may be because I'm very timid about making excursions into the unknown. I dislike judges who start preaching philosophy, making moral lessons, and decisions. When judges don't tend to their knitting, do what they're supposed to do, go out of their way to reach difficult conclusions because this is the way "it ought to be," regardless of what the law said, that's what bothers me. The Warren Court, for instance, which has been so much criticized, is one of my anathemas, because I think the Warren Court did more to destroy the stability of this country than any other court we've ever had or any other institution we've ever had. They actually usurped the powers of Congress. They didn't respect the fact that they were a separate but independent branch of government.

You think of the term "activist judge," a term that appalls me. I don't think a judge has the right to be anything like an activist, or a pacifist. He's not there to mold the community into doing this or that. I think of a judge as a man who is given charge of a piece of highly complicated and precious machinery that was there long before he came. He comes with an oil can, and he's given a set of tools—his knowledge, his work in law—and he's told to keep this machinery running. Every now and then, a spare part may have to be changed, a part that needs improving, but the legislature is going to do that. You keep the machinery going— that's your job. If any wheels come off, or start scratching each other, or breaking, you fix them so they will work. I think that is the job for a judge. It is not his job to design or construct a new machine.

[It is the nature of values that we are aware of their existence only in others, while our own seem merely descriptive of the natural order of things. Judge Stone, of course, is an "activist judge," at least in one sense of the word. He does not merely do the law's bidding. No one knows the law's bidding. He defines the law's bidding according to his value system. It is difficult merely to "keep the machinery running" when the nature of the machinery is constantly being redefined and one's concept of proper running is as abstruse as such contingent concepts as justice, mental health, normalcy, or the good life.]

*One last question. What do you think about capital punishment?*

I've given it an awful lot of thought. I agree with the English system, which has selected cases where they impose it. I think that where a person deliberately shoots down a policeman, a jail guard, or a judge, he should be executed. Because there I think the individual is declaring war on constituted authority, and where he declares war on constituted authority, he's got to accept capital punishment, both as a means of deterrence, and also as a means of justifying and reaffirming the assertion of authority by the murdered official. But where it's a case of Joe Blow killing Joe Blow's wife, I think capital punishment is wrong. Because it generally occurs long after the crime, when the person has completely changed, and there is something so irrevocable that I find it terrible. I don't think that a human being should take another human being's life when he can possibly help it.

*You would reserve it for those who undermine the very structure of authority and government?*

     Yes.

*As a religious man, would even that not bother you?*

     No. Not at all. I was prepared to impose it in several cases. I had a maritime murder case; I had a kidnapping case involving harm to the victim. I would have been ready to impose it in either case, if the jury had found them guilty.

[The jury didn't find them guilty, and Judge Stone did not have to condemn them to death. I left with the conviction, however, that had he done so, it would have been a decision free of guilt, a decision that had, for him, the moral certainty that comes from a faithful performance of duty.]

# CHAPTER VII

# Judge Nicholson

Judge Nicholson is short, athletic-looking, handsome in a puckish way; fidgeting and active throughout the interview, his speech had a similar pell-mell quality, with ideas spilling rapidly out of incomplete sentences. Despite the Brooks Brothers country-tweed clothes, there was a loose, swinging aura about him. Perhaps it was the incongruous long hair, which came irreverently close to the shoulder. He had the uninhibited, poised charm of someone who had always confidently and unaware assumed his position as a member of the Establishment.

I suppose I am one of the judges that has sentenced more people than anybody here. I figured out last year that I sentenced 1,600 people, all serious misdemeanors or felons. When I started out, I sort of had no idea that it aggravated the situation by putting people in jail for long periods of time. I dealt out long sentences here and there like I was scattering trash in the yard. And in all of them I begin to see the people who had been given a year for a misdemeanor come back. And I'd wonder, "What's wrong? I gave him a year, that's supposed to straighten him out." And you find out that it doesn't. I think that the thing that really struck me the most here in the last year or so is a recognition that, like almost every other person who gets to be a judge, I had no background or training or expertise in what it's all about when it comes to sentencing.

In my own case, I had an undergraduate degree in business at the University of X. I didn't take any psychology, no criminology, none of that sort of thing. It was all political science, economics, math, and that sort of thing. I went in the navy for four years. Came out, went to law school, studied under the case-books method (been for many, many years the accepted way to do it), only now are they moving away from it, making it a little more open, giving a little more realistic idea of what is going on. In fact, in the middle fifties when I was coming through law school, it was really very cut and dried. There were torts, contracts, estates, and all that. Criminal law was taught in one semester during the whole course of law school. That was it. And even then, nothing about sentencing—none of those things—nothing.

I came out; was a prosecutor for a couple of years; went into a private firm for seven years practicing law, trying a variety of cases, some criminal cases, civil work; then I get appointed a judge. And only then did I discover that anywhere from 75 to 90 per cent of my dealings with people would involve sentencing. I had a six-month assignment in felony court—270 cases I cleared, 175 of those were on pleas of guilty. Only twenty-seven of them went to a jury trial. Now, granted that trying those jury cases—there were twenty-seven jury cases and another eleven or twelve non-jury cases—consumed more than three quarters of my time. But in terms of the number of people I deal with, those actually consume very little of my time. In the day-to-day operations, your time is spent with that tremendous number of people you have to sentence.

So I wind up out of 270, sentencing maybe 190 of them, 175 on plea. Now, a plea of guilty doesn't require me to do much of anything. It doesn't require me to put into operation all those things that my legal background, my legal training, my expertise in the law have presumably equipped me to handle. But I don't have any background or training at all in sociology, psychology, penology, criminology, any

of these things. Most judges know precious little about
what's going on in correction, or what the institutions are
really like. We may read a lot of the press releases, all the
"cover your ass" kind of reports that come out of all the
various places. When you go around and talk to the people
in the prisons, go down to the warden, and talk to the inmates, you don't recognize the place. A real eye-opener for
me was to spend a day and night in there as a prisoner, as
part of a conference put on here by the X Association. Suddenly I was on the inside, if only for a couple of days. But
on the inside as a prisoner looking around. And spending all
that time as a prisoner with prisoners. It seems to me that
every judge ought to get locked up for a week in jail before
he's ever allowed to sentence anybody. Because then he begins to get a realistic idea of what goes on down there. A
recent conference we had down here, a prison administrator,
a former warden from the X state prison system, came down.
He said, "You know, judges send all these people down
there with sentencing recommendations for psychiatric
counseling, to get themselves together so they won't do
all these terrible things. So they send a man to jail so
that he can receive psychiatric help while he is there." Well,
as he pointed out, he had one psychiatrist for six thousand
inmates.

It's an absurdity. I have two people to sentence here in
just a little bit—one for armed robbery, one for straight robbery—they're young people who were sent down for evaluation to the youth center. There is the possibility of giving
them youth-correctional sentences. And I'm about to send
both of them back down there to the youth center under
special new commitments. Under this program, they're expected to get job training, therapy, counseling, and all of
the rest of it. Well, I know that 80 per cent of that can be
discounted as poppycock. They say what they're going to
do, and that's what they're supposed to do, but the actual
doing of it falls far short. But I also know that some of that

counseling and job training and that sort of thing *is* available down there.

It's a dilemma because I also know that the indeterminate sentence will put them out under parole supervision all the way for four, five, six years, after a short period of time down there. With these two particular cases—neither one of them is that aggravated; they are young men (eighteen years old); it's their first adult conviction, and I'm not ready to put them on probation. Because I know that probation isn't going to do just a whole lot. What it really comes down to, why the program is so bad, is they have too many people to take care of and they don't have that many sharp guys who are available for hire for the kind of money they can pay. That's what it comes down to.

You know, the workload is terrific, it piles up, most of the people who are to be supervised are black, and an effort is made, rightly I think, to get black probation officers. That means you've got to go around and find sharp, qualified black people with social work degrees and with that kind of experience and expertise. Let's face it, pragmatically speaking—realistically speaking—the blacks have been disadvantaged in terms of education, they have been disadvantaged all along the line, so the result of it is there just aren't that many sharp, well-trained blacks available to do the job. But the drive is on to hire black people, so you've got to take the best you can find—and the best you can find just aren't good enough. This is a fact of life, it's got nothing to do with prejudice or anything else. It is something that goes way back to the way we've been dealing with people in this country for a hundred years.

The hell of it is that I have to face it now. Complicating the tremendous workload is the fact that people don't really cooperate, they hide from the probation officer. Even when you get a real sharp young gal as a probation officer, who's got all the skills, all the finesse, and all the expertise, and is really smart, and could do the job, she's really up against it when it comes down to going back into some of these ghetto neighborhoods, trying to get around and make house visits to check on some of these young dudes. So you've got *that* problem. We've got a couple of probation officers over there who simply will not go out into the community. Yet they are perfectly good people. The result of it is they send for the probationers to come to see them. Now, since John Doe has taken over our probation office, it's I'd say 100 per cent better than it was when he came in. But he can't work miracles overnight. And the number of people being sent over there has been increasing and increasing and increasing all the time. So there are problems there, there are problems in prisons and corrections, problems everywhere.

When you come down to it the promise of corrections is great, but in actuality what occurs isn't worth a damn. You put them in halfway houses—we've had a lot of problems with the halfway house operations. The concept is the greatest thing in the world. I think community corrections is probably the one thing that's going to save us all. But the problem is, once again, that it takes the extremely skilled, knowledgeable type of people with good experience that you can really trust to staff those kinds of institutions. The problem is that you just don't have those kind of people around to put in there to operate those places. One of the problems with corrections is the assholes that are running it. They're dummies. Once again we are up against the same problem. They look around and the best that they can find just aren't good enough. So the result is that you get well-meaning people, but they're incompetent.

*Your sentencing attitudes are obviously going to be influenced by your feelings that correctional facilities are pretty bad.*

There isn't really *any* worthwhile, viable alternative. What you've got to do is sit here and figure out something that's going to do the best you can for society, the victim, and the defendant. To satisfy everybody in the best possible way, recognizing that every alternative you've got really isn't all that good. They're all alternatives, they're viable in the sense that they're there, but every one of them has its weaknesses and every one of them unfortunately doesn't live up to the paper promises that they published by way of justifying their requests for funds.

*You implied early in the interview that when you first came on the bench you tended to be more aggressive when it comes to sentencing than you are now. What made you change?*

Well, I'm still tough in many cases. But I'm not as tough in many cases. I think the difference is, over a period of time, I've not only been at it a little longer, but I've made it my business to try to find out these things that I didn't have any experience in, didn't have any training in. My wife is perhaps the one that has helped me the most. She's helped a great deal. She's a graduate of Y with an undergraduate degree in criminology and then went ahead and did her master's thesis. She's worked with corrections, on a variety of projects; she's worked on a bail project; she's been a probation officer in this court for a long period of time; and now she's working in public safety, dealing with drug abuse, and working over in police and corrections. Her whole background and training is all these things that I really need to know when it comes to sentencing.

And one of the things about it is that she reads a lot and has a lot of books, so that all of these books that I'd be reading if I were taking courses are there and available. I can pore through them and read them, and keep up with it. Not only that, we do a lot of talking about it. Then, once involved and interested, you get an opportunity to make friends and to get to know people like John Doe of X, he's head of the project at X University and is probably one of the leading experts in the legal profession. He's very bright, about my age. And you get to exchange ideas with people like that.

These kind of people—they are up on what's going on and where we ought to be going. Where we are, and *why* we're where we are, and why we ought to be going someplace else. You begin to develop a little greater awareness. You begin to understand. You study and you find out that sentencing isn't something you just do off the top of your head on Main Street. You're supposed to have certain reasons, you know —punishment, deterrence, rehabilitation (although I don't like that word; I think "socialization" is the word we're looking for, not in the political sense, but in the sociological sense). And ultimately we're trying to satisfy society's requirement that the wrongdoer be punished or dealt with in some fashion to satisfy the eye-for-an-eye thing that society demands, even though it is questionable that it ought to. I suppose that if you had a program to compensate the victims of crime out of public monies, then a lot of this eye-for-an-eye or tooth-for-a-tooth business would melt away.

*Is that something you regard as a serious possible solution?*

Well, I think it would take a lot of this away, that is, society's urge to punish, to get even with somebody because he did something to us. If you got that sort of thing going, you might not have all these people, the law and order types, clamoring "Lock them up, put them in jail and throw away the key." That's all fine and dandy. But that is only the angry roarings of a wronged society that has no other remedy for itself. If some guy holds you up, or knocks you down, or breaks your arm, or shoots you, you can't very well sue him to recover damages. You're left without a remedy. Another thing that leads to a punitive attitude, I think, is the frustration that occurs when so many crimes go unsolved. You also get resigned. The public gets to the point where it throws up its hands. And figures, so somebody broke into my place or broke into my car and stole my stuff out of it, what can I do?

You know what happened to me in Nassau? Somebody broke into *my* car and stole something out of it. I've never been the victim of a crime in Chicago, Washington, Detroit, Philadelphia, or in New York City, the great crime capitals of the world. I've lived in big cities all my life. I go to Nassau, use a rented car, and somebody rips me off. But then I didn't even bother to report it! I'd have to go down to the police station, report it, spend a lot of time, and it's gone; and there's no way to find out who did it, so forget it!

So I understand how it is with a great many minor offenses—people just don't bother to report it. And even the ones that get reported, only about 20 per cent of them get solved. So what happens is that both the wrongdoers and the victims know that the system isn't really all that efficient in the first place. We talk about sentencing people for a deterrent effect, you know, we're going to give a guy a long sentence for robbery? But 80 per cent never get caught and the people out on the street know that—the guys that are committing the robberies. You don't have to worry about deterring the good people. The people you want to deter are the guys who are going to go out and commit the robberies. You don't need to deter you and me, presumably. You should deter some young dude who is walking around out there and is very much tempted to stick a gun in somebody's face and take their money. Now, what you want to do is presumably keep him from doing it. Mr. Nixon believes that the way you do that is by giving some guy a life sentence for armed robbery. That's what Mr. Nixon believes. But he hasn't got as much training as I do and I haven't got any at all. So he's condemning social theorists: "What we don't need is a bunch of social theorists here coming up with all this business about not wanting to hand out the death sentences. I don't want anything to do with social theorists. I know in my heart of hearts that it does deter people, therefore we will have it." Well, he's immediately becoming a social theorist himself. Only without a portfolio. So, everybody operates in that kind of a vacuum.

*Along the way, you said your wife had the kind of training you should have had, and also that she has a strong influence on you. Maybe she should be sentencing and not you?*

No question about it.

*It's been suggested that sentencing be done by other than trial judges.*

No—well—no. I'm not sure that that's a good idea. It's a great idea in one respect, but yet again the judge is the guy who has got to bite the bullet. Let me put it this way. I think you can't turn it over to other groups unless they are going to sit in on the trials. Because the judge sits there; he hears the defendant; feels the defendant's attitude. Say he gets up there and tells outrageous lies, everybody knows it's a lie. The jury must figure he is a lying son-of-a-bitch, so they convict him in ten minutes. He's in a way aggravated the situation. Not only has he demonstrated that he has absolutely no sense of guilt, and no sense of shame, no contrition. He's not only *not sorry*, but he'll brazen it out, and under oath commit perjury, so the upshot of the whole thing is that it becomes another thing for the pot, an aggravating circumstance, that is bound to influence my sentence.

The court, in many instances, takes it into consideration. Now they tell you you shouldn't do that—balancing the courtroom behavior into the facts of the crime. You aren't supposed to do that. Hell, there is no judge on the bench that *doesn't* take that into account, from the human aspect. When you're dealing with somebody, he's all of one piece.

You want to know if he is ever going to get to the point where he's not going to go out and do that sort of thing over and over. That he's capable of becoming a better man, or better woman, or whatever the situation.

But I don't think that some sentencing counselor would have quite the sense of responsibility to society or the public. You would, I suspect, tend to get all social workers, or all probation officers, into those new positions. And they are all rehabilitation-oriented. They are all oriented to the individual point of view. Their concern is, what can we do for the criminal, not society.

[Judge Nicholson is already a paradox. In personality, unlike any of the over forty judges that I interviewed, he has the earnest, excited, impassioned mien of a college undergraduate. In the jaded group of the judiciary, his presence is like a rock interlude in a chamber music concert. More than that, there is a sense of a groping, changing, confused but still curious man. He is a man in process, and it is that which reminds one of the undergraduate and explains much of the contradictory quality of his statements. His emotional and intellectual judgments are not yet in balance. One sees this specifically when, despite his having talked of the inadequacy of his background and the admirable training of his wife, he greets the suggestion that perhaps she should be the sentencer with an instant, emotional protest. It is the judge who is "the guy who has got to bite the bullet." He catches himself up and begins to give justifying reasons for what is patently a reluctance to abandon the power of authority.

His humanistic concern and passion for the deprived remind one of Judge Garfield, but Judge Garfield is a scholar and Judge Nicholson is not. Because he is not, he is still confident of what experts may do. Judge Garfield, himself an expert, has no such illusions. One notes from the immediate encounter with Judge Nicholson that his emotionality and his identifications will drive him to compassionate concern, but one also knows that because he will be intuitive he is capable of seeming contradictory. One would predict that he would be unafraid of the impulsive gesture, and have the courage to do what is right, as he sees it, independent of public comment. To that degree, he has the security and self-confidence that often accompany an Establishment upbringing.]

Well, I count deterrence out completely. I don't think that sentencing has any deterrent effect on anybody, because, as I've said, the people we're trying to deter know damn well they have an 80 per cent chance of getting away with it anyway, so their immediate presumption is that if *they* do it, the odds are they are not going to get caught, so the sentence isn't going to apply to them anyway. There's a much greater specific deterrence that comes from immediate apprehension, immediate trial, and prompt sentencing. If the guy gets caught within four weeks, and he's been run through the whole thing within six weeks, and the judge passes fast sentence—you know that's swift retribution. That's swift application of the system to the wrongdoer. It seems to me *that* would be a great deal more of a deterrent than giving some guy a long sentence.

But, still in all, there are certain societal demands by the "good" people of society, and they have some rights, too. The judge really has a responsibility to consider that, balance that. I mean that has to be an input. If you turn it over to somebody who doesn't have to sit here, doesn't have to see all these things—the entire picture—the clues, the policeman, the victims, and everything else, then you lose one essential ingredient that has to go into the sentencing process.

There has to be, in many instances, a certain degree of punishment that goes into this thing. If for no other reason than to satisfy what is a societal demand that hasn't been eliminated yet. Perhaps compensating the victim will eliminate that demand for retribution by way of punishment, and if that happens we may have to rethink the punishment aspect. But if you deal with a set of kids, like the five I've raised, you discover early that there is the carrot and stick approach, and there is sometimes when a swat in the ass is in order. Certain punishments, certain takings away of privileges have got great value at times. We can't always treat each wrongdoer by paying more attention to him, playing more games with him, or sending him to the psychiatrist and all that sort of thing. Sometimes a swat in the ass has the same effect and is better.

The problem is *what* punishment. Here, it seems to me, long sentences defeat themselves. Maybe after a year, maybe after two years—at a certain point, the punishment aspect of it achieves its maximal function. By then, whatever it is you're trying to teach this guy is over and done with, and after that all you're doing is alienating the guy. You're making him angry at society and removing him farther from it. If you're going to give long sentences, you've got to try and sort out that 10 per cent of all the people that come before you who really are an institutional problem. I doubt that there's even that many. Those who, through a long period of demonstrated misconduct and perhaps psychological evaluation, are diagnosed sociopaths. These individuals, by and large, are probably going to have to be salted away for the protection of society. We simply don't have that much available to deal with them. And unfortunately, we're going to have to put them away.

But I've had experts tell me that in order to find that individual, to get the true positive, you end up getting two false positives. So essentially you end up locking up three people for long periods of time, up to life, in order to get one of them! Do we adopt a system that punishes those two that shouldn't be there in order to get the one that should? Again, again . . .

*You feel that, for the most part, sentences are too long?*

There's actually no reason to give people long—you know, fifty-year—sentences, that sort of thing. I think that, at most, the minimum sentence should be at two or three years. Three to ten, or twenty, years is a good sentence because that leaves it up to parole, up to corrections. The people who are the experts in rehabilitation. In other words, certain aspects of it are a punishment, and I think we ought to tell a guy that when we sentence him. We ought to say, "Look, I'm giving you three to twenty. The first three is punishment, and after that it's for rehabilitation, so from there on it's up to you and the parole board how you hack it. From that point on, you have some chance of getting out."

[Again, one is reminded that words have meaning only within context of the value system of the person using them. Judge Nicholson, like every other judge interviewed, wants a "fair" sentence, a more moderate sentence. But it is, as it always is in the courtroom, the sentence that is the payoff; and his definition of a moderate sentence is amazingly high. More important than being high, it carries that broad spectrum of discretion (three to twenty years) that reveals Judge Nicholson's continuing trust in the discretionary powers, the abilities and good will of such institutions as the parole board, the probationary system, and so on. In his trust he is closer to Judge Stone, and it is here that one senses the conservative base of Judge Nicholson's liberal beliefs.]

*Do you trust the parole board?*

I think the judge has got to be able to set some kind of maximum beyond which you can't hold them. I don't trust them the way they have it in California. I think that George Jackson is dead because of that sort of system. I mean, there's a guy who was an extremely bright but undereducated black. He became educated, he began to read, began to develop his potential; but given the setting in which he was developing it, there was no choice but for him to become an angry militant.

Now, that theory is belied immediately by John Doe, who spent eight and a half years on Death Row here, became self-educated, and really got himself together. He comes out, and has dinner at my house, and rides my horses, and is a friend of the family. And here's a James Smith, who my wife deals with all the time, convicted for a felony, also comes out to the house and we get along fine. Who knows? One of the guys that came to my wedding reception ultimately got picked up, tried, and convicted for wasting some guy up on the street, and is now down in X for a life sentence. You never know—some of your best friends may turn out to be killers!

*What about the dilemma of indeterminate sentences? Is it an open door to bias and prejudice? Would we be better off with a rigid sentencing structure?*

No, no. I don't think so. I'd almost rather trust a parole board than I would myself. You know a judge, with 1,600 sentencings, can't possibly keep track of these people and know when to let them out. They're not around for us to know. Look at the arrogance, look at the total arrogance, of the system that puts so much power in the hands of the judge, who has no more qualifications than I do. Maybe less, in many instances, because I suppose a lot of judges do a whole lot less studying and trying to find out about this thing than I do.

I tell you this—it's a whole lot easier the way I *used* to do it. Because I never agonized or worried over these things. I never used to worry. I never saw all these various elements that fit into the problem. But when you don't see all that, when you just sit up there, somehow or other you listen to the clamor of the crowd in the background. I suppose it's like when it was going to be Barrabas or Jesus and the crowd said, "Give us Barrabas." Jesus and a couple of other wrong-doers wound up getting crucified. It was all being done by some guy who sat there, listening to the crowd, and not doing what he knew he ought to do but just satisfying the crowd. And in the doing of that—he just deals it out, makes his fine pronouncements about law and order, and everybody buys that! The losers are the people that you have to deal with. So to do it otherwise involves really agonizing over it. And there is a lot of pain involved in that.

[Throughout the interview, I found the psychoanalyst in me more intrigued by Judge Nicholson than by his opinions. He constantly refers to a dramatic change in his behavior and while at first I tended to discredit this, it became apparent that indeed he had undergone a metamorphosis, the nature of which is beyond what most men experience merely by growing up. But Judge Nicholson seemed unaware of any acute precipitating event; at least, he said he was unaware. It was tantalizing because he very clearly, without necessarily recognizing he did so, tended to perceive this not as a continuity of change but as a precipitous, discontinuous event starting three or four years ago. I, as will be seen, continued to press on what caused this seeming "re-evaluation of values" in him. Even without knowing the causes, the fact of the change has broad implications for this study. Judge Nicholson prior to "the change" was a different man with different values, harsher and less sensitive than the emerging liberal of today. He was the conservative law and order man, dealing out "long sentences here and there like scattering trash in the yard." A whole generation of criminals, at the rate of 1,600 a year, are the current recipients and beneficiaries of those fortuitous events that precipitated the change.]

*How did you change so much? Obviously, your wife had a great part of it.*

Just being in and around it. You can't be in this business without your developing certain sensitivities. If you're any kind of a sensitive person, you recognize that you're not dealing with so much merchandise in a grocery store. You're dealing with human beings—persons, people caught up in the problems of society. These are the "actings out," these are the paroxysms, of the disadvantaged. Those that have somehow been left behind the door have come out for a variety of reasons and committed these offenses, not the least of which is that it's a striking out. A striking out at a system that makes a lot of promises to them and never produces anything! And they're frustrated and they're angry and they feel cheated, and by God they are cheated!

My own feeling is that it is television more than anything else, really. The whole concept of television, paid for by advertising, has a great deal to do with it. The advertisers tell everybody in this country, pictorially, that the material things in life are necessary; you have to have pretty girls, big cars, fancy clothes, or you're *nobody*. And similarly, the stuff in between the commercials convinces everybody that life is just a bowl of cherries. Nobody is ever poverty-stricken, nobody is ever out of work, nobody ever really has any problems. You know it's all one big cheery, glossy, smiling, wonderful American dream type of thing. And it isn't long before the disadvantaged, the undereducated, the ones that *can't* get jobs, are all sitting around looking at the TV, and having all this stuff fed into them subliminally, and they come out and look around at reality and realize that they have been cheated. And some turn to drugs to ease the pain; and if that doesn't work, the next thing you know they turn around and strike back at this society of which—if you are not in the mainstream—you're not really part. And they may strike back at these people by holding them up, robbing, whatever. And they aren't concerned, don't care about them. How in the hell is putting them in jail going to solve any of that?

[Judge Nicholson was such a unique combination of conservative and radical, Ivy League and hip, that he seemed an amalgam still in process. The diverse elements, rather than fusing into a new homogenous compound, were still evident like discrete and occasionally contradictory pieces floating unmelted in the mold. Beyond this, his dramatic turnabout did not seem merely a part of "seasoning" on the court. It made me, as a viewer, particularly searching, anticipating the exposure of some trauma, conversion, revolution—anything that might weave together these rough irregular threads into that whole cloth of personality that unifies a man's behavior. It was this which made me turn, at this point, to his past.]

*You commented that most of your education occurred after you became a judge.*

Of course.

*Could you tell me a little bit about yourself before you became a judge, where you came from, what you were like?*

There's pictures of me up there [on the walls] over the years. My dad was a judge for thirty-four years. I grew up in a lily-white area, went to good schools; married early; had a flock of kids—sort of came along. Doing the right things; doing what you were supposed to do. Never had to get into a situation where you really had to deal with people on a broad spectrum, the people that you deal with in the courtroom.

My mother came from the Midwest, and my dad was a lawyer there when they were married. Both of his parents were lawyers, my grandmother and grandfather both. I grew up initially in a small town in a farming area in the Midwest, a small town of about five thousand people. No blacks there when I was born forty-two years ago, and no blacks there yet. It's an area in whch there's tremendous prejudices, not so much religious as racial. Everybody hates the "niggers." Won't have any in town, and that's the reason they're not there. At one time, the Klan was very big there. Still a lot of it left. My dad was a prosecutor for ten years and then began to rise in local politics and came here. You know, he was a Republican, and I grew up in a conservative Republican family with a Midwestern background. My dad's a Methodist, my mother is the same. I was educated in good private schools and then prep school, and from there went on to X university, and by and large grew up in a fairly conservative sort of atmosphere. I've got one sister and one younger brother. Always had plenty of money. 'Course, during the war years you couldn't spend it. I don't think there was really much I wanted that I couldn't get. When I was a kid I once wanted a set of drums in the worst way, so naturally I got a set of drums that Christmas. The fact that when I started playing them, they made me stop, tells you something else.

I got to be sixteen, got my driver's license, had a car available to drive around, always had money to spend. I worked as a kid every summer in high school and college. Soon as I was big enough, I got a hardworking, full-time, physical labor summer job all summer long. Not sure whether I was pushed into it or just did it. I worked in lumber yards, delivered coal; at that time people ordered coal in the summer time, we shoveled it on the truck and shoveled it into coal bins all over town all summer. Might as well have been working in the mines.

You know, repairing roads, stone buildings, construction companies, that sort of thing; I think I learned probably more about people doing that than I did any place else.

That's one of the few places where I really got exposed to the lower class, if you will, the workingmen, by working with them. 'Course, I was just a kid at the time, but I didn't have any real experience. Those people were, all of them, of course, very solid, hardworking people. Now a lot of them weren't terribly well-to-do, but hard-working people and they were solid Republican conservatives. Making up what Mr. Nixon calls his Silent Majority. I'm not so sure what's happened to that right now.

*When you were in college, were you a typical conservative?*

Oh, was I ever! To the point where I took a course from Professor Doe [a world-famous liberal political scientist], and I argued with him so much that he finally told me I was a disruption to the course. I was such a hard-bound reactionary, he'd give me a C+ if I'd never come back again; I didn't have to take exams, just get out of here and you've got a C+. I told him there's no way! I stayed in the front row and baited him all semester and got a B. But you know, there was that sort of thing. I thought that every professor at X was, at least, in the Communist Party.

I got out, and the first job that I had when I got out of the navy was working on an internal security subcommittee in the U.S. Senate. I was a witch hunter. And I felt, ideologically, right at home. I think my dad had a lot to do with my change, in many respects, although he claims there's this great ideological gap between us now. I don't really think there is that much. I think the political figures of his generation really understood, and cared about, human beings. I came to understand about men like my dad, you know, real politicians regardless of party or ideology. Those people really cared about human beings. I remember one day when my dad was in politics riding down the street back home; he'd call on people in every district, call people by name, stop in the street and talk to them. He had the feel of the people. It took a long time to realize what he meant. You don't just sit up here and sort of operate out of statements that you read, the theoretical stuff. It ultimately must somehow, whether you're a politician or a judge or whatever else you are, deal with people as human beings. You've got to get out and travel around. You've got to get to understand them; know what they're all about; get the feel of them.

*When did you begin to sense that you were being trans-formed from your conservative, Republican, Midwestern image?*

About three or four years ago. You know, it's funny—I talked to a friend of mine about something or other on the phone and I reminded him, I said, "You know I'm a Republican," and he said, "Oh, are you?" So I don't know, maybe I'm like Justice Frankfurter, who suddenly became a conservative in the context of where he sat, you know, as measured by those around him.

*Four years ago you were still a conservative?*

Oh yes, I still am. I feature myself as a Jeffersonian conservative.

*You still are a Republican?*

Oh yes, of course. And I still like to think of myself as a conservative in the real sense of the word. I don't fancy myself a radical or liberal. Labels bother me a lot. I'd rather be a realist.

[My incredulity was obvious. To hear this with-it, hanging-loose, jive-talking long hair describe himself as a conservative Republican made me wonder whether he was speaking tongue-in-cheek. He was not. This did not mean that he was what he thought, any more than that's true of any man. But it is part of his self-image, part of where he came from, and certainly part of any value system he would have in this transition period. It was also a caution to me not to be deceived by manner, not to confuse the package with the content.]

*But when you say three or four years ago—what happened?*

If you're looking for some kind of dramatic shift, I don't know what it is. I am just . . . like I am. I can look back and see how some of these things occurred. I guess maybe it's a process of education in the court. I'm forty-three now. I was just thirty-four when I came to the bench, and only because I was a qualified, good lawyer. Most judges are nothing but qualified lawyers who know politicians.

*So you're telling me then that even the first five years on the bench, you had an entirely different attitude?*

Well, it isn't like half-time, where the teams changed sides. Perhaps it represented a shift of ideas, perhaps really it represents a little better understanding . . .

*Well, what's terribly interesting to me, you say it's a matter of growth. But as a psychiatrist I am aware of how few people do grow, how few people do change, in adult life. Whatever their ideas are, they tend to get more and more fixed as they go along into middle age. If they do change it's with their social milieu, rarely counter to it.*

Well, my feeling about that is, when I get to the point in this job that I become so set in my ways that I become fixed, it's probably time to leave. The court's response in its dealing with society necessarily has to be a growing, living thing. I think it's one of the things that disturbs me about Chief Justice Burger's viewpoints which, in many instances, probably differ from how he feels. How can anyone say that we plant our feet firmly here, turn 180° around, and walk back a hundred years into the law? Precedents are fine, in terms of showing where the changes come, how they come, and in terms of guiding you along reasonable, legitimate shifts. I don't think the law ought to become ossified, a solid sort of thing.

Of course, in the larger context there must be a fixity. Change must be reasonable and sensible. You must be able to count on the law. But you simply can't take rigid fixed attitudes and say here is where we're going to follow these guidelines. Society changes; the problems change. Who would have thought ten years ago that we'd have all this concern with the ecology movement? Who would have thought three years ago that we would be concerning ourselves with the problems of an energy crisis? Way back, we were talking about what was going to happen if we kept on and had too many people. We talk now about the changing projections, because we can't even see what's needed in certain places. But all these things shift and change, and while you may understand wherever you are by looking behind, you cannot project where you're going to go. Quite frequently you are fooled, just like with projections on how big a jail you'll want. You suddenly find out that, the way things are going, one thing and another happening in the system, you don't need as big a jail, so you have to change the projection.

I just don't think that we can make the law or courts so rigid or inflexible that they are unable to respond to the changes that society demands. There's a contest right now about sexual laws with many people saying, for example, that sodomy ought not be a crime among consenting adults. Others say, "It's absurd. This is a standard of morality. A fixed morality that goes back to biblical times." You know it was fine 150 or 200 years ago, when people came around and had all these *fixed* ideas. But the public's attitude about these things is such that these laws applied in those fashions today simply don't make sense. I think we become hypo-crites at that point.

*Are there other crimes that you think ought to be "de-crimi-nalized?"*

I think it's absolutely absurd to spend the time of the police, prosecutors, and courts going after people so extensively in all of the victimless crimes. And by that I mean crimes of which there is no complaining witness. There is no person wronged, no one who can come in and say that this individual did harm to me.

*Would you include pornography in that?*

Sure, sure. I don't think we ought to be blazing it up and down the streets, there ought to be some limitations on it . . . In other words, you don't want to open the doors on the gin mills while some guy is balling some chick on the stage. Obviously, you don't want that. But within limita-tions, I suppose, if a man has obscenity or pornography in his own home and wants to look at it himself, that's *his* business. We shouldn't be going around prosecuting people for that unless we can establish that some real, definite harm is going to come out of it, and essentially we can't. We've eliminated locking up drunks, and one of the few places that has. You know, I suppose a third of all the police time in the major cities is spent locking up drunks. Now we quit that. The police find somebody that's down, that's drunk, we haul them to the city hospital, turn them over to the medical people. There are fewer drunks on the street now than there were when we were locking them up, so when you come down to it—when you actually do—it's fine.

Sometimes you get this great clamor. What happens is a lot of people come out and make these public pronounce-ments, the great puritanical sort of approach to things. The fact of the matter is, what they're doing in their own lives is totally different. You get a situation where, for example, they go around locking up all these kids for having a marijuana cigarette. And at these parties around town, among young professionals and the prosecutors themselves, they're all smoking dope! Absurd! You know, Judge Doe up north got all bent out of shape a while back here with a couple of those cases and issued an order that every assistant attorney that was prosecuting cases in front of him had to file an affidavit that he never possessed or smoked marijuana in his life. It caused a panic. Hell, all those young guys in the D.A.'s office smoke! There was a great brouhaha about it, and ultimately the prosecutors went up there and talked to the judge, and the judge backed down and said, "I won't make them do it." But he sure made his point. Now I suppose they struck a bargain: If the judge doesn't do that, they'd quit bringing in all those kids for possession of a roach.

I suppose it would be all right if we had all the money in the world to go around and do that, but we don't. So maybe we ought to be putting our resources in the places where we need them: for armed robbery, burglary, assault, things like that that terrorize people in the city streets, and spend less of our time cruising up, trying to get these prostitutes. We've got fifteen policemen every night doing nothing but going around in plain clothes, cruising in their own private cars, trying to get solicited for prostitution, so they can lock some gal up, bring her down here. It's absurd.

*What about white-collar crimes and criminals? Do you think they ought to be sent to jail?*

Sure, some of them. It depends on what they're doing. If they're really cheating the system, you know, that's the punishment aspect of it again. Where is it?—in *The Mikado*, where?—I forget, where it says, "Let the punishment fit the crime." Let's accept there's punishment—you ought to view the crime and how it affects the framework of society. What it really does in those terms. To a certain extent, it's like all these people who have been involved in this awful Watergate mess. They're undermining our faith in our institutions! To that extent, they're going to deserve a lot more punishment than some poor devil, some poor kid down here, that's got no father, no job and no chance for one, no education, and who winds up breaking into somebody's house and stealing a television set he's been led to believe he simply has to have. You know, he's far less culpable than some guy who prostitutes an office of trust. That guy doesn't need to be rehabilitated, he needs to be punished.

*Do you predict most of them will end up serving time?*

Oh, I don't know. I'd like to be the judge and sit up there and read them back all of those public pronouncements about law and order that have been coming out from that bunch in the Administration. All those things about "soft-headed judges," "lenient probation officers." Read them all, get it all down, and then say, "Given all this stuff you have been responsible for putting out, and accepting this as what you believe in, what do you feel now is my duty?" Let them tell me; let them be real hypocrites. That's what gets me—the hypocrisy.

*There's a difference when you read something and when you're sitting here a week or two with a defendant who is flesh and blood. Do you have any idea what sort of things influence you?*

Well, attitudes, generally. If a guy comes in, and his wife is there all the time, sitting in the front row. During the recess he goes over—some relationship exists, you can't help but see that. There's some sense of responsibility, some sense of caring about another person, you know? I suppose to a certain extent, we all of us assess people's attitudes, we look at them like psychiatrists—we have to encroach into your field and look very carefully at the individual: how he testifies, what he says, whether he's evasive, hiding things, lies to you; whether he's a real smart ass or comes through as a reasonable guy. All of that becomes important when you assess what the probation officer says.

[At this point, the reader does not have to be told that the relationship between husband and wife is a crucial and rewarding one for Judge Nicholson. To him in his personal life the individual relationship is what counts, and this personal experience will extend into the courtroom, where he will value the individual relationship between the judge and criminal, too.

The sense of the person, of the criminal—how he relates, and how that relationship is experienced by the judge—is ultimately a conclusive factor in sentencing. I suspect that, with most judges, the personal impression is important. The smell, the feel, the gestalt, the identification with or the revulsion to, these are the hidden determinants of the sentencing procedure, and they operate on Judge Nicholson as they did on Judge Garfield (who admitted it), and as they will with all judges, whether they deny it or not.

This process of identification is probably essential and decisive to all the decision-making mechanisms involving human behavior. The intellectual reasons marshaled often are only supports and justifications for a decision made on the basis of the experiential. This is shaped by past experience, and we are aware of the uniqueness and individuality of each man's experience. This, more than any other factor, may be the argument against broad discretion. The experiences of the judge and judged will never be the same; therefore, their aspiration will not be the same, their values will not be the same, indeed, the "facts" as they view them will not be the same. Similarly there are broad differences in the backgrounds, therefore values, of judges, so that like criminals committing like crimes will receive disparate sentences because of the irrelevant factor of unlike judges.]

You know, it's interesting, I've got two sentencings coming up. One of them, a guy pled guilty . . . and yet he swore to me that he never did it. He didn't have anything to do with it but that he doesn't want to snitch on anybody. Later, when the probation officer's report came in, the guy told the probation officer the truth: he was just wandering around that day, didn't have anything else to do, went over to this kid; wanted his coat so he took it away from him. But when he got arrested, he gave the coat back.

*Now* I know he did it. I know exactly what happened. But he lied to me about it and that's something to consider. On the other hand, he finally came clean and told the probation officer and that is a point in his favor. All of it is hard to put your finger on. It's the same way with anything—like running a business. You have to decide who to hire and who to employ, and a lot of factors go into it that are not in the book. I'm honest enough to say it. Any judge who tells you it doesn't is trying to give you the kind of answers he thinks you ought to be hearing.

*Given that case, the one you mentioned just offhand. Supposing we were back to that small town in the Midwest from where you came, and this were a black kid, what . . .*

Never gets a fair shake. Gets crucified! They're going to lock him up, stick him in jail. How's he going to get a fair jury trial? If he gets a jury, he's going to be tried by twelve prejudiced white men and he's an outlander. He's going to get it. There are flaws in the system. If I were out there defending him, or being the judge or anything else, I'd understand that, but they don't.

*What can be done about it—anything? Is there any protection against bias in judges?*

Well, you've got to recognize the judge is a human being, just like anybody else. The probation officer who has to deal with this guy must be a human being, there has to be some personal input. It can't be computerized 'cause it's human beings dealing with each other. It's interaction, that's part of this. I don't know what you can do about it. Unless it becomes 1984. Where it's all worked out. You just punch these buttons and nobody has any identity any more.

*You won't like that? Even though you recognize the prejudice, you feel we're safer with this system?*

Yeah.

*Some people are recommending a catalogue of offenses, where you have to give specific sentences, with no discretion.*

Oh no. You can't do that! That's one of the reasons, in many respects, I'm a great believer in leaving wide options in terms of sentencing and then letting other people take a look at it. But there are problems because you are turning the power of decision over to other people. Who are you going to have for people reviewing? The same sort of people who are in California, or here on the parole board, or someplace else! Those kind of people are going to be the ones. When the judge says, "I'll give him one to ten," he's saying, "Look you can't keep this guy longer than ten years but you can let him out in one year." He gets his one because that's his kick in the ass. From there on, it's kind of up to him about how he does. The problem is, of course, that when you do that you're dependent upon the other part of the system to do those things that they promised to do. But the hell of it is that they don't! So then you wind up putting more people on the probation, or you wind up just saying to yourself, "Oh my Lord, it's really a terribly imperfect system. There isn't a hell of a lot I can do about it except go around and do everything I can to try to get them to do something about improving the correction system." Or, I suppose I could take some dramatic step like suddenly announcing that from this point on I'm going to suspend the balance of the sentence of everybody I've put in jail; or refuse henceforth to send anybody to jail till they get that damn thing into some sort of shape so it does what it's supposed to do. Then they'll put you down as some sort of an idiot, or some wild-eyed radical, and file a complaint and impeach you.

*Let me ask you a couple of things more about your personal life. You've really been most helpful. What about your kids? You hear a lot of how parents influence kids. How about their influence on you politically and ideologically?*

[I was still groping for the factor that turned Judge Nicholson around. By this time it had become apparent and explicit (later research confirming it) that Judge Nicholson was in a profound transition in life-style, political orientation, and judicial philosophy. This raises another kind of disparity in sentencing. There may be not only a difference between Judge N and Judge P, but equally a difference between Judge N prior to fact X and post X. It doesn't matter what X represents. It may be a mugging of his neighbor, the theft of his car, or more profound unknown factors which influence his attitude about muggers, car thieves, and other offenders.]

A lot of them are pretty much the way my first wife was. [This was my first conscious awareness that Judge

Nicholson was married for a second time. In retrospect, though, there were many indications that the "wife" referred to in the discussions of criminology was not the childhood sweetheart he married originally.] My oldest and my present wife are just at each other all the time. My eldest is a bit spoiled, problem of the first one—all the stuff that goes with it. He's a good kid, but he's having a lot of problems. My sixteen-year-old son, on the other hand, is sort of in the middle. He's got some pretty good ideas. Writes some of these papers about corrections that could have been written by Karl Marx. He's groping, and trying to find out. He voted for Nixon, though—I influence him more than he influences me.

I suppose one of the things they do is to make me more aware of their peer groups, what they're up to, their associates. It isn't that *they* influence me so much, as it is the people they have around. The people they deal with cause me to begin to look at other segments of society; consider them and their viewpoints and what they want. These kids come home and they're sort of exuding in many ways the culture of their peers. You can't help but absorb a little of that, if you look at it with some sort of an open mind. If you don't just sit back and act like a "father figure," an Archie Bunker, and command this and that. I used to do that, and all it got me was my kids hating my guts. When it came down to the divorce from my first wife after eighteen years, they wound up generally against me. It's taken about four years for this thing to kind of go back to the point where I quit being a tyrant, a son-of-a-bitch, where I began to sit and listen. It's still my house, and I'm still basically in charge. I reserve the right to ultimately veto decisions. By and large, they're getting to be the sort of adults I like.

I was divorced about four years ago—I've been married about three years. She's a very different person. She comes from New York. She's thirty-six. She's had a completely different background, her parents are European. She's an only child. Her father's an artist. They're very gentle people. Very different from mine, they're not hard drivers, they're not aggressive. My old man was the most hard-driving, aggressive, whip-cracking guy I ever met. Still is. I guess *I've* got a lot of that.

My first wife was from back home. Her dad was in the life insurance business, an agency manager. Her parents were aggressive, moneyed, Eastern types. My ex-wife was a great mother, ran the house, kept the kids in great shape, kept animals, horses, everything was kept super, but somewhere along the line the personal relationship lost out. There it went.

*So this is a whole new kind of relationship?*

I think what really happened is that my present wife sort of stuck the key in the lock and unlocked it and sort of encouraged and allowed me to get out of the mold— get to look, think, explore, find out what it's all about.

[Finally, and almost incidentally, an explanation emerges. The change did occur three to four years earlier, with the break-up of his marriage. The marriage to a new wife, unlike many, was not a replication of the previous one but introduced Judge Nicholson to a whole new set of experiences, a whole new set of friends, a whole new set of aspirations, and a whole new set of values.]

*It must have been there before, but I'm sure it was a crucial influence in the way you now have of thinking about things.*

I must sound like I really believe I've got all the answers, that I know what I'm talking about, but I really don't. I'm still always open. Some new idea, some new concept comes along. Like your talking to me about turning sentencing over to other people, it's an idea that comes along that needs to be refined and examined. I wouldn't jump into it—maybe that's why I'm a true conservative. In other words, I wouldn't jump in to try it, to see how it works. My feeling about things like that is: Let's examine it, look into it, refine it, and then if we get to the point where we're pretty damn sure how it works, let's try it on a small scale and see what happens. Let's approach it from the point of view that it's *going to work*, not just that it's something new.

# CHAPTER VIII

# Other Judges, Other Views

None of the four judges presented would seriously qualify as a bigot, although it would not have been difficult to present four alternatives who certainly do. Yet each has a point of view, a set of standards and values, a bias, if you will, which will color, influence, and direct the nature of his verdicts independently of the specific condition of the criminal being charged. It might even be that the more intelligent, the more intellectual the judge, the greater the likelihood that he will have a formed and predictable bias representing a personal philosophy. His point of view may or may not be defined, may or may not be explicit, may or may not be self-admitted; but it is there and it influences his decisions. This value system is created in memories lost as well as lessons recalled. It is shaped as much by the judge's emotion as it is by his logic; by the nonverbal and the nonintellectual; by people known and experiences endured as well as by principles adopted or concepts crafted with deliberate reason. We act from what we are, and we are what we have endured as well as what we have been taught.

Judge Ravitz will be seen by many as the most political of the judges, which of course he is not. To be a Marxist is no more political than to be a capitalist. But to be a Marxist in a capitalist society *seems* to be more political (as would a capitalist in a Marxist society). To share a common majority political view allows for the conceit of being nonpolitical. The common heritage of the majority is more often seen as a matter of fact than an opinion, a position, a point of view. It is so much a part of the common culture that it assumes the form of the natural order of things. This is what makes it so difficult for most men to comprehend the political writings of the women's movement. (Indeed, it is just as difficult for many women.)

No, they are all political judges, each representing his point of view. As a minority member, Judge Ravitz is required to enunciate his views and must define his political intention. The political intentions of the others are equally there but less explicit. There is no question that the simplest computer program could define a consistent pattern of sentencing which would separate these four judges. That means that any one defendant, independent of his personal history and his particular crime, will be meted out a punishment based on the idiocyncrasies of the particular judge into whose hands he is delivered. There will be considerable differences.

All of the judges, operating on the basis of their own convictions or beliefs, are doing precisely what the law would have them do. It is the purpose of discretion to allow the judge to exercise his best judgment about the special considerations of the individual before him. There are, however, certain tacit assumptions by which we operate which are simply incorrect. One is that somehow or other the judge represents the community and that when he introduces his specific value judgments they will be those of the community.

But what is a community feeling? And does community feeling have meaning in as heterogeneous a society as ours? What is a community, even? Whatever the community of the judge, it must assuredly be different from that of the defendant. They are not peers, nor issue of a common class.

The "judgment of his peers" has for two thousand years been considered the glory of the judicial system. In the *Oresteia*, Aeschylus, in passing, pays tribute to the birth of trial by jury in Periclesian Athens, and its basic innovation is the specific renunciation of the role of authoritarian judgment, even when the authority was the Goddess of Wisdom. It is Athena who decrees that there is a greater justice in the wisdom of one's peers than in wisdom itself.

It may be that a trial by jury approximates the democratic ideal. But as has already been stated, the jury only decides guilt or innocence. In our modern criminal justice system, these have become almost irrelevant. The vast majority of cases plead guilty anyhow. It is *how* we deal with the guilty that will decide even the nature and meaning of the word "guilty" and the quality of justice. It is the sentence that is important and that has been relegated to an authoritarian, privileged minority. (Some sentences are love pats, others crippling blows.)

There may be an essentially "anti-justice" principle in the fact of an authoritarian judge who, in America, almost by definition must come from a different class (and therefore a different consciousness and a different sensibility) from the convicted. It means that the biases of these judges, formed in the nature of their lives—their parents, their experiences, their aspirations, their griefs, their frustrations, and their hopes—will be dominant factors in the lives of other men who may share none of these factors with them.

The argument will be used that judges are no more biased than any other professional group. That of course is true. But the engineer, the architect, the teacher does not have such immediate direct influence or so much awesome power. The judge has the right to set a man free or to imprison him for the rest of his life. It may be argued that there are other groups with such power. The physician also holds life-and-death decisions in his hands. Rather than arguing against restriction of the power of the judge, this simply implies that sooner or later this other power too will have to be re-evaluated, shared, and controlled.

It is not just the fact of discretionary power, but the *breadth* of that discretion which makes the problem so devastating. Five years is a maximum for Judge Garfield; it is seen as a minimum for Judge Stone. Crimes against property are a rectification of the order of things, political actions, to Judge Ravitz; they are profound threats to the fabric of civilization to Judge Stone, and will be dealt with accordingly. These sets of values constitute bias in a nonpejorative sense—but bias nonetheless, and a bias that will influence equity and fairness in exactly the same way as naked bigotry does. Wiser judges are no solution. Objective judges are impossible. It is imperative to understand that; to recognize the inequity that co-exists with decency and good intentions. To the victim of such inequity, the purposes of the punishing authority are unimportant. That is why I have chosen for my examples four decent, concerned, idealistic men.

I have presented these four judges so far as possible in their own words, and as uninterruptedly as possible within the limits of understanding. I have often hesitated from commenting even when sorely disposed to, since I assumed that whatever illumination my comment might offer would not warrant the sacrifice of continuity. This is based, again, on the conviction that "getting to know the judges" is the best way to understand the complexities of the decision-making process. Obviously, my preference would be to present all of the judges in this way. But since this is not feasible, I have decided to devote some space to a horizontal, rather than a vertical, approach; to take excerpts from many other judges in an attempt to expand the sense of contrast and conformity, common problems and individual differences.

To that end, I have assembled a melange of extracts from other interviews which demonstrate some alternative opinions and personalities from those presented in detail in the previous chapters. These comments are organized around the principles of sentencing: confinement, general deterrence, specific deterrence, rehabilitation, and retribution.

One aspect that emerges throughout the entire study is that while general deterrence—that unprovable but assumed concept—is the balance point on which the sentencing scale rests, retribution or punishment on the one hand and rehabilitation on the other are the polar points which shift the balance. To accept one is generally to deny the other. Most judges prefer the philanthropic implications of "rehabilitation" to the retributive implications of "punishment." If we must hurt someone, we prefer to think of it if not as "hurting us more," at least as "for their good." It is understandable that judges prefer to identify themselves as the teacher rather than the flagellant. But the patent failure of rehabilitation is causing an identity crisis in these good men. The gradual stripping away of the elaborate costume of rehabilitation exposes the naked form of punishment.

[Compare these two statements from one particularly brilliant and concerned judge:]

Rehabilitation can work. Young people who have no family, no love, no job, etc., can be helped when put in the proper center for a short period, e.g., Danbury. They can be taught skills, etc. Some of my bleeding-heart friends tell me it's outrageous to feel this way, but I tell them they're full of baloney. The truth of the matter is that there are some people who respond to short terms in jail, I believe.

[Now, eight months later from the same man:]

I submit that one of the real problems today, to say that rehabilitation is the only objective in sentencing—indeed, even an important objective of sentencing—is cant and immoral, simply because we all know that our present jails and workhouses are unworkable in rehabilitating anybody, even if he has a Rhodes Scholarship and a few degrees from law school.

[Since the philosophy of an individual can vary this directly in so short a time, very careful attention to the process of reasoning that leads him to one conclusion or another is needed if we are to understand the complex forces that move a judge to a specific position.]

---

*Do you believe in rehabilitation?*

Yes. Well . . . sometimes people expect miracles to occur. It strikes me as rather strange what people expect. An individual who is in society, let's say, between twenty and twenty-five years; has committed numerous crimes; and has revealed himself to be an antisocial person . . . suddenly receives a sentence in prison. Usually the average length of time one spends in state prison is somewhere in the neighborhood of twenty-two months. In that short period of time, to expect some miracle to happen in an individual whose whole life has been buffeted around and molded and now is pretty much directed in a certain course of conduct—to expect sudden change is foolish.

I think they try. More than people wish to give them credit for. When one goes up to state prisons, one sees some miracles which are wrought. One sees individuals who never painted suddenly becoming great artists. I mean truly great artists. One sees individuals suddenly furthering their education and being motivated to further their education. Innately intelligent people, who have never been motivated in the society in which they found themselves, now really being motivated to go forward. I hear a great deal of criticism with respect to the Narcotic Addiction Commission facilities. Those people who like to classify themselves as liberals make weekly or monthly jaunts to those facilities and as soon as they find a cockroach immediately condemn them, not recognizing they were a start in the right direction. And not recognizing that if these facilities failed, the hysteria which exists in society would allow the demagogues in positions of power—important power—men initiating legislation, to take over. They are already calling for life sentences for these selfsame adolescents. Suddenly these sick individuals, who would have formerly had a chance, now find themselves faced with possible life incarceration.

In those facilities, cockroaches notwithstanding, I saw fifty-odd youths, mainly black and Puerto Rican, in a class studying for a high-school equivalency exam. In one center a teacher was reading *Paradise Lost* by Milton (which is not one of the great poems of the world as far as I'm concerned, rather boring) and these youngsters, all overage, all problem kids who never attended school regularly—I'm assuming they were not the best students in the school—listening attentively. You could hear a pin drop. The teacher who was teaching them was blind and was reading by Braille. I would think people would look for that rather than the cockroaches.

———————

[The cynicism, bordering on hypocrisy, that begins to infect many judges is perhaps the most depressing aspect of the failure of our system.]

*What do you think about rehabilitation—do you believe it works?*

Well, if all the programs which are announced were properly funded and staffed then these programs would have a working chance of success! But since they are not properly funded and staffed, then whatever success they have comes by happenstance. Of course, I can only go by the statistics that are given to me, and cannot go into the validity of the figures they use or the ability of the individual who is compiling them. I must take them at face value. Since the state says it is spending twenty million dollars on a particular project, and it has indicated that it has attained a certain degree of success in that particular matter, then I'm for giving that program a chance to continue, be more vibrant and viable. If it isn't so, and they're fooling the public and fooling the people, then we still are compelled to live the lie. That's all.

---

*What about prisons? Do you think that as now constituted they serve a rehabilitative function?*

Well, prison, with the programs they *say* they have initiated, and *say* are in existence, serves a useful purpose in the rehabilitation of the individual. It causes the individual to involuntarily partake of learning a trade, schooling, or various other activities which the penal institution is involved in so as to take up the person's time. If that again is not a truthful picture, then what we are doing is merely containing an individual.

*What do you think? You've been around a long time in this area—you're a pro.*

Every time we go on inspection tours, we see people engaged in industrial achievements—we also see what they do in their spare time on their own. All of which indicates superficially that the programs do work for those persons who are motivated to aid themselves. We cannot foretell if what we see in our inspection trip is actually what takes place in common-day occurrence.

*Don't you have an impression after all these years? You're a thinking person!*

My impression—prison is merely a containment— every program they give us is a lie. But you've got to protect society, too. No judge can say that a program enunciated by the state is a falsehood because then he would have to set up his own system, and no individual judge can set up his own system. We have a choice of one or two things: either trying to rehabilitate within the confines of the program, or say the program is not so. Since I don't believe in cruel and inhuman behavior, I can't just say, "This man has committed a crime, we have no place in society for him, we've got to send him up until we learn how to reform individuals who commit antisocial actions." Nor can I simply say, "The demand of society is containment rather than social rehabilitation." That would be cruel.

*But if that's what we are doing, then shouldn't we at least say it instead of playing games?*

Well, I'm not in a position to say that in all facets of the penal system they're playing games.

*But you personally don't believe in rehabilitation—you just said you had to go along with it.*

I do believe in it. I only say we don't get the tools to effectuate it in the proper manner. We don't have enough funds, we haven't got the proper program. If you need a psychiatrist for four hundred men, and you've got two men on the staff and you pay them half of what they make on the outside in their private practice—they're not going to devote their time to the needs of prisoners. If they were properly funded we'd get the competent help to come in, but we don't.

We need remedial reading for some of our inmates, who can't even look at a joke book without looking at the pictures, and we don't provide sufficient teachers for them to learn how to read and write, so their time is being spent idly.

Now we have all these paper programs, and they'll give us a statistic saying they've got fourteen teachers in a particular institution in which maybe two show up. I don't know, I'm not over there, but they have statistics which show they are achieving education achievement, industrial achievement. That being so, it stands the community well.

If they're interested in punishment alone, why don't they go back to flogging! You flog an individual, that's sufficient, that's corporal punishment! He'll remember. Next time he does something he'll get the same thing—it may be a deterrent. But that's not our social philosophy, and since I'm a creature of the state and I must go along with the thinking of those who set down the rules of conduct, then I'm going to comply with those rules. That's all! Treat the individual rather than the crime! (Pause) Of course . . . weighing both at the same time.

[I had managed to bait this cautious political man to a point of some real emotion, although by the end he once again gathered himself together and presented the neutral stance that he felt was appropriate to the image of a judge. His primitive logic was that since nonrehabilitative incarceration is cruel (therefore illegal), we must pretend that it *is* rehabilitative to make it less cruel. While the conscious expression of such an absurd position was perhaps unique among the judges, the process of reasoning is typical of the unconscious maneuvering, rationalization, and self-deception that every individual will selectively utilize. It permits people conveniently to ignore the presence of data inimicable to their interests and prejudices. This way we reinforce our goals and satisfy our desires without compromising our self-respect.]

---

[As I said before, to deny retribution is to embrace punishment. The judge above was recognizing that, and discomfited by it. It was difficult to find any judge who truly and overtly acknowledged the concept of punishment in any of its forms. Occasionally, a particularly intellectual or philosophical judge would grasp its importance.]

If there isn't something left to retribution, can it be said that we as judges have a commission from anybody to impose sentence? . . . I feel without the concept of retribution the whole system we operate under is illogical and wrong.

———————

[This, however, was a very atypical response. More often than not, the judges were so conditioned to avoid thinking about the moral role that the concept of punishment or desserts simply could not be grasped.]

Punishment is a deterrent which is quite negligible in my opinion, because the typical individual who commits these crimes is not concerned so much with punishment as with "Can I get away with it?" That's his motivation. Of course, if the punishment was sufficient, then even if he thought he probably could get away with it, he might not be so inclined because of the risks; punishment in and of itself is generally not a deterrent. It may be in some but not in all.

*But what about punishment independent of deterrence—the concept that some people ought to be punished—do you subscribe to that?*

No. That's not our penal system philosophy. You don't punish a person because he should be punished. That is not what we are now engaged in. It is not the sphere of our actions. We are told by the acts of our legislature, by these various organizations set up to do the social thinking for the courts, that punishment itself is not the aim or goal. It is rehabilitation. We have all these programs, albeit they are really just paper programs, but they claim this is the program we have, and if that is what they give us to work with I don't think we as judges should ignore it. You can't say, "I've got my own private ideas—I'm a law unto myself—anybody who comes before me who is a bum—I'm going to give him fifty years no matter what the statute provides for. That's what he is going to get."

*Notwithstanding all that, the legislature gives you an awful lot of leeway. How do you decide whether it's going to be two years or seven years? Doesn't punishment come into that decision?*

That's based on this man's history. Of course, taking into consideration the act that he committed. Some acts are more vicious and more heinous and deserve a bigger outcry. But I just can't equate sentencing two individuals for the same crimes on the same basis; what I have learned from their past means more to me than that which they have done at this particular moment. I have an insight into their actions because of what I have learned.

If punishment is what we're looking for, I could act blindly. Both would get the same, even irrespective of the nature of the crime, and how it was committed . . . it's grand larceny in the second degree, no matter how it is committed or what means is used; but grand larceny in the second degree can be committed in various ways under the statute. The crime is the same, but there still is a difference.

[Without recognizing the fact, this judge is articulating the very reasons why discretion is attacked by many. Are we punishing the transgressor or the transgression? Is it the nature, the state, of the individual or the nature of the crime that must be attacked? Which is the legitimate concern of society? Should we judge a man for what he is or what he does? Can we fairly and specifically define what a man is independently of what he does? Should what the judge has "learned from their pasts" mean more to him than "that which they have done at this particular moment"?]

———————————

[The arguments about deterrence fall into almost predictable patterns. Individual or specific deterrence, that is, the concept that if you punish or incarcerate a man it will deter him from committing the same crime again, is accepted or rejected invariably according to the judge's faith in rehabilitation. General deterrence—the concept that by publicly punishing a man caught for committing a crime, you deter *others* who might be contemplating that same crime—is a principle that is generally accepted unquestioningly. It is never really examined, I suspect for fear that it may prove to be a fantasy. In the same way, retribution is never examined for fear it may be a fact. With most judges, general deterrence is simply assumed to work and is one justification for the fact that we apprehend and, therefore, punish only a small percentage of the individuals that commit crimes.

In general, the judges felt that white-collar criminals dramatize the point most eloquently. Here, specific deterrence was seen as unnecessary; rehabilitation is a concept not associated with the middle class; and retribution is never admitted. Therefore, general deterrence stands out most dramatically. Indeed, it may be most effective with this group.]

With a prominent person, no one is going to think the person is going to be corrected, in the rehabilitation sense, in a penitentiary. Also the chances are that we don't have to worry about specific deterrence with that man; his career has been badly smashed so he should learn. Very often then you wind up with only one possible rationalization for your sentence, and that's general deterrence. If these men don't get punished, the system has no credibility whatsoever.

———————

[Or, from another judge:]

Mostly, I'm in the rackets bureau part. If I have an organized crime figure who has led an antisocial existence for most of his life, I will give him a stiff sentence, in order to deter others from entering into this. Also to control them. If his whole life has been one of violating the law, I'll give him a stiff sentence. If I have a white-collar crime, the breach of a fiduciary relationship, a one-shot Joe type of thing—usually because the man has marital problems or a drinking problem or gambling, etc.—who has already been fired and been disgraced publicly, it would be vindictive to inflict more suffering. What more punishment is there? You don't have to control him; he's not going to do it again; you want to deter others. Certainly this individual who has gone through this type of punishment doesn't need more. Let's say he gets a year in prison. A year to a type like this may be like ten to one who is used to being in prison. It's not the same thing.

*You would not suspend sentence even though you might think he's been punished enough?*

Oh, sure, I might. But I feel we have a proliferation of white-collar crimes because punishment all too often is not imposed. I feel it is necessary to impose punishment so that people who commit this type of crime know they will go to jail. He has to recognize that if you commit such a crime, the mere fact that you come into court with a necktie and a shirt and are most polite and courteous to the court doesn't mean that you won't receive any jail time. Otherwise these types of crimes will continue to increase. In addition, it has the effect of causing individuals who commit the kind of crimes that occur within the ghetto (and usually against ghetto inhabitants) to feel that justice is evenhanded. They must not be led to feel that if a fellow is wealthy or educated or not a member of a minority group he doesn't get time. It keeps individuals who try to look upon criminal justice as a problem which can be solved in a simplistic fashion from capitalizing on this by saying, "Why should someone who is black and poor get it while another fellow with so much money gets probation?" So part of it is to show there is evenhanded justice with regard to these white-collar crimes and also to deter others.

With respect to crimes of violence, it is twofold. One, to control, and two, to rehabilitate.

---

[Most individuals examining our system of justice would tend to agree with the judge who says:]

If you take away deterrence, you have removed the principal underpinning of the whole criminal justice system as we know it. If we think we have a system built on the premise and principal cornerstone of rehabilitation, then we're bigger blithering idiots than I think we are. Our entire criminal justice system would crash in a heap if you take away the idea, or purpose, of general deterrence. It just doesn't make sense without deterrence.

---

[When it comes to prevention or protection of the society by isolation, there is an obvious and indisputable need in a certain class of offenders, as expressed by the quotations from the following two judges. First, a judge who is very anti-jail:]

Should anyone go to jail?

Yes, I certainly have no trouble sending to jail people who are going to rob, kill, or maim. It is clear to me at that point that the purpose of jail is a custodial one. It aims at prevention of these actions by the individual who predictably is going to do them. I would say that that limits it to 10 or 15 per cent of the cases we see. In these cases there isn't any recourse. For that reason, recidivists are the easiest people to jail. There are certain numbers of individuals in every society who are vicious nonconforming types. They must be controlled and the primary concern here is not some concept of justice to them but the rights of the normal people in society to be protected from the abnormal and the irrational. That, however, is a totally minor aspect and is the easiest part of the problem.

[And:]

The truth is that there are people who must be put somewhere so as to protect society. Some call them psychotics, some call them dangerous offenders. We all know there are people who in the present state of human knowledge must be removed from the scene in which they have been operating and doing the dastardly deeds for which they are being punished.

---

[In addition to the five basic considerations in the sentencing process (confinement, general deterrence, specific deterrence, rehabilitation, and punishment), there was throughout all of the interviews a distinct concern, defensiveness, or ambivalence about that peculiar phenomenon known as plea bargaining. To generalize from so small a sampling as I have is always hazardous; such generalizations are best left to the statistical studies. With this disclaimer, let me just say that it does seem that those working judges on the state and local level seem more predisposed to a benevolent appraisal of plea bargaining than their more leisurely federal counterparts.]

Recently, I've been concerned with plea bargaining. That's a very essential element in sentencing. I initially did not like plea bargaining. I thought it was immoral. Even though the Supreme Court upheld it, there was something about it I didn't like. I would still rather give a man his day in court. There may be some cases where it is indicated; maybe the district attorney doesn't have a strong case; or maybe it's a case that requires some leniency because of what the defendant has done. But to utilize it just to dispose of cases where the defendant bargains on sentence is repulsive to me.

*What do you think about these new proposals—the stiff sentencing, mandatory life, and so on?*

Look, as a practical situation they can't work out. We have a great deal of difficulty *now* coping with the problems we have. The reason we can't cope is because we are understaffed and underfinanced. Also, the incidence of crime has risen to great proportions. As a classical example, if you've got 10 per cent of 100, you've got 10. If you've got 10 per cent of 200, you've got 20. You've still got only 10 per cent of crimes committed, but you've got a greater incidence.

Now, what happens if the defendants *all* decide to go to trial? I'm trying a case now, this is the second day we're working on a jury. We haven't got past the first panel. This case took a week and a half to try the first time, and it'll take the same week and a half to try it again. That, in contrast to disposing of the matter in plea bargaining. You can dispose of it in fifteen minutes, albeit a lesser sentence. I think it is the better way of handling it. You can't ever have enough judges in any particular county to try all the cases that come in without plea bargaining.

Take the case on trial now, a hung jury in the first trial. The district attorney will take an E felony [lower charge] on a robbery case because of the mistrial. The defendant says, "I'll take the E, but I want only a year." The district attorney says, "I can't assure you a year, the sentence is up to the court." The defendant wants assurance of one year. But I'm not going to give him assurance because I don't know anything about his background and I want to look into it. Why should I give him special assurance? If he wants to go to trial, he must take his chances. If he shoots crap and loses, shouldn't he be punished? He's taking the chance. If the jury says he's convicted of robbery one, then he's not entitled to consideration of zero to four, which is the maximum under an E felony.

I'd rather dispose of it on the plea than go through a week-and-a-half trial. Will society benefit more by putting him away for fifteen years if he is convicted of robbery one?

What this guy was arguing about was really only two months. So far as time is concerned, if he is given an indeterminate sentence (0–4), they keep him no more than a year at most. Then he's on parole. So what is he fighting about? If I give him the one year, he has to do eight months. He's shooting craps for two or three months. He's willing to go to trial, have the court waste time and effort, and chance a conviction on a grade B felony. Do you treat this man in the same way you would one who is willing to cooperate? One who is willing to admit his guilt and dispose of it?

---

[Another example:]

Yesterday I had a matter where some of the witnesses are deceased. It made it quite tenuous whether a conviction could be attained based solely on the testimony of the remaining one. The defendant took a plea for a misdemeanor. I asked him, "You say you committed a crime?" He says, "Yeah." I ask him, "You're sure you held up this man?" And he answers affirmatively. Now, isn't that a horrendous situation? I would rather have the district attorney try this case and *lose* it than take a plea on a *misdemeanor* when this man admits he held up a man. But that's what we are faced with. If I were to try this case for a week or a week and a half, we'd get the same results. So I took the plea to the misdemeanor. The only reason they can't prove the case is because one of the witnesses died. So here's a man who admits to a serious crime, armed robbery, but the people couldn't prove it. So far as I'm concerned, he's still the sinner.

*Is it pretty much up to the prosecutor?*

The prosecutor can only recommend the degree of crime.

*But do you usually go along with him?*

Yes, I do. In the interests of justice. I don't care what he recommends so far as sentences are concerned. I give no guarantees. But if they say they want to take a plea to E or B or C charge, I go along.

———————

[And another judge:]

I still take the attitude that I'd rather not plea bargain and allow the defendant to tell me how much time he will go to jail, that he will "settle for five years." I'm amenable to his pleading guilty to a lesser offense so long as my hands aren't tied. I make no promises. I take no part in the bargain. In other words, I wouldn't tell him I'll give him five years provided the pre-sentencing report will support such a sentence, or otherwise I'd let him withdraw his plea. That, in my opinion, could be exploited by the other party to the bargain. So, only if they want to plead guilty to a lesser offense without curtailing my powers will I agree to plea bargaining. I think in the county we are encouraged to participate in plea bargaining by the Judicial Conference. We are asked to take a part in it. I think they mean for us to take a part in all phases of it, not only to encourage it, but also to participate in limitations in respect to sentences. We refuse to follow that here.

---

[Even a federal judge can be sympathetic to plea bargaining.]

Do I factor in a guy who cops a plea? Yes, not always, but mostly. I think that's important. After all, a truly uninhibited plea of guilty is probably the best step toward rehabilitation and should be considered. Most of the time the plea is simply a mass of total irrelevance—you know you've got to do those things that will warm the cockles of the reviewing panel's hearts, the kind of thing that has nothing to do with rehabilitating mankind, things you've got to worry about in a plea. But there are pleas that are heartfelt and there I like to give credit and I think I should.

# CHAPTER IX

# The Discretion Problem

While sentencing in the criminal courts is a crucial problem in its own right, it should always be remembered that it is only one narrow aspect of a much larger, broader field known as discretionary justice. This is one of the most poorly researched areas of law, whereas it should be the most examined. As Kenneth Culp Davis has said:[1]

> The greatest and most frequent injustice occurs at the discretion end of the scale, where rules and principles provide little or no guidance, where emotions of deciding officers may affect what they do, where political or other favoritism may influence decisions, and where the imperfections of human nature are often reflected in the choices made. . . . The further we go toward the rules end of the scale (of justice), the greater the quantity of useful literature; the further we go toward the discretion end of the scale, the fewer the books and articles. Indeed I know of no systematic scholarly effort to penetrate discretionary justice. Writers about law and government characteristically recognize the role of discretion and explore all around the perimeter of it but seldom try to penetrate it.

Plea bargaining, deterrence, retribution—all of the previous considerations, whether of definition, of process, of sentencing, or of disposition, have relevance only within the concept of discretion. A rigid and automatic sentence-for-crime system would change drastically the implications and uses of these concepts of discretion. What it comes down to is whether the individualization of justice serves justice. Does discretion bring an equity into judging the complex nature of human interaction that is not possible by mere behavior description? Or is it simply an open door for the introduction of prejudice and the personal bias of the judges? This is the question I put in one form or another to all of the judges. More illuminating than the yes or no responses (to a man they supported discretion) were the extended associations that came to mind, offering not only answers but instances of their discretionary powers in operation. Six specific examples follow.

# Example I

Now take your narcotic crimes, your marijuana, for instance. A first offender, who's trying it for a kick or is caught in an automobile riding down with his buddies, or coming home from school, no prior record, no selling, and no recent involvement in the drug game—that person might be eligible for the Youthful Offender.

*How do you feel about the broad open-ended kind of sentencing that goes with that?*

I think it is good in the case of the first offender, somebody who has technically violated the law, but who may never go off the deep end again, and is not stigmatized by this criminal conviction. I think it better, again, to spank and not horsewhip.

*But often they are detained longer under the open-ended sentence.*

Yes, we lose control of the disposition. It shouldn't be.

*But since it is, wouldn't we be better off by ruling out discrimination?*

You can't be that arbitrary! Maybe a review board. I'd have no hesitance in discussing proposed sentencing with any of my colleagues. I discuss it with the probation officer; I discuss it with other members of the bench; I discuss it with the district attorney; I discuss it with anybody who I think would help to test my thinking."

*But you don't like the idea of a nondiscretionary system?*

No. I think there are too many variations there. We're dealing with people, not things. I think we could probably get some better guidelines, but I don't think you can just make it arbitrary. Why have us here then? Anybody could do this job. Then it just becomes like a computer. I don't think you *can* do that with human nature. I don't think you should.

# Example II

Some people think I am too light in sentencing. I had some kids come in here from the newspapers and ask why I only gave a certain defendant one year. I hadn't even given it to him yet, but in taking a plea I had said what the sentence would be and that he could withdraw his plea if not satisfied. It was a young man who worked for his father, a law-school graduate, who at the insistence of his father forged some checks and delivered them to his father, who profited from them. He, himself, as a result of this exposure can no longer be a lawyer. He carries the stigma of a criminal conviction. He's a young man in his twenties. He had not profited from his crime, but had been manipulated by his father. It was a huge sum—more than half a million dollars. They, the press and all, were impressed by the sum; but

I'm impressed not only by the facts of the case but the individual. You take an individual, completely destroy him, he'll be of no use to society or himself ever again. You have a dual purpose: one, to the individual, and two, to the society. They're both on an equal plane—not more, not less. That individual is an important object to me, just as society is important.

# Example III

A judge may, after looking at a report, see that a defendant, while charged with a heinous crime, still has been through some real problems: a neglected child, placed in foster homes, not having had the benefit of any parental love or care, always been a charge on the society. He is arraigned before you for sentence for a particular crime. The evaluations by the social worker and psychiatrist indicate how his traumatic experiences in the past were contributory; they then say that this last experience has taught him the lesson that he can't be antisocial. Now, you can't deal with that individual in the same manner as you would one who comes from an intact home who commits the same type of crime in a vicious manner. This second individual had all the benefits society can confer upon him, and if he does this, his problem is different from the one we had before.

We evaluate these two individuals in a different order. That's how I operate, in any event. Punishment isn't the sole scope of my adjudication, or judgment. If it were, I wouldn't need a probation department.

# Example IV

*From the way you talk, you're a great believer in sentencing according to the individual's actions. I'm sure you're aware that there is a whole movement, particularly in the black community [the judge was black], against discretionary justice?*

It's a mistake. I really think so. In other words, they want to go back to punishing the crime. They say that whether he's black or not, he'll get three years because the crime calls for it. But the same complaint will be there; I don't think you can ever eliminate that. If all the judges in the county were black, I think there would still be a hue and cry that the blacks get tougher sentences.

*Why should that be? Suppose the sentences were fixed?*

They're not asking for that. They're asking for mandatory *minimums*. For instance, an E felony is punishable by no more than four years in the state prison. The judge now has the discretion. He could go for one or not at all. Suppose it were fixed so that for this particular crime he must be sentenced for two years in a state prison. The mandatory minimum. How does that affect anybody?

*But supposing we also said that he could spend no more than two years. Then you couldn't use any sentencing discretion?*

That's ridiculous. What about the first offender?

*You would take all that into account, in writing the law. You simply would not allow the judge to use his own discretion.*

But that's what we're here for—not just to direct traffic in the courtroom. We're supposed to reflect society's attitudes.

*But what about a society like ours where there is a bias?*

I don't see how you're eliminating it by saying he must get two years. It may have been the first time he stole;

it may have been the tenth time. O.K. Maybe *that* can be written in. But what about all the rest? You don't know the real reasons why he stole. You can't understand a person in a paragraph. You could never put into place all those many factors that might mitigate against a fixed sentence. We might win the battle and lose the war!

# Example V

There was this father and son, they had an argument. It was one of those tense, emotional things, there was no intent to kill. It was one of those unfortunate things. Of course, you could see the impact there. The father killed the boy, and he should have been sent to prison. And yet, the *feeling* was that the father loved the boy, and was trying to do the best thing for the boy, but was driven to this incident which caused the unfortunate accident when he fired a warning shot and the kid moved into the line of fire. The question was whether this man was to be sent to prison. I gave him probation. He was a physician, an outstanding physician, and I received hundreds of letters on his behalf. But some said I was still too generous. Others said I shouldn't have, the father was hurt enough. So you're damned if you do and damned if you don't.

# Example VI

I make lenient sentences. I consider it a very grave responsibility when I take away a person's liberty for the first time. I certainly don't want to add more years than one needs. I like to give the benefit of the doubt to a defendant who is going to be sentenced. Take the case of two youths who, with three other youths under sixteen, came upon a young married couple, terrorized them, kicked the man, threw him to the ground, stole his wedding ring. Then they threw the woman to the ground, beat her, and then took her to the park and raped her. They had a gun.

That's an atrocious crime! The psychiatric report revealed one went into the army while still under age and stayed two months and wasn't in any trouble (apparently he responds somewhat to a structured society). His background showed he had five felony arrests since he was sixteen. He had conflict with his mother and hardly saw his father. He no longer went to school and used narcotics. Now an individual such as that has to be placed in a structured society for some period of time, not forever. He could have received up to twenty-five years. I sentenced him to a maximum term of twelve, but I further stated he could not be eligible for parole until after four years—so it was a four to twelve. The other young man with him had a very low IQ, but because he had this low IQ, was easily led. He had to go for a considerable length of time too, so he could be controlled, so he couldn't commit these crimes. He got two years to seven, because he was not the ringleader and had cooperated. Hopefully, they'll be rehabilitated while in there but my purpose was not rehabilitation but controlling them so they can't do this again. You have to protect the young married couple on the streets. As a result of this incident, the marital relationship had become strained. The woman was unable to go out on the street alone, she needed someone with her, she was under psychiatric care. A traumatic experience like that is horrible.

*What made you decide on the sentence—why not twenty-five?*

When he took a plea, the plea that was obtained was a C felony. He was indicted for B, but with C some consideration must be shown for the defendant who shows contriteness in that he takes a plea. It saves the court the expense of the trial. It eliminates the necessity of this woman having to recount again the experience on the stand, which probably would have added to her burden. Also his age—he was seventeen. Certainly, even in a person with his record, one hopes that as he matures in a structured society he would somehow improve. You have to have hope. With a C felony, I could have given him fifteen. I shaved it to twelve and therefore could only give one third of the maximum for my minimum, which was four years. I had written down five to fifteen, but looking at him and seeing him—seventeen years old—I changed it.

It was an atrocious crime which revealed the necessity for control. But still, I thought four to twelve would be enough since he would go to a structured society where a parole board would be able to assess whether or not he was fit to go into society after he had done a minimum of four years. They would have the advantage of psychiatric testing, of seeing how he adjusted to jail. They would be in a better position to judge if he would be a good or bad risk.

If you make the sentence too severe, a person loses all hope. What's the point in changing, it's too discouraging. I had two youngsters who committed a robbery in Central Park—a nothing kind of robbery—but the victim had his neck stepped on and change taken from his pocket. And the two were addicts. The district attorney recommended a misdemeanor plea for one, but he insisted the other take a felony—the younger one. Originally, he wanted a felony from both, but I indicated that the older one already had one felony, and asked him if he wanted to give a youngster who was only eighteen two felonies. They were both addicts. As a result, since I could give them misdemeanor time, and they had already done seven months waiting trial, they would then only have two more months to go.

I wanted to send them to the Narcotics Addiction Center, where they wouldn't stay more than a couple of months either, but would then be under supervision for twenty-seven months which could hopefully straighten them out by getting them jobs, watching them. I wanted to give them *that* opportunity and still give society some control over them. During the course of the trial, the district attorney made some statements that these individuals were going to wind up doing life imprisonment anyhow because they were so bad. He was glad that one took a felony and one a misdemeanor because I would have to impose different time limitations. The defendants were brothers and the district attorney felt they should be separated. I felt differently— one brother should help the other—so I gave them the same three-year sentence and directed they be sent to the same center. And I told them what I was doing. I told them that they had better get a job, start going straight, living like human beings, having enough hope to have children whose lives might be better than their own. I told them to straighten out so that every Christmas they could send the district attorney a card telling him to go to hell—that they were still out and hadn't gone to prison like he said.

[If we are thinking merely in terms of the illegal act, disparity of sentencing is not needed. In a humanistic, individual-oriented society such as ours, however, it is not the act but the relationship between the act and actor that is important. The purpose for allowing a range and option in sentencing is, again, to serve that poorly defined concept of justice. It does not at all serve security. It is an attempt at individualization of justice by allowing for the introduction of mitigating, exculpating, modifying conditions. This discretion, however, can be drastic, and it is questionable whether it is ever justifiable to allow it to cover so broad a range as zero to life imprisonment. Such discretion does now exist.

A range of sentences, therefore, establishes for humanitarian purposes discretion at the time of judgment at the trial. There are other alternatives to allowing any discretion to the judge. Discretion is already introduced at various other stages. For example, in decisions of the parole board a sentence of the judge can be further modified. The indeterminate sentence places all the discretion at a later point than sentencing. Its justification has always been that it will allow for evaluation of the individual where it counts most. It will test his response to imprisonment and, if our purposes are reformation and rehabilitation, we can tailor the sentence to that end. The abuse of discretion here, however, has been demonstrably more flagrant even than discretion in sentencing.

Discretion in sentencing, at least, is not an essential to a system of justice and was not always as fundamental a part of our judicial system.

> Because of unhappy experiences with judges in colonial days, early American State legislatures severely restricted judicial discretion in sentencing. The law frequently specified the penalty for each offense, so that the judge served mainly to preside over trial proceedings. When a man was found guilty of a particular crime, he generally had to serve the penalty prescribed by statute for that crime.[2]

One way, therefore, in which sentencing discretion can be limited is by gradation of crimes. That is, rather than allowing the judge to take into account the various extenuating circumstances which might permit him to give anywhere from five to fifty years to an individual, the statute itself will indicate its limitations. For example, take the case of one man killing another man. In the state of New York, that may be defined as murder if it fulfills any of a number of conditions (intent to kill, depraved indifference to human life, etc.) without any of the legislated mitigating factors (extreme emotional distress, etc.). Murder is a grade A felony with a clearly circumscribed range of penalties. Other conditions will clearly define manslaughter in the first degree (a grade B felony) down to criminally negligent homicide (a grade E felony). Each offense involves the taking of a human life, but the conditions dictate different degrees of punishment. The specific provisions are given in the Appendix (p. 235).

For every crime, there are similar distinctions. What the layman calls "robbery" in the law is selectively divided into a set of crimes with varying prescribed ranges of penalties. It is theoretically possible, therefore, to remove discretion from sentencing altogether by extending the concept of gradation of crimes to something that would resemble a catalogue. Critics say that in order for gradation to be equitable, it would have to more closely resemble an encyclopedia than a list. Gradation allows distinction but not discretion. Or to put it another way, value judgments would still be introduced, but at the legislative, rather than at the judicial, end of the process. So, for example, rather than allowing a judge to decide that he wants the age of the offender, his history of previous offenses, his intentions, or his cooperativeness with the court to influence the sentence, all that would be written into the definition of the crime. First offense stealing of a certain amount, by a criminal of a certain age, with a guilty plea would carry a different punishment from that same offense by a criminal of a different age. Or same age, but different history, etc., etc. Since the distinctions would be made independent of knowledge of the criminal, it is assumed they would be "objective" rather than subjective. What is really meant is that they would be independent of a specific judgment of one man (the judge) on a specific individual (the criminal). They tend to be heavily oriented toward the acts done rather than the nature of the doer, although that is not essential. Recall "extreme emotional disturbance" as a mitigation or defense in manslaughter and murder.

While discretion could be completely removed from the

sentencing process, it is certainly impossible to remove it from the entire apparatus of justice. Discretion operates at almost every point: whether an individual is picked up on a charge; whether the police officers decide to book him; whether the district attorney decides to prosecute—and at what level of prosecution; the crowding of the calendar; the pressure to plea bargain; and combinations of these factors. The knowledge of what the sentence might be, for example, is one determinant in the decisions as to whether to prosecute and under what charge.

It is important to remember that sentencing is a paradigm; it is only one prototypic example of where discretion enters law. Therefore, whatever is said about bias in the sentencing procedure has a broader and more profound meaning when it is extended and expanded to all the other areas where bias and prejudice may equally influence discretionary decision making. To remove discretion from the judges only to give it to the policeman or jailer is not likely to enhance the quality of justice. Consider the evidence in those cases where we have already done so. Much of the current discouragement about discretion evolves from the experience with indeterminate sentences practiced in California, esteemed by many as the most progressive, advanced state in terms of penal reform. The California system has been dominated by the rehabilitation model. Here the judge abdicates the privilege of sentencing by making it indeterminate. The intention is clear and admirable. To determine sentence at the time of trial is to place it on a punitive base, and punishment has no place in a rational system. Imprisonment should be an educative experience. The length of sentence should be only so long as is necessary to reform the individual.

Too often, however, precisely the opposite has occurred. With the indeterminate sentence, rehabilitation was used as a rationalization for heaping punishment on punishment. While there may be a useful role for punishment in a judicial system, it must never be disguised as reform. When clearly defined as punishment there is the decent limit set by our own standards; but if we convince ourselves it is for the patient-convict's own good, then we are free of guilt, and there are no limits. There is little concern for "too much" where a "good" is involved. The discretionary process was at one time the pride of the liberal reform movement. It assumed that human beings were individuals and that the law, with its rigidity, must bend compassionately to the considerations of each individual case. Now the whole question of discretion is being attacked from the same humanistic forces that spawned it. They are saying, and for good reasons, that discretion has failed; that in all aspects it must be removed from the law; that the only protection for the downtrodden, the disenfranchised, the poor, the black, is in a rigid set of laws which demand equal treatment for every offense—and where the only allowable extenuations will be those in the definitions of the offense. It is, in a sense, a vote of no confidence in human compassion and fairness. While certainly understandable, I personally think that this, too, is a dangerous position. More important, I think it is unworkable.]

# CHAPTER X

# Conclusions

Clearly, something must change. The inequity of the current system is an affront to conscience made particularly offensive since it is part of a process called justice.

The solutions offered generally fall into three major categories. First, the argument that says, maintain the current system of open discretion but remove the conditions that lead to its abuse. Second, remove discretion entirely. Or third, the inevitable compromise, a constriction of discretion. The current system of discretion has its strong defenders. The judges interviewed were without exception supporters of the discretionary system, for discretion is a fundamental component of the humanistic tradition. (Although the extent of discretion as we now know it is a relatively new phenomenon.) To abandon discretion is to return to an earlier, though not more equitable, or charitable, time. Of course, this does not mean that an earlier procedure cannot, by serving a better political philosophy, be used to a better political end. But those earlier times should not be forgotten. In an autocracy, or a strongly class-oriented society, discretion was not necessary. The masses of people controlled by the criminal law were simply perceived as a mass of like beings. The "dead souls" of nineteenth-century Russia or the black slaves of nineteenth-century America could be differentiated by "objective" standards, size, weight, sex, strength, and so forth. But there will

always be fewer variables necessary to distinguish among
"things" than are necessary to distinguish among people.
In a strongly hierarchical society, that class which defines
law and enforces its use for the most part on the other class
will not perceive the distinctions, as much as the common-
ality, of that alien mass. Discrimination is therefore less
necessary.

It is in our imperfect progression away from hierarchical
structure that discretion has been expanded. The progression has accounted for the introduction of such concepts as
intention, duress, and the allowance for the unseeable and
ill-definable that may demand extenuation and mitigation.
It is the imperfection of that progression that has led us to
what should be an intolerable state of injustice, where class
judgments and class bias still prevail.

One of the solutions, therefore, is to maintain the present
system and to move closer to that ideal which alone will
effect its aim of equity. If we could live in a prejudice-free
society, presumably this current system would work.

We cannot wait that long. To remove prejudice from a
society we have to know its causes and roots, which we do
not. However, even were we to discover the very causes of
prejudice, it may well be that they are inextricably bound
into the nature of man and his social institutions, and, in a
limited form, an inevitable product of moving from small-
group living (the extended family or tribe) to large-group
living (the city, state). The small group, in its isolated territory, can be perceptually encompassed; can be identified
with; can be viewed amiably as an extension of one's self.
The "other" is not present in the community, not a part of
its law, its justice or compassion. It may be enemy or friend,
but it is "other."

In the large group, the "us" and the "other" share the
same territory and the same laws. Unfortunately, there is
no assurance that the judge and the judged will emerge from

the same group. The interviews clearly demonstrate that the opposite is far more likely.

The fact that we know so little about the nature of bias is an indictment of the social responsibility of psychiatry, psychoanalysis, and psychology. It is incredible that, in this day, when so much of man's suffering is the product of psychological aberrations (uncontrollable violence, institutionalized violence as in war, racism, sexism, drug addiction), so small a percentage of the research attention of these psychological fields has focused on the social problems. Psychoanalysis, it seems to me, has been particularly guilty of neglecting its social applications. This magnificent tool, this unique body of thought, whose very theory enunciates the primacy of irrationality in motivating man, has devoted itself almost exclusively to the application of that knowledge in limited treatment of a privileged few individuals, neglecting even in theoretical and research considerations its applicability to the social problems that may destroy us all.

There has been a considerable literature about certain specific types of bias. Shortly after World War II an interest in the nature of anti-Semitism flickered, although even here the most interesting work was by a literary figure, Sartre in his *Anti-Semite and Jew*. There have been careful individual case studies of bigots, some studies of the meaning of anti-Negro bias, but very few studies on the *nature* of bias, bigotry, and stereotyping itself. It is ironic that to this day, far and away the most up-to-date, comprehensive, and knowledgeable study is Allport's twenty-year-old work, *The Nature of Prejudice*.

If we could root out the gross prejudice that leads to stereotyping individuals by race, sex, and so on, that of course would be immeasurably contributory to a fairer system. While it may be true, as I suggested earlier, that our natural growth process, in identifying the self, must also identify an "other," and that man's biological constitution is almost calculated to the establishment of group loyalties, and group loyalty by inference defines a nongroup—what still must be investigated is whether the concept of nongroup has to bear the connotation of enemy.

Man's prolonged dependency period early impresses him with his excruciating vulnerability. The impotence of the young is a potent conditioner (particularly in an animal-like man who is "young" so long), searing into his consciousness an awareness of his helplessness and vulnerability in a world that is full of dangers and pitfalls. His earliest defense is in the recognition of the role of dependency in survival. "If I am weak there are those (parents) who are strong and who will protect me." Safety is with the group.

But we know that even the strongest biological imperatives can be modified to the needs of social living. After all, the biological competence for parenthood, which occurs naturally in the early teens, has been deferred to the twenties for the convenience of an industrial society. Solutions can be found. It is inconceivable, however, that the current inequities should be maintained while such solutions are sought, particularly if, accepting Allport's thesis, we recognize that the American society is almost designed to encourage group prejudice:

> On the basis of what is now known, we may say that prejudiced personalities will be more numerous in times and in places where the following conditions prevail:
>
> Where the social structure is marked by heterogeneity
> Where vertical mobility is permitted
> Where rapid social change is in progress
> Where there are ignorance and barriers to communication
> Where the size of a minority group is large or increasing
> Where direct competition and realistic threats exist
> Where exploitation sustains important interests in the community
> Where customs regulating aggression are favorable to bigotry

Where traditional justifications for ethnocentrism are available
Where neither assimilation nor cultural pluralism is favored.[1]

Another alternative, a short-cut method, suggests that we may not have to wait till we improve society as a whole but merely that sector which will be doing the discriminating; so, in this case, we merely improve the quality of the judges. This was an essential part of Judge Ravitz's interview, his temporary solution until such time as his more optimal solution—the abandonment of the capitalist system—could be fulfilled. Judge Ravitz was not so naïve as to ask for the introduction of less biased judges. What he was asking for, in effect, was more judges with a different bias. In his request for more "peoples' judges," he tended to lump black judges, politically radical judges, and proletariat judges into one classification.

Certainly, there can be no objection from anyone to increasing the heterogeneity of the court, making sure that it does not represent either one point of view, one class of society, or one subgroup of our social structure. It should be evident, however, that by introducing numbers of different judges with different opinions and biases, you only guarantee a greater *statistical* equity. In terms of any individual, justice will be even more disparate because as judges become more polarized, the luck of the draw becomes even more monstrous. It is one of the dangers of statistical evaluations that such a system would indeed balance out, as in a society of two in which one has everything and one nothing; both the median and the average are at the point of perfect statistical balance.

And, of course, the results of opening up the court are not all that predictable. People are different. They will insist on defying the stereotypes of even the well-meaning. It has been suggested, for example, that those who have been prosecution-oriented prior to appointment will be prosecution-type judges. This is far from the case, although it did represent my original bias, and was responsible for the following dialogue.

*You came up through the district attorney's office. Another judge might come from legal aid. Do you think it makes a difference?*

My own opinion is that district attorneys on the whole appear to be more lenient than the legal aid.

*(This was not the answer I expected): Why do you think that is?*

Well, to begin with, a district attorney's training is such that he is not strictly speaking the adversary like a defense attorney. He is a quasi-judicial official. He's imbued with the desire to do justice. There was one case of a man convicted for murder, where our investigations revealed he had a brother who may very well have committed the crime. We didn't know that he didn't commit the crime, but his brother might just as easily. After the conviction, we went to the appellate division asking them to set aside the verdict. This was for an individual with a record as long as your arm, a guy who will never win the man-of-the-year award, and who, I'm almost certain, is out on the streets committing more crimes today.

But that wasn't my function. My function was to make certain that no one was convicted unless his guilt could be established beyond a reasonable doubt. It was just as much my duty to uncover evidence which exonerated an individual of a crime, or even merely established a reasonable doubt for which he is entitled. A district attorney is quasi-official and as a result that carries over when he moves to the bench. I've found this true of almost everyone who served as a district attorney. As you go down the line, Joe Kerr, who's my colleague, is considered a lenient sentencer. You'll find fellows in the criminal court who are from legal aid who are considered tough—very tough. Take Bob White—who was head of legal aid down there. It's their reputation. I don't know if they are or not. I have here over 140 pleas, people *want* to plea before me—defense attorneys and defendants. I have more pleas than any other trial part.

------------

[The judge's explanation need not be considered definitive. It obviously serves his self-image more than sociological truth. What is important is to recognize that defense attorneys when elevated to the court often become prosecution-oriented, and erstwhile prosecution attorneys defense-oriented. The reasons are multiple; it is likely that cynicism and expiation play a part, but any generalization is difficult.

Certainly, the introduction of more black judges in a system where so many of the defendants are black is an absolute imperative. But to assume that this will lead to less disparity, or even a greater compassion for the black criminal, is to be just as guilty of stereotypic thinking as the racial bigot. The following five examples illustrate this.]

## Example I

I was extremely sensitive after Attica, which occurred just before I got on this bench. Then there was something else I was concerned about. I happen to be the only Negro judge in the area and I think about it when I sentence, particularly when I sentence other Negroes. I'm sensitive to it.

*How does that work? Does it make you harder on them, different, easier?*

No, I don't think I'm harder. I won't tolerate any aggressiveness in the courtroom—the type of aggressiveness that's associated with street behavior. Where they use bad language and accuse me of being "part of the Establishment," a "prosecutor" and a "persecutor," I don't stand for it. I say to them: "Listen here now, it's just you and me— you know what I mean?" They know what I mean. They know I've been through it. That's the way I look at it. I either say it orally or with some gesture. I don't think it's made me more lenient, but I think I consider my sentences considerably closer—I have that factor with me.

# Example II

*You said you think it's good to have a Negro judge for the effect it has on the community and other judges. Could you tell me some ways you think it does this?*

I really can't but I do sense it makes a difference. I know the failings of my own race, also their desperations and hopes. I sense that. A very successful drug pusher was arrested a few months ago. He had an IQ of 129 and he was Negro and he had fifty thousand dollars at home. I sent him to jail for seven years and told him I should send him for ten. Not only did he "kill" every Negro boy in the community that he contaminated but he has an IQ of 129, and with that kind of advantage he should be on this side of the bench. I took race into consideration. *He understood me very well!* I try to establish rapport with everyone I sentence.

# Example III

My fellow judges—I feel I have influenced them. I placed a woman on probation who had committed a homicide. A manslaughter, and I don't think it had been done before in years around here.

*What was the nature of it?*

The woman was a Negro. She had been living with another man. By the way, some of my attitudes on human relations I bring with me from the family court where I had previously served, my whole outlook on crime and what have you. Certain interfamilial behavior doesn't shock me. Anyway, this woman was in effect taking care of this man and had been for years. He found a girl friend and they had a relationship right in the apartment. The woman discovered it and went to pay a visit on the other woman and, not intending to kill (that, at least, was my way of looking at it), she stuck her with a nail file; she ran out, dropped the nail file in the nearest gutter she came to, and then went *directly* to the police department. She announced she had just stabbed a woman. By the time the police got there the woman had died.

The defendant was in her fifties, she worked three jobs —worked around the clock. She worked in the church. She had been separated from her husband, and living with this man for three years. She had a daughter about twenty-four years old. All of her difficulty centered around this man. I didn't think she belonged in the State Prison for Women, which was all I had to offer her, for a period of fifteen years. I couldn't see myself sending this woman, at this age, under these circumstances to a state institution. In my opinion, the state institutions really are for hard-core criminals.

# Example IV

I'm known as a lenient sentencer. They say I was lenient with respect to a gambling case. It was the stiffest sentence that gambler ever got in this community, surprisingly. I've been criticized in a rape case because the defendant was black. I listened to all the evidence and dismissed the case after the prosecution had finished his case. I thought that the people hadn't proven their case and I was criticized for that. That was the time there was so much agitation in the Capitol—changing of the statute in respect to corroborative evidence. I think they felt I may have injected race into it. I was written up in the local papers, although a couple of months later the court of appeals in a very similar case took the same position I did. This is the kind of pressure a black judge is exposed to. I say that to let you know I don't sentence according to the newspaper. I haven't changed my attitudes.

*You don't let that bother you?*

Not at all. I look at the case. I look at the individual and I sentence him.

I was never sympathetic to the idea that Negroes are political prisoners. I felt Angela Davis could have put her brains to better use. I think the fact that Bobby Seale and Newton are out on the streets on bail is proof that Negroes can get a fair trial. I think it's just jive talk. The guys with the biggest mouths and ability to do all the confrontation are the ones who get the press notices. Ninety per cent of the Negroes they never hear from—the ones making it every day. I don't believe this bit that there are two forms of justice. Maybe I'm parochial, my world is too small. I don't see the double standard now. I think there was in the past, but now I think if the judges around here have prejudices they try to submerge them when they come to work here. That's my personal feeling. . . .

# Example V

I feel this way. I have the greatest respect for the judges that sit with me on the family court. My appointment helped change attitudes, though. A good number of the people who came to us were black. The judges reflected their community, and the attitude was very undemanding with respect to support orders where Negroes were concerned. I felt I took a very realistic attitude, and the other judges fell right behind me. I feel you have to make the Negro male shoulder up to his responsibilities, and I'm tough on them. The white judges were easier. It was patronizing. The hidden assumption was that Negro children could subsist on lesser amounts than the white children. That changed since I've come. Maybe the other judges thought, God, he's awful tough on Negro males—something we didn't want to do before. I think introducing more black judges on the bench does have an effect on the other judges, since a large percentage who come before the courts are Negroes. A considerable amount is for dope addiction and related crimes. I don't think their attitudes [the white judges] are like ours. We hate narcotics, because we really know what it does to people. It's taking black manpower and destroying it.

[The variety of influences that go into disparity of sentencing extend well beyond generalization or categorization. Even with a selection procedure which attempted to bring the best of men into the judiciary, there would be unpredictable individual biases which would cause large swings in sentencing because of the infinite variations in the moral judgments people make on individual behavior. Take, for example, the following article from *The New York Times*. In this case the judge ordered that a three-and-a-half-year-old not be allowed to set foot in her mother's residence or even be allowed "in the presence" of a man whom he described as the "paramour" with whom the mother was "cohabitating." The mother, aged thirty-four, and a social worker, had been living these past two and a half years, unmarried, with a thirty-five-year-old graduate student in education. They were living in a two-bedroom, fourth-floor walk-up in the East Village in New York City.]

The judge did check out the "inadequate living conditions and character of the neighborhood" on an "extremely rare" trip to the city from his home on Sandy Hill Road, among the wooded estates that rise above the beaches of Oyster Bay Cove. (Three telephones are listed, one under "children.")

He wrote his decision with the air of one who has seen strange sights in a far country:

Although the couple has rented a second apartment next door and taken down the intervening wall, Judge Delin said, "The small, antiquated apartment leaves a great deal to be desired."

There was no "fully equipped bathroom, as such," he reported, since the plywood-topped bathtub is situated—as in a generation of old buildings—in the former kitchen of the second apartment and the toilets are separate.

"Furnishings are very modest and the decorations quite meager," he wrote.

"This," said Mrs. Brienze, is "the judge speaking for society but with the voice of what he is personally—conscientious to the utmost but rigid and conventional."

What is he more specifically? Like all judges, even those in the supersensitive family courts, he is many things:

A former chief assistant district attorney of Nassau County (chief of homicide, deputy chief of rackets) . . . a Republican appointee to the bench in 1970 and "good party man" without previous experience in family law but since elected for a 10-year term . . . 49 years old, a "good father" . . . a Catholic and graduate of St. John's University Law School . . . an Elk, a Legionnaire, a Levittown Volunteer Fire Department member and leader in the Massapequa Boy Scouts.

"Any judge is the product of his whole life experience," said Judge Florence M. Kelley. "In Family Court, in particular, you have to hope we have enough breadth, and enough sensitivity to values that are foreign to our own, to detach ourselves somewhat."[2]

If one thinks in terms of individual values, shaped by individual experiences, beyond the coarser and grosser concepts of stereotyping prejudices it becomes apparent that bias is inevitable. There probably can never be a bias-free individual, any more than there can be a value-free judgment. Even in the "objective area of the sciences, the impact of values is everywhere apparent in what are misguidedly thought of as nonsubjective, scientific, or technological decisions. If we recognize the concept of bias as a part of the heritage of each man's growth, exposure to circumstances, and so on, it may lead us to abandon attempts to eliminate it and content ourselves with disarming it.

To say that there are no "objective" or value-free judgments does not imply that all "subjective" decisions must be considered alike and condemned. Referring once again to another problem in psychology and law, even if we were to accept the concept that all behavior is determined, we still can, and ought to, distinguish between the kinds of determination. Despite its illogicality in a puristic sense, we can, indeed must, arbitrarily assign responsibility to some behavior, and not others. The purposes of justice demand such "illogicality." We excuse the man who, unwitting and unwilling, commits an act of aggression as a result of a toxic delusional state; we do not excuse the hired "enforcer" of a mob, even though his behavior may also be an involuntary end product of a chain of life-circumstances over which he had no control. The law will and should draw those lines necessary to its ends, and define its logic, for its own purposes.

An excessive, across-the-board use of sociological and psychological excusing conditions will only drive the law-abiding majority to reject them all. Perhaps the judge in

*Erewhon,* that topsy-turvy world where only illness is punishable, summarized the position best:

> You may say that it is not your fault. The answer is ready enough at hand, and it amounts to this—that if you had been born of healthy and well-to-do parents, and been well taken care of when you were a child, you would never have offended against the laws of your country, nor found yourself in your present disgraceful position. If you tell me that you had no hand in your parentage and education, and that it is therefore unjust to lay these things to your charge, I answer that whether your being in a consumption [tuberculosis] is your fault or no, it is a fault in you, and it is my duty to see that against such faults as this the commonwealth shall be protected. You may say that it is your misfortune to be criminal; I answer that it is your crime to be unfortunate.[3]

There are certain "faults" in judges, also, which can be defined as crimes and declared intolerable. And while it is true that there is an inevitable continuum of subjective distortion between a paranoid obsession at one end and "taste" or preference at the other end, we are obliged to draw an arbitrary line and say, "To this side is bigotry and prejudice, and not allowable; the other side is permissible human variation." To dismiss the problem by saying, "all decisions are biased," would represent the kind of theoretical truth that requires equating Roy Bean with Solomon.

It is incredible how cavalier we are in our selection or election of judges. Professor Harold J. Rothwax, then of Columbia Law School and now himself a judge, said, "A basic problem of the court is the quality and dedication of its personnel. We do not select our judges wisely or well; we do not train them sufficiently; we do not monitor or value their performance." Mr. Rothwax noted that the judges in New York City were appointed by the mayor after being screened by the Committee on the Judiciary. Mr. Rothwax continued,

> Although the members of the Mayor's Committee are estimable and honorable men, they have consciously approved men whom they know to be unqualified. . . . A large and continuing flow of unqualified appointments will mock and impede for years to come all our other efforts to rationalize, humanize, and systematize the operations of the court.
>
> The judges and the prosecutors are often experienced but they usually are poorly trained for the position they occupy. They are "room-wise" but either unaware or indifferent to the larger human and social implications.[4]

To attest that man differs from the machine is not always to claim the superiority of the machine. Biases will, of course, shape judgments, but this subjectivity need not imply injustice. It may be precisely that which defines human compassion. Indeed, a decent case can be made that such subjective compassion ought to be an essential ingredient in the law, provided, of course, there can be some way to protect against those extremes which cross the border from reasonable concern to irrational exploitation. To that end, I think it important to examine some examples in which judges, while indicating clearly how their judicial behavior is influenced by their past, still would not necessarily be excluded from the criterion of fairness.

Judge Tracy had a cocky manner and a jaunty walk. Sandy-haired, blue-eyed, cigar sticking out of the corner of his mouth, he was the prototype right down to his name of the typical Irish politician. He happened to be Jewish. He kept me waiting for one hour in his waiting room. When he did show up he had a couple of cronies with him, didn't remember who I was, and then assured me that he could handle the whole thing in ten minutes. I assured him that it would take longer and he said, "Don't forget I'm a fast talker."

I was prepared to dislike him. In the end I found a concerned man. And I liked him. At the time of the interview, he was involved in a case which was attracting a great deal of publicity. This explains the opening question.

*Don't you think there is a kind of political pressure, with the public and press watching?*

I take a great deal of pride out of being a dissenter. I fight the government if I think it's wrong. For example, I think this mandatory minimum sentence is outrageous. I think the governor's policy is outrageous, and I've been rather outspoken about it—to my detriment. But I continue to be outspoken because I feel it very strongly. I made a speech Saturday before four hundred assistant D.A.'s. I stated that in the name of humanity you must always react to the particular person. As a public official, in the justice system, you will quite often be hit by the squalls of opinions of the moment. If you can't take that kind of storm and weather it, you have no business being a public official. You have to act on your expertise, that's why you're elected. If you're going to merely take polls and find out what 51 per cent of the public want every time you act, you don't need a judge—all you need is someone from Lou Harris or Gallup. You're put in because you have a degree of expertise which you have developed over the years. The one thing that bothers me most about this period of hysteria we're now undergoing is that, with the heavy criticism of judges and the justice department, some of my colleagues have just folded. They have the balls of tsetse flies, and instead of giving a youngster probation when they should, and formerly would have, they now take the safe way and sentence him to five years in prison. That's one of the evils of the current hysteria. They play it so the press or governor can't criticize. My attitude is, let them criticize! I welcome it! I enjoy it! I love a fight! I will do what I think is right.

*Why are you that way? Can you tell me a little about yourself, where you come from, what's your background?*

Well, I grew up in the city, was a competitive youngster, played ball in school, in college. Always played ball. Made my way through school playing ball. Somewhat competitive as a result. Went into the army—was in the infantry in World War II. Confronted while I was in the army with anti-Semitism. Fought it. Tried as a result to exhibit myself as braver and better. Not too great a student at college level, not motivated to be—playing ball, athletics. Went to law school. Extremely motivated to do well, and there did very well. In law school roomed with a young man who was black—in those days it wasn't such a popular thing to do—Pete, he's still my good friend. Always took positions which I thought were right, whether they were unpopular or not, maybe for ego satisfaction, maybe because I truly believed it—I truly believed I could fight my way out of it. I was an Assistant D.A. here and got a break to become Chief Assistant D.A.

*Why did you go to the D.A.'s office?*

We applied—both Pete and I—we didn't know where we should go, we applied here. I was going to be a labor lawyer, that's what I was studying. I wanted to represent unions—better working conditions for people, but came here, worked, did well, became Chief Assistant D.A., because they needed someone to improve the image. Out of the blue it came. Went in, revamped the entire office—changed it completely. Removed the political chairs from it. No more private practice. Hired kids right out of law school. Made it a very fine office. During the first years hated, but respected, by everyone—regulars, party people, reformers, people in the office who felt threatened. But changed that around—changed it so everybody got to like me—everybody. Made it a hell of an office.

*Are you still a competitive guy? Do you play competitive sports?*

Oh yeah, tennis.

*Are you a hard man on the courts?*

Oh yeah. See that cup? Our office beat Smith's office. They were the champions of the legal baseball league and we played the final. Last inning we were behind 4 to 1. We finally got one run, and then a second, and third. Then, with 2 out, I'm the guy that comes up, and bang—a double into left center—we won. I'm competitive!

*You imply more than that—you imply you like being Peck's bad boy.*

Yeah. I enjoy it. Sure.

*Where were you in your family?*

First. Two other brothers and a sister. My father died when I was still young.

*So you were very early the man in the family, so to speak?*

Yes, we lived with my grandparents and my mother had to work.

———

[Judge Davis, soft-spoken, almost gentle, contemplative, conservatively dressed—and black. Throughout the interview he was most often moved to passion, anger, resentment, and a bitterness, which was inconsistent with this most untendentious of judges, when the subject of drugs was discussed. Toward the end of our interview came the following interchange:]

. . . As to my attitude about the people who come before me on drugs. I'll admit that I had a lot of hope for the Narcotic Control Commission until it was sabotaged by those people in the city. They threw everything into it. All the hardened criminals who just happen to use dope were coming back every six months—with serious crimes like mugging, rape, robbery. The Commission couldn't cope with it. You've got to be hard on them, even though they incidentally happen to be drug users. I don't want to send *them* to the Commission, because they turn them loose too soon regardless of the seriousness of the crime—anything short of murder. They say they'll treat them and dry them up in five months, then turn them back to the community, and they go right back to the same thing.

*Do you feel you can tell between the criminals who are narcotic addicts and addicts who happen to commit crimes?*

Yes. I rely upon pre-sentence reports. If I'm not satisfied, I'll resubmit it. I don't know if I'm harder than my fellow judges.

*What do you think of free distribution of heroin as a concept of control?*

I'm opposed to it. I don't think even if it's controlled that society needs it. I'm even opposed to marijuana. By keeping it in society it's accessible. What does society need it for?

*What about methadone?*

If a young fellow says, "Send me to methadone instead of jail," I will. I don't like that either—it's just a substitute drug. But I insist that he go down every day for his methadone. I'll do that before I'll put him in jail. Until we get something else, however, if he won't go on methadone, I'll jail him. I have to protect society. I had a son I "lost" through Vietnam—I lost him through addiction. That rides me too. I have had those nights where I'm afraid for the telephone to ring. I have empathy for parents who have been through it. He's [the son] been put away—he's in the military. But the army can't help him. Eventually they'll release him but I'm not hopeful. The cure rests with the individual. He has to want to do it. . . .

*How do you explain what happened to him?*

I have to blame myself. He was a good boy. I get kind of carried away but I neglected him. He didn't do it on his own. You've got to excuse him. I have a daughter—a very good girl.

*Why are you so despairing of your son, so hopeless?*

He's twenty-eight. He's been on drugs about seven years—I'm guessing. It may not be that long. But I don't thing there's enough out there to help him. The President has cut back on all the programs that might help him. These addicts need a lot of help. We don't have enough facilities, enough psychiatrists. That's my own personal opinion. We're trying a young boy today—his name is John Doe— I've known him since he was fifteen. He killed a store owner. He kept coming back—they repeat. A lot of them were nice boys, but drugs are terrible. There's something in a Negro neighborhood, where you're pressed to try it. You've got to "go along." I don't know how to cope with that. I've got a lot of friends in the same position as I'm in. I went to a drug rehabilitation center the other night and saw a lot of my friends there. We're fighting it this way. If there's anything they want from me, I always help these halfway houses. When it doesn't work, they send me the nicest letters saying they tried, but they couldn't make it. They surrender. I don't know what it is in the Negro community. There's not the resistance against it that ought to be there. Our middle-class Negro children are under a lot of pressure, with parents who so badly want them to succeed.

---

[Judge Robinson was the classic tough guy with the heart of mush. He demonstrated enormous empathy and compassion for the deprived and the underprivileged, yet seemed totally insensitive, indeed resistant, to the idea that this could relate to his own past. It would be presumptuous on the basis of the short time with him to indicate *how* it related, but that it did so would seem unquestionable. Yet consider the following excerpt:]

Let me give you one case. A fellow comes up who was sort of glum. He comes from France, his family was exterminated during the Hitler holocaust, he escaped as a youngster—he was eight or nine. He settled in Argentina. Got a job in a brokerage house; two people he met there asked him to carry some securities to a transfer agent. He did. Then they asked him to do it again. The first time he didn't know it was stolen but the second time he became wiser and knew it. As a result of this there was a $59,000 loss suffered by the brokerage house. He, himself, is a patsy. He got $2,500 as his share.

Came time for sentence, and I'd read the probation report. He has a wife and a couple of kids here so I was going to give him a minimal sentence of six months. I was also going to fine him. Then I read further in the report. He lost his job and couldn't get a job in a security house anymore and I decided this guy suffered plenty. Society hasn't treated him any too well. So I just gave this particular individual probation, and recommendation against deportation. I figured he had a credit card for what society had done to him. That's true of many of the young black and Puerto Rican kids that come up. On the other hand, you're worried they can hurt other blacks or Puerto Ricans; you've got to protect the community. You have the whole thing to think about.

*You don't feel that the fact that you come from poverty, out of a ghetto and are Jewish, has affected certain values and attitudes you have?*

I don't think so. I don't believe so. I haven't discovered that a judge because of his ethnic strain will be a certain way. I really haven't found it that way.

———————

[On balance, I believe the present discretionary system is a product of our conceit. We would like to think that we are better than we are, and while we certainly can be better than we now are, the ideal necessary for so broad a discretionary system to work seems unfortunately remote. Painful as it is to abandon cherished dreams, the time may have come for us to do so.

Now, what about the possibility of moving to a totally nondiscretionary system. Is that desirable? As I have stressed, almost to a man and across identifying barriers of age, race, and political outlook, the judges have been opposed to a nondiscretionary system of sentencing.

Judge Harold R. Tyler, Jr., said recently:]

. . . If the death sentence is deemed cruel and unusual punishment because the same crime receives different sentences in the same jurisdiction, most punishments should be ruled unconstitutional. For almost all offenses against the law seem to be treated differently. If just punishment must fit the prisoner and not only the crime, it can be argued that no two cases are the same. *That is why laws must be applied with discretion.*[5]

———————

Here are some of the interviewees' comments:

Uniformity of sentences is the bunk. Ununiformity of sentencing is what is really required. I think recently of a case of three bank robbers. I gave these three different sentences because three different sentences seemed indicated. Unless one thinks of sentencing as a deterrent, which seems totally unprovable, and I don't believe [it] at all, I see no sense in the establishment of uniformity. I do believe in punishment. I do believe that certain crimes deserve or even demand some retributive acts, but that will never be definable by a statute. In addition, the judgment of punishment will vary from one individual to another. In some cases, probation can be punishment. Thirty days also can be a serious punishment. I think of a young boy I recently saw, a graduate of Hotchkiss and Yale. He was not working. He was supported by his girl friend. His father was paying him a regular allowance to stay away from home. He was brought in for selling narcotics. I gave him five years' probation with thirty days to spend in jail. I felt that he had to have a sample of what he might potentially have for five years—to understand what the choice was for him. I demanded that he receive no more money from his father and leave his girl friend. He is now working at a magazine and he's had three promotions. He's highly regarded there. He's going with another woman in a much more stable relationship.

---

A greater problem, of course, is mandatory sentencing. I've sent numerous people to jail who shouldn't be there, because of the inflexibility of the mandatory sentence and its inability to anticipate the marvelous complexities and intricacies of human behavior. I also have cases where I did that which I was not legally allowed. There is the case of a black man from a very good family who committed armed robbery, certainly a serious offense. It seemed to me obviously an aberrant action. By every indication he seemed to be a potentially rehabilitative individual. However, the offense is nonprobationary. Nonetheless, I ignored it and put him on probation, sent him to college and psychiatric treatment. I violated the law to do that! His family, however, have resources and understanding and were obviously going to take responsibility for the rehabilitation.

---

A first degree murder case is a mandated twenty years. Obviously I have no problem with this with a presidential assassin or a recidivist. That kind of case doesn't bother me, or I presume anyone. But I recently had a case of a man forty-eight years old, a responsible decent person involved in an unhappy, and what seemed irreconcilable position with the woman he loved. They decided on a suicide pact. It was clearly established by fact that he killed her and then seriously wounded himself. By all the definitions of first degree murder, he qualified, and therefore I had to assign a mandatory twenty-year sentence.

---

Two men commit the same crime. One is twenty years old and one is twenty-one years old. Equally guilty and the conditions are the same. One gets three months and one gets ten years. The statutes constantly hem us in. To follow the law, I am forced to do things that by almost any standard in the individual case would be seen as morally obscene.

---

To go back to the main issue, one of the things that worries me about having a legalistic catalogue of sentences is that you will lose sight of the human and moral problem. I happen to believe there ought to be a colloquy with the defendant or at least between the judge and defendant's lawyer designed for the ears of the defendant, so he could respond if he chooses to. In fact, most of the time I tip my hand as to what route I'm thinking about, so they can get after me if they don't think it's right. I'm chagrined to find how often lawyers, most particularly private lawyers, don't take advantage of that opportunity.

[Time after time, drawing on personal experience and with considerable passion, the judges defend the right to discretion. The rhetorical counter to such sensitivity by judges is the traditional one: those in power will always find rationalizations for the perpetuation of their power. While I do not dismiss this, and recognize it as a significant fact of inertia built into any system, I think it an oversimplification and an injustice if offered as the basic and even exclusive explanation. I suspect, as a matter of fact, that its psychological roots stem less from the vicious and ignoble aspect of man than from his hopes and his ideals. It is an essential element of the humanistic tradition that needs to see each individual as *sui generis,* distinct and unclassifiable; our pride and vanity that insists that the distinctions from one man to the other must be greater than the distinctions among penguins. It is the tradition of individualism which forces us to defy pigeon-holing, and is threatened by any categorization of punishments, since this implies a categorization of behavior and people.

It may indeed be only a conceit of man. B. F. Skinner specifically states so, that freedom and human dignity are two dangerous illusions which must be abandoned if man is to preserve himself,[6] an argument with which I do not agree.[7] Nonetheless, discretion in terms of individualizing sentences is an idea that has been given its time and not worked. The reluctance to abandon it, in myself as well as others, is the reluctance to abandon the aspiration to full understanding and total fairness, which may merely represent clinging to innocence.

The answer, however, is not necessarily to turn to a nondiscretionary system. First off, such a system is no more practically possible than it is desirable. Of course, when you are simply thinking of the sentencing process, you can remove discretion. You can demand that a judge impose $\underline{X}$ number of months for offense Y. But the sentence is only one part of the interlinked process that begins with the commission of a crime and ends with the person's release from jail. It has been traditionally known that there is a closed-system effect, as in some huge interconnected hydraulic circuit: constrict it in one area and you increase the pressure in another. When sentences are mandatory, the discretionary process increases at every other level. The determination to arrest an offender will be influenced. The police, after all, only arrest a certain number of "criminals." They exercise a moral judgment; they decide what they wish to consider a crime and what they do not wish to consider a crime. Certain crimes are rigorously prosecuted in certain communities and left alone in others. The treatment of prostitutes is a prime example. If there is mandatory sentence with no bargaining, then the number of trial cases with which the police will be embroiled will influence them and force a discretion in whom they choose to arrest. The factors of economy and expediency will always triumph over the technical law.

Perhaps the widest discretion we now have is at the level of the police officer. The next widest discretion is at the office of the district attorney and prosecutor. How many will be prosecuted and to what charge is at his discretion. Again, mandatory sentences will vastly expand *his* discretion. For moral or humane purposes, the prosecutor as a human being will be reluctant to see someone charged because of a technical violation of the law, when he knows that extenuating factors are present which can no longer mitigate the fixed sentence. In addition the very practical, less philanthropic fact is that the prosecutor wants a conviction; and he is aware that with mandatory sentences certain convictions will be much more difficult to get from juries. When discretion is removed, plea bargaining will be enormously expanded and the judge will express his discretion this way. If, as part of this system, plea bargaining should be eliminated, then the decision to prosecute or not to prosecute will play a greater role in the criminal process. You will, inevitably, be squeezing the discretionary process down from the judge to the arena of the local district attorneys, sheriffs, police—not necessarily an improvement in discretionary sensitivity.

And even were it possible to eliminate discretion, is this desirable? Every model of absolute nondiscretion that I have examined, even in limited areas of criminal law, has always seemed unmanageable in its gargantuan dimensions, unfair in its arbitrary cutoffs, and silly in some of its specificity. I remember particularly a model to define pornography in the law, rather than in the minds of the judges (although I will grant that it's perfectly silly there too); by the time I got to a moral line being drawn through "the lower limit of the upper perimeter of the areola of the nipple of the female breast," I had given up.

There is, and always will be, a place for the undefinable in law as well as in life. We are left then, I am afraid, with the inevitable compromise, a constriction of discretion from the current excessive level. How to locate the correct point of compromise is the question.

One novel suggestion is that we strip the sentencing procedure from judges. The arguments for this were eloquently and colorfully marshaled by Judge Nicholson, who then rejected the suggestion. However, even so severe a critic of his fellows as Judge Marvin Frankel is also opposed to this. He states: "In proceeding, then, to consider possible roads to improvement, I start with the assumption that sentencing not only will be, but probably should be, left in the hands of judges."[8]

The argument on which he bases this goes in part as follows:

The point is not simply, or mainly, that other professions are inadequately qualified. Rather, for all the wretchedness of our performance to date, I think vital aspects of the sentencing function are particularly legal, and peculiarly within the special competence of people legally trained. Granting that psychiatrists and other professionals have much to contribute, the eventual judgments as to criminal responsibilities and the penalties for offenses are squarely within the legal order. They are judgments that must turn in the end upon the weighing of values, interests, and choices in the everyday province of legal rather than psychiatric study.[9]

I am inclined to agree with Judge Frankel that turning over sentencing to psychiatrists or sociologists would not improve the matter. As legal purposes and psychiatric purposes differ, so do legal perceptions and psychiatric perceptions differ, and it may be best not to confuse these two areas any more than they already have been. On the other hand, it is not necessary that sentencing be transferred from one ultraspecialist to another. It is conceivable that a distribution of power away from an increasingly focalized élite is in order here as elsewhere. The judgment of an ombudsman, or community standards expressed through a community committee (a separate sentencing jury?) might have a refreshing impact. It is not an impelling consideration but an interesting one.

Even if such a system did not work in terms of sentencing fairness, it could serve ancillary, worthwhile goals. Anything that opens up the institution of government to the impotent mass of people excluded from participation in their own destinies is worth trying. Something must be done to allow our disenfranchised a participatory role in society. The vandalism, the gratuitous destruction, and the graffiti mania that seem ever-increasing are not only signs of alienation but pleas for attention.

Another suggestion has been to use sentencing tribunals. Judge Talbot Smith, who called sentencing a "baffling" and "gray area of criminal administration,"[10] feels that one man is not competent to do the job. He favors a three-judge counsel, which would review pre-sentence information, psychiatric reports, the elements of the charge and criminal offense, and then discuss the case. In his model, each judge first decides upon the sentence he would give, then a discussion follows in which the judgment of each judge is challenged by the others. This conference discussion would produce the sentence. One judge interviewed approved of this scheme, but with little enthusiasm:]

I had a case to decide which involved the death penalty. It troubled me very much. If ever a death penalty was justified, it was here. We have the procedure of the tribunal so I utilized it. After a long discussion with the tribunal one said yes and one said no. So, once again, it was up to me since I was the one who saw the man.

Another judge disapproved vehemently:

I don't agree with the panel approach at all. It's the good old American dodge of appointing a committee when you don't want to make a tough decision. I think the judges who don't have to make the decision, even though they're on the panel, won't really think about the case thoughtfully. I deplore and abhor the committee idea for this.

[My personal bias is against a sentencing committee. As a man who has always seen the ideal group for the vast majority of human activities as two, except for a minority of cases in which the ideal group is one, I am wary. A committee more often becomes an excuse for sharing blame rather than responsibility. It also affords the anonymity that protects from shame of consequence, so that people tend to do in groups things they would be reluctant to do if singly accountable.

I am reinforced in my bias against group decisions by my experience with another dreadful example of discretionary justice, the Federal Parole Board. In another place,[11] I have discussed in detail the nature of this pursuit of charity, and how this model of "group process" has in action deteriorated from its stated methodology and whatever aspiration originally inspired it. At that time I reported that, while the published rules stated that a majority of five members made each decision, it had in fact been operating under an "emergency procedure" which had been going on for six years before my study. The actual procedure was a five- to ten-minute interview, which was referred to as "the hearing." Afterwards, the interviewing member called a colleague in Washington who had presumably reviewed the record. If the colleague concurred, parole was granted or denied and the matter ended there. Only if there was a disagreement would the third member be consulted. That was the process they referred to as a "majority decision." Of course, when the decision was reached, no justification or rationale was made and no argument presented.

That "emergency procedure" was recently made official; and in typical Madison Avenue style, where each deterioration in a product is advertised as "new and improved," this compromise was not announced regretfully as a necessary expedient, but was extolled as evidence of a new efficiency. It seems to me that more often than not this kind of deterioration is the inevitable result of committee work. A group performance, particularly in a bureaucracy, is generally below the median of its individual judgments. Nonetheless, we do have decision committees on whom democracy depends; the jury system and the Supreme Court alone could support an argument alternative to mine, so there is no reason not to experiment with this idea.

Finally, in addition to these suggestions, which ought to be considered, there are certain modifications to the present procedure which appear long overdue for adoption. It would seem to me that a minimum program to restrict the influence of blatant bias, to enhance the sense of fairness, and to introduce a greater measure of justice into "the processes of justice," must include the following five processes.]

# 1. A Sentencing Follow-up Procedure

[The remarks below are typical of what I was to hear from many judges:]

*Do you think that jail or penitentiary serves rehabilitation generally?*

They're supposed to rehabilitate, but who knows? Now, for instance, the only follow-up we have is that if someone we sentence commits something again, then that's called to our attention, but the parole people take over from there on. We lose all control over the case once he has been sentenced, and we don't know how they turn out. With probation it's different. We do know when they are discharged from probation because we sign the discharge and read the report recommending the discharge.

Some follow-up report, at least on those cases with significant periods of incarceration, should be returned to the courts. Whether a judge will take advantage of the opportunities present for assessing sentencing procedures is of course open to question. But the conscientious judge should have an opportunity to be as decent and effective a sentencer as possible.

## 2. A Statement of Sentencing Reasons

When a judge assigns a sentence now, he is under no obligation to explain why he imprisoned a man for the maximum sentence, imprisoned him for a minimum sentence, let him go on probation, or whatever. There is almost a consensus of feeling that nothing so provokes bitterness among offenders as the disparity of sentences. Particularly when this is unjustified by argument, it will be assumed by the prisoner, in fact, as unjustified. But in addition, if the judge is forced to present reasons for assigning sentence, he will have to document the facts which influenced him rather than the prejudices. Either in the presentation of his argument or in anticipation of it, a judge will have to examine and weigh the real considerations. Further, if there is to be a review of sentencing, this will facilitate intelligent review. One can compare the stated reasons with the actual conditions. Professor A. R. N. Cross, speaking of the determination of sentences states:

> . . . In the main, it is necessary to rely for this purpose on intuition and common sense. I think these are singularly poor substitutes for a statement of reasons for sending a man to prison for a long time, and I would like to make the tentative proposal that . . . a judge should be obliged to state the reasons for doing so.[12]

Sol Rubin, who is a strong defender of individualization in sentences, feeling that individualization and equality complement each other, said that there is a need to require the judge to give reason for sentence; to require pre-sentence investigation; and to gather and distribute information on sentences. He feels that this material would then give a base from which to challenge a sentence that has not adequately been exploited. Rubin says:

> The appellate courts everywhere have the power and obligation to apply the Fourteenth Amendment test of equality to sentences, and if the sentences do not meet the test, to reverse. . . . It is a general power to review error, the obligation to protect Constitutional rights.[13]

# 3. Appellate Review of Sentences

Many of the judges interviewed felt that the absence of an appellate review for sentencing was a serious omission in the judicial process. The American Bar Association has recommended it. Numerous organizations across the country concerned with legal and judicial matters have seen this as a particularly glaring omission from our federal system. But even within the state system, less than half the courts have an appellate review of sentence available, and where they are written into law they are often not properly used.

In print, at any rate, it is very hard to find anyone who still offers a rational public argument against sentence review. Judge Lawrence E. Walsh (former judge and former Deputy Attorney General of the United States) said in a sentencing seminar that he did not feel sentences and the appellate review thereof were of "public interest." He stated, "Anybody who is worthy of being a district judge should be left alone with his judgment. . . ."[14] In that same seminar, Judge Leo Brewster also expressed his opposition to appellate review of sentences:

> It is better to have one man with the advantage of having observed the particular defendant and others appearing and giving information, and with the further advantage of hav-

ing theretofore observed many other defendants appearing
for sentencing, than to have a panel of three judges, none of
whom has ever seen the particular defendant involved during the sentencing proceedings, and most of whom have
never seen any defendant during any sentencing proceedings.[15]

Nonetheless, the official hierarchy in the law field has en-
dorsed the need for review in the strongest terms.

Among the ironies of the law there are many surrounding
the manner in which sentences are imposed in the majority
of our jurisdictions. One of the most striking involves the
methods for determining guilt and the methods for determining sentences. The guilt-determination process is hedged
in with many rules of evidence, with many tight procedural
rules, and, most importantly for present purposes, with the
carefully structured system of appellate review designed to
find out the slightest error. Yet in the vast majority of criminal convictions in this country—90 per cent in some jurisdictions; 70 per cent in others—the issue of guilt is not
disputed.

What is disputed and, in many more than the guilty plea
cases alone, what is the only real issue at stake, is the question of the appropriate punishment. But by comparison to
the care with which the less frequent problem of guilt is resolved, the protections in most jurisdictions surrounding
the determination are indeed minuscule. As has been observed, "the whole intricate network of protection and safe-
guards which were [the defendant's at the trial] . . . van-
ishes and gives way to the widest latitude of judicial discretion . . . nine out of ten plead guilty without trial. For
them the punishment is the only issue, and yet we repose
in a single judge the sole possibility for his vital function."*

It is not an overstatement to say of these jurisdictions
that in no other area of our law does one man exercise such
unrestricted power. No other country in the free world permits this condition to exist.[16]

* Remarks of Judge Simon E. Sobeloff.

The public statement differs from the private view. Several years ago, the chairman of the Criminal Rules Committee of the American Bar Association surveyed the Federal District Court judges and found that 90 per cent opposed the concept of a review board. Recently, however, the same committee has proposed a mandatory review of all sentences.

This ambivalence between official and private views, coupled with the pervasive apathy of the general public, has defeated an overdue reform. It *is* overdue. The need is not debatable. It is the minimum which must be done, and it must be done quickly.

In considering appeal of sentence, the question always arises whether this should be a privilege of the defense only or, as in some countries (Canada, for example), the government should also be free to appeal. In other words, should we allow sentences to be reviewed up as well as down? There is no reason why bias and partisanship cannot operate to grant a defendant too *low* a sentence. Some of the scandals in New York City suggested an excessive empathy with Mafia figures by certain judges. Logic would seem to imply that fair is fair, whether up or down. I feel myself that allowing review upward would probably be unwise. It would threaten inadequate defense attorneys and defeat the automaticity which is essential for serious and successful review. While it might permit some unfair sentences to slip by, the weight of injustice at this time is most grossly felt when *excessive* incarceration is assumed. The bulk of pro-defendant injustice is usually in the processes (arrest, charge, conviction) prior to sentencing. The presence of a routine review procedure will at any rate illuminate all sentencing and serve to put all judges on their company manners.

## 4. Constriction of Sentencing Discretion and Increased Gradation of Punishments

The open-ended, often freewheeling discretion that is written into much law now, though well intended, has simply not proved out. It is essential, therefore, that the range of options be reduced drastically. In order to do this with fairness, a marked increase in gradation of crimes is necessary; that is, to ensure justice, the discrimination between one individual and another must be maintained. We, of course, will want to allow a mechanism for granting leniency for the youthful first offender; we, of course, will want to allow for all sorts of other extenuating, mitigating, justifying, and excusing conditions. But since we find that too much discretion in the hands of too few individuals is readily abused, it is essential that some of this discrimination be legislated in. By the process of grading crimes, some of the discriminating factors will be defined by the legislators and mandated with the charge. It is an unfortunate fact that too often judical discretion has been used to serve the specific needs of the judge, and not the defendants. In all fairness it should be realized that these days the judges are the "fall guys" for other defects in the current system. Many times, a judge's intention in giving an indeterminate sentence is clearly to allow for the early release of a prisoner who "proves out." Unfortunately, after 120 days, he loses jurisdiction and his intentions mean nothing. The offender is then at the mercy of punitive prison personnel, and a parole system that has often been political, paradoxical, petty, and persecutory.

# 5. Massive Decarceration

At the present time, with our inability to control a rising crime rate; with severe frustration at the failure of traditional methods; and with mounting fear and impotent rage, encouraged by cynical and exploitative politicians, the public is demanding more of the same. If the medicine hasn't worked, use more of it. But one result of using more of a bad medicine is death.

In our frustration we are progressively sending more and more people to prison for longer and longer terms. Every rational study has shown that these extended imprisonments are ineffectual. The deliberations of the Committee for the Study of Incarceration (soon to be published) will come out for across-the-board reduction of sentencing. This disparate group, interdisciplinary and cutting across both political and legal philosophies, was from the beginning united on perhaps only two convictions: the ineffectualness of our current system and the need to move toward the lowering of sentences.

If we do move toward reduction of discretion, it is crucial that the mandated sentence should range in most cases closer to the current minimum than the current maximum. This is not simply out of compassion for the prisoner, although compassion is a scarce commodity in his world; we take much too lightly what five to ten years locked in a cage does to the human condition. The primary beneficiary may be the nonoffender, the general public. Prisons may not be criminogenic institutions, but they are certainly not crime-curing. It is imperative that the members of the public be educated to what doing time really means, in terms they can understand, so that they will not be so vulnerable to the cant and rhetoric of elected public officials who cover every conceivable ineptitude and inadequacy on their part by a call for a greater lock-up. To abandon discretion without a simultaneous re-evaluation of prison length and a gradation downward would be an unthinkable cruelty and a frighteningly dangerous move.

Ironically, a more humane and effective prison system would probably have to have its equivalent of a "Devil's Island," a hard-core isolation center. Whenever "open" prisons or marked decarceration (lowering of sentences) are suggested, one always hears, "What about the Specks and Mansons? Are you going to turn them out in two years to repeat their crimes?" No, I do not think we can turn them out in two years to recommit their crimes. These bizarre and psychotic criminals, who constitute such a tiny percentage of the criminal population, dominate the news media and haunt the mind of the average citizen. Their leverage is ugly and disproportionate. For the sake of one Speck, thousands of young offenders may be crushed in the confining arms of the prison mold. Both for the protection of society, and to remove an inappropriate $X$ factor from considerations about the general problems of criminal offenders, it may well be that some total confinement facility must be established. Even that need not be cruel. Cruelty does not redeem either the victim or the perpetrator. Although their punishment may be essential for us, it probably has less meaning for these eccentric few than for most prisoners. A near-lifetime of imprisonment, even were the prison a palace, is burden enough. They would be punished and we will feel safer.

And still, when all this is done, we will have an imperfect system. And still, *if* all this is done, we will have those other areas of discretionary justice where bias may be packaged and sold as individualization of justice. Yet justice in the affairs of man *is* an individual business. Each compromise forced by our narrowness, our meanness, our sense of the other as alien, and alien as enemy, each compromise with compassion will exact a cost. We must mechanize justice because we are not yet up to the love and understanding that is essential if discretion is to serve justice. But we will pay a price. Each retreat from individuality diminishes the individual—it matters not whether the area is criminal justice or the practice of medicine. In the crush for space, food, pleasures, we are progressively being reduced and regimented, homogenized and dehumanized. Security, safety, survival may be the ultimate values, but there are limits. As in individual life itself, we may win the battle of survival only to be appalled at what has survived.

It is only in defense of the "other" that we protect the "self." The struggle against prejudice and bigotry will ultimately be won or lost not in the institutions of man but in his perceptions.

# APPENDIX

# Categories
# of Offenses<sup>*</sup>

125.00 Homicide means conduct which causes the death of a person or an unborn child with which a female has been pregnant for more than twenty-four weeks under circumstances constituting murder, manslaughter in the first degree, manslaughter in the second degree, criminally negligent homicide, abortion in the first degree or self-abortion in the first degree.

125.05 Homicide, abortion and related offenses; definitions of terms

125.10 Criminally negligent homicide—A person is guilty of criminally negligent homicide when, with criminal negligence, he causes the death of another person. Criminally negligent homicide is a Class E felony.

125.15 *Manslaughter in the second degree*—A person is guilty of manslaughter in the second degree when:

1. He recklessly causes the death of another person; or
2. He commits upon a female an abortional act which causes her death, unless such abortional act is justifiable pursuant to subdivision three of section 125.05; or

* Taken from McKinney, *New York Penal Law*, Sections 125.00 ff.

3. He intentionally causes or aids another person to commit suicide.

125.20 *Manslaughter in the first degree*—A person is guilty of manslaughter in the first degree when:

1. With intent to cause serious physical injury to another person he causes the death of such person or of a third person; or
2. With intent to cause the death of another person, he causes the death of such person or of a third person under circumstances which do not constitute murder because he acts under the influence of extreme emotional disturbance, as defined in paragraph (A) of subdivision one of section 125.25. The fact that homicide was committed under the influence of extreme emotional disturbance constitutes a mitigating circumstance reducing murder to manslaughter in the first degree and need not be proved in any prosecution initiated under this subdivision; or
3. He commits upon a female pregnant for more than twenty-four weeks an abortional act which causes her death, unless such abortional act is justified pursuant to subdivision three of section 125.05.

Manslaughter in the first degree is a class B felony.

125.25 *Murder*

A person is guilty of murder when:

1. With intent to cause the death of another person, he causes the death of such person or of a third person; except that in any prosecution under this subdivision, it is an affirmative defense that:
A. The defendant acted under the influence of extreme emotional disturbance for which there was a reasonable explanation or excuse, the reasonableness of which is to be determined from the viewpoint of a person in the defendant's situation under the circum-

stances the defendant believed them to be. Nothing contained in this paragraph shall constitute a defense to a prosecution for, or preclude a conviction of, manslaughter in the first degree or any other crime; or

B. The defendant's conduct consisted of causing or aiding, without the use of duress or deception, another person to commit suicide. Nothing contained in this paragraph shall constitute a defense to a prosecution for, or preclude a conviction of, manslaughter in the second degree or another other crime; or

2. Under circumstances evincing a depraved indifference to human life, he recklessly engages in conduct which creates a grave risk of death to another person, and thereby causes the death of another person; or

3. Acting either alone or with one or more other persons, he commits or attempts to commit robbery, burglary, kidnapping, arson, rape in the first degree, sodomy in the first degree, sexual abuse in the first degree, escape in the first degree, or escape in the second degree, and, in the course of and in furtherance of such crime of immediate flight therefrom, he, or another participant, if there be any, causes the death of a person other than one of the participants; except that in any prosecution under this subdivision, in which the defendant was not the only participant in the underlying crime, it is an affirmative defense that the defendant:

A. Did not commit the homicidal act or in any way . . . cause the commission thereof; and

B. Was not armed with a deadly weapon . . . and

C. Had no reasonable ground to believe that any other participant was armed . . . and

D. Had no reasonable ground to believe that any other participant intended to engage in conduct likely to result in death or serious physical injury.

Murder is a Class A felony.

# NOTES

## Introduction

1. Glendon Schubert, "Judicial Behavior," *International Encyclopedia of Social Science* (New York: Macmillan Co., 1968).

2. Edward Green, *Judicial Attitudes in Sentencing* (London: Macmillan & Co., 1961).

3. John Hogarth, *Sentencing as a Human Process* (Toronto: University of Toronto Press, 1971).

## CHAPTER I: Disparity

1. Willard Gaylin, *In the Service of Their Country: War Resisters in Prison* (New York: Viking Press, 1970).

2. Marvin E. Frankel, *Criminal Sentences* (New York: Hill and Wang, 1972).

3. Henry Coe Lanpher, "Length of Sentence & Duration of Detention of Federal Prisoners," 9 *Federal Probation*, pp. 13–14 (1945).

4. Mathew F. McGuire and Alexander Holtzoff, "The Problem of Sentence in the Criminal Law," 20 *Boston University Law Review*, pp. 423–34 (1940).

5. Judge Edward Lumbard, "Sentencing and Law Enforcement," 40 *Federal Rules Decisions* 406, p. 409, at First Philadelphia Judicial Sentencing Institute, October 29–30, 1965.

6. George Everson, "The Human Element in Justice," 19 *Journal of Criminal Law and Criminology*, pp. 90–9 (1919).

7. Sam Bass Warner and Henry B. Cabot, *Judges and Law Reform* (Cambridge, Mass.: Harvard University Press, 1936), pp. 165–8.

8. Harold E. Lane, "Illogical Variations in Sentences of Felons Committed to Mass. State Prison," 32 *Journal of Criminal Law, Criminology & Police Science*, p. 171 (1942).

9. William A. Lunden, *The Courts & Other Criminal Justice in Iowa* (Ames, Iowa: Iowa College, 1957), pp. 42, 43, 47.

10. Shepard v. U.S., 257 F.2d 293 (6th Cir. 1958).

11. *As a Matter of Fact . . . An Introduction to Federal Probation*, The Federal Judicial Center, Washington, D.C. (1973).

12. Glynn Mapes, "Unequal Justice: Legal Experts Troubled by Sentence Disparities," *Wall Street Journal*, September 9, 1970.

13. *Sentencing Aims and Policy*, Seminars for Newly Appointed United States District Judges, The Federal Judicial Center, Washington, D.C. (1970–71).

# CHAPTER II: The Sentencing Process

1. Report of the Royal Commission on the Penal System, London, 1967.

2. Sigmund Freud, "The Psychogenesis of A Case of Homosexuality in Women," *Collected Papers*, vol. 2 (London: Hogarth Press, 1950), pp. 226–7

3. David Rothman, *The Discovery of the Asylum* (Boston: Little, Brown & Co., 1971).

4. Karl Menninger, *The Crime of Punishment* (New York: Viking Press, 1968).

5. *Wall Street Journal*, September 9, 1970.

6. Erving Goffman, *Asylums* (Chicago: Aldine Publishing Co., 1961).

7. Leon Radzinowicz, *Ideology and Crime* (New York: Columbia University Press, 1966), p. 110.

# CHAPTER III: The Intrusion of Bias

1. Justice Hugo Black, dissenting opinion in Green v. U.S., 356 U.S. 165 (1958).

2. Henry Coe Lanpher, "Length of Sentence & Duration of Detention of Federal Prisoners," 9 *Federal Probation*, pp. 13–14 (1945). McGuire and Holtzoff, "The Problem of Sentence in the Criminal Law," 20 *Boston University Law Review*, pp. 423–34 (1940).

3. Harold E. Lane, "Illogical Variations in Sentences of Felons Committed to Mass. State Prison," 32 *Journal of Criminal Law, Criminology & Police Science*, p. 171 (1942). William A. Lunden, *The Courts & Other Criminal Justice in Iowa* (Ames, Iowa: Iowa College, 1957), pp. 42, 43, 47.

4. Henry Allen Bullock, "Significance of the Racial Factor in the Length of Prison Sentences," 52 *Journal of Criminal Law, Criminal & Police Science*, p. 411 (1961).

5. George Everson, "The Human Element in Justice," 19 *Journal of Criminal Law and Criminology*, pp. 90–9 (1919). Emil Frankel, "The Offender and the Court," 41

*Journal of the American Institute of Criminal Law and Criminology*, pp. 448–56. Sam Bass Warner and Henry B. Cabot, *Judges and Law Reform* (Cambridge, Mass.: Harvard University Press, 1936), pp. 165–8. Edward Green, *Judicial Attitudes in Sentencing* (London: Macmillan & Co., 1961).

6. Thorsten Sellin, "The Negro Criminal: A Statistical Note," 140 *Annals of the American Academy of Political and Social Science*, pp. 52–64 (November 1928). Edwin M. Lemert and Judy Rosberg, "The Administration of Justice to Minority Groups in Los Angeles County" (University of California Press, 1948), p. 19. Edward Green, "Inter- and Intra-Racial Crime Relative to Sentencing" 55 *Journal of Criminal Law, Criminology & Police Science*, p. 348 (1964). Henry Allen Bullock, "Significance of the Racial Factor in the Length of Prison Sentences," 52 *Journal of Criminal Law, Criminal & Police Science*, p. 411 (1961).

7. Stewart Nagel, "Judicial Background & Criminal Cases," 53 *Journal of Criminal Law, Criminology & Police Science*, p. 333 (1962).

8. Leon Thomas Stern, "The Effect of the Depression on Prison Commitments & Sentences," 41 *Journal of the American Institute of Criminal Law and Criminology*, p. 696 (1941).

9. Edward Green, *op. cit.*, note 5.

10. Donald H. Partington, "The Incidence of the Death Penalty for Rape in Virginia," 22 *Washington & Lee Law Review*, p. 43 (1965).

11. Edward Green, *op. cit.*, note 6, p. 351.

12. John Hogarth, *Sentencing as a Human Process* (Toronto: University of Toronto Press, 1971).

13. George Everson, *op. cit.*

14. *Time* magazine, vol. 64, no. 19, November 6, 1964, p. 44.

15. Lucear v. State, 221 Ga. 572 (1963).

16. State v. Roberts, 47 N.J. 286 (1966).

17. State v. Belk, 268 N.C. 320, 150 S.E. 2d 481 (1966).

18. Green v. State, 97 Miss. 834, 53 So. 415 (1910).

19. Ex Parte Mary Hamilton, 156 So.2d 926, 275 Ala.574 (1963).

20. Smith v. United States, 273 F. 2d 462 (10th Cir. 1959).

21. Willard Gaylin, *In the Service of Their Country: War Resisters in Prison* (New York: Viking Press, 1970).

22. Lason v. State, 12 So.2d 305 (Supreme Court of Florida, 1943).

23. State v. Start, 65 Or. 178 (1913).

24. Glover v. State, 179 Ind. 459 (1913).

25. Cunningham v. United States, 311 F.2d 772 (D.C. Cir. 1962).

26. Strand Amusement Co. v. Commonwealth, 43 S.W. 2d 321 (1931).

27. Commonwealth v. Tompkins, 265 Pa. 97, 108 A. 350 (1919).

28. In re Adoption of Richardson, 251 Cal. App. 2d 222, 59 (1959).

29. State v. Muraski, 69 A.2d 745. Castleberry v. Jones, 99 P.2d 174 (1940).

30. Hoff v. Eighth Judicial District Court, 378 P. 2d 977 (1963).

31. Tumey v. Ohio, 273 U.S. 510 (1926).

32. Connelly v. U.S. District Court, 191 F.2d 692 (9th Cir. 1951).

33. Dennis v. U.S. and Sacher v. U.S., 343 U.S. 1 (1951).

34. Offutt v. United States, 348 U.S. 11 (1954).

35. Crosby v. State, 97 So. 2d 181.

36. State v. Bellah, 311 P. 2d 264 (1957).

37. Silverman v. Silverman, 162 A.2d 773 (1960).

# CHAPTER IX: The Discretion Problem

1. Kenneth Culp Davis, *Discretionary Justice* (Baton Rouge: Louisiana State University, 1969), p. v.

2. Daniel Glaser, Fred Cohen, Vincent O'Leary, for National Parole Institutes' *The Sentencing and Parole Process* (Washington, D.C.: U.S. Printing Office).

# CHAPTER X: Conclusions

1. Gordon W. Allport, *The Nature of Prejudice* (Garden City, N.Y.: Doubleday Anchor Books, 1958).

2. Laurie Johnston, *The New York Times*, February 23, 1972.

3. Samuel Butler, *Erewhon* (New York: New American Library, Signet Classic, 1960), pp. 93–4.

4. David Burnham "Columbia Report Assails Judge-Selection Method," *The New York Times*, October 19, 1970.

5. Judge Harold R. Tyler, Jr., "Some Guideposts for the Complete Sentencer," Speech Given in New York City, April 1973.

Notes

6. B. F. Skinner, *Beyond Freedom and Dignity* (New York: Alfred A. Knopf, 1973).

7. Willard Gaylin, "Skinner Redux," *Harper's Magazine*, October 1973.

8. Marvin E. Frankel, *Criminal Sentences* (New York: Hill and Wang, 1972), p. 58.

9. *Ibid.*, p. 56.

10. Judge Talbot Smith, District Court of the Eastern District of Michigan, from "Proceedings of the Seminar on the Sentencing of Offenders," Queens University, Kingston, Ontario, 1962.

11. Willard Gaylin, "No Exit," *Harper's Magazine*, November 1971.

12. A. R. N. Cross, *Paradoxes in Prison Sentences* (Oxford: Clarendon Press, 1965), pp. 13–14.

13. Sol Rubin, "Disparity and Equality of Sentences—A Constitutional Challenge," 40 *Federal Rules Decisions* 55, p. 69.

14. Judge Lawrence E. Walsh, remarks in 32 *Federal Rules Decisions* 276, p. 277.

15. Judge Leo Brewster, "Appellate Review of Sentences," 40 *Federal Rules Decisions* 79, p. 82.

16. American Bar Association, *Standards Relating to Appellate Review of Sentence*, Project on Minimum Standards for Criminal Justice (1967).

# INDEX

age
  criminality and, 83
  mandatory sentences and, 218
alcohol offenses, 9, 19, 36
Allport, Gordon W., 197
American Bar Association, 227, 229
animosity, emotional, 40–2
*Anti-Semite and Jew* (Sartre), 197
appellate review, 64, 123–4, 227–9
appointments, judicial, 111, 208–9
assaultive crimes, 109–10, 202–3
  bail acquittal, 77–9
  geographical disparity, 8
  gradation of, 191–2
  mandatory sentences, 191–2, 218
  plea bargaining, 77–9
  political bias and, 50–2, 55–7
  racial bias, 30

bail acquittal, 77–9
behavioral psychology, 21–2
Bennett, James V., 11
bias, judicial, 28–43, 162–5
  acceptable level of, 208–16
  blacks as judges and, 201–5
  heterogeneity of court and, 199
  morality, 36–7, 117–18, 120–1,
    205–7
  property crimes, 29, 30
  protection against, 63–4, 122–5,
    157–8, 226–9
  psychology of judges and, 10,
    38–42, 68–71, 118–19, 121–
    2, 126–8, 138–40, 144–52,
    154–61, 210–12
  researches, traditional, into, 28–
    32
  *see also* political bias; racial bias;
    religious bias
Black, Justice Hugo, 28, 39

blacks
  bias against, 4–5, 29, 30, 33–4,
    156–7
  as judges, 201–5, 212–14
  narcotics use, and, 212–14
bond, pretrial, 62–3
Brewster, Judge Leo, 227–8
Brown, Hayward, case of, 62
Burger, Warren, 61, 150

calendar, 79–80
  assignment of judges, 72–3
  bail acquittal and, 77–9
  plea bargaining and, 3–6, 178–9
California, 12, 29, 61–2, 124–6,
    193
Canada, 229
capital punishment, 65–6, 100–1,
    128–9
committee, for sentencing, 64,
    222–4
Committee for the Study of In-
    carceration, 26, 231
community standards and feelings,
    8, 163–4, 186
Connecticut, 12
conservatism, judicial, 103–29, 142,
    149–50
Court Employment Project, 85
Cox, Judge (of Mississippi), 33
crime
  categories of, 233–5
  desensitization to, 80
  detection and reporting, 86, 137
  evaluation, social, and punish-
    ment, 6, 16, 18
  gradation, 191–2, 230
  hierarchies, personal judicial, 88–
    93, 173
  prevention, sentencing and, 17–
    20
  prosecution, failure of, 109–11

crime (*cont.*)
  responsibility for, societal vs.
    individual, 46–67
  victimless, 152
  white collar, 105–9, 153–4, 174–
    6, 215
  *see also* criminals
*Crime of Punishment, The* (Menninger), 20
criminals
  age and criminal activity, 83
  deterrence, individual, 119–20,
    172, 174–6
  *see also* deterrence
  ex-convicts, bias against, 37, 46
  habitual vs. occasional, 9
  nonculpability and medical/
    psychological model, 20–4
  recidivism, 18, 46, 81–2, 86
  rehabilitation, *see* rehabilitation
  responsibility, societal vs. indi-
    vidual, 46–60, 119–20
  *see also* crime
Cross, A. R. N., 226
cynicism, judicial, 168–9, 201

Davis, Judge (pseudonym), 212–
  14
Davis, Kenneth Culp, 182
defense attorneys
  evaluation of severity of judges,
    72, 94
  plea bargaining, 71–2
deferred prosecution, 109–10
*Dennis* v. *U.S.*, 38–40
determinism
  psychic, 22
  responsibility, societal assignment
    of, 207–8
  socio-economic, 46–67
deterrence
  discretion, judicial and, 54–5,
    82–4, 112–14, 140, 173–7
  general, 18–19, 166, 174, 176
  individual, 19–20, 174
Detroit, 44 *passim*
discretion, judicial, 6, 162–5
  abuse of, 63–4, 191
  bail acquittal, 77–9

black judges and black defendants, 201–5
calendar and, 74–80, 178–9
constriction of, 230
desensitization, 80
deterrence and, 54–5, 82–4, 112–
  15, 140, 173–7
experience and perspective, 96–
  7, 135–6, 144–6
imprisonment and, 84–9, 105–8
individualization of justice and,
  58–60, 88–97, 173, 183–90,
  216–19, 226
law vs. justice and, 52–3
leniency, 55–60, 107–8, 184–5,
  187–90, 200–1
opposition to, 60–3, 122–5, 157–
  8, 184, 186, 191–3, 219–25
plea bargaining, 71–9, 177–81
pre-pleading investigation, 71–2
pre-sentence reports, 99–100,
  103–4
psychology of judges and, 10, 38–
  42, 68–71, 88–97, 118–19,
  121–2, 126–8, 138–40, 144–
  52, 154–61, 210–16
punishment factor, 55–7, 117–18,
  140–1, 171–6
reappointment or re-election and,
  111
reform of system of, 196–233
and removal of sentencing from
  judge, 88, 124–5, 221–4
selection of cases, 81–2
sentence length, *see* length of
  sentence
sentencing reasons, proposed
  statement of, 226–7
training for sentencing, 130–2,
  135–8
*see also* crime; *specific biases*
discretion, other than judicial,
  220–1
disparity, 3–14
  "community standards," 8
  defense of, 12–13
  discretion, judicial, and, *see*
    discretion, judicial; *specific
    subjects*
  emotionality and, 10

disparity (*cont.*)
 federal courts, 6–8, 10–12, 35
 geographic, 6–8, 12
 habitual vs. occasional offenders,
  9
 local courts, 9
 plea bargaining and, 74
 probation office and, 12–13
 purpose of sentencing and, 6,
  12–13
 social climate and, 13–14
 state courts, 9–10
district attorneys, 76–7, 94
 discretion, and mandatory sentencing, 220–1
Douglas, Justice William, 39–40
draft resisters, 4–5, 6–7, 35–6
drugs, *see* narcotic offenses

election of judges, 61, 111, 208
Elliott, Judge J. Robert, 33
emotionality, judicial, 10, 38–42,
 139–40
*Erewhon* (Butler), 208
Everson, George, 9, 31

family court, 203, 205–7
Federal Bureau of Prisons, 7
federal courts, 104–5
 disparity in sentences, 4–5, 6–8,
  10–12, 35
 interview with judge, 103–29
 review of sentences, 229
 sentencing institutes, 11
Federal Parole Board, 224
follow-up of sentencing, 224
Frankel, Judge Marvin E., 6, 221–2
Frankfurter, Justice Felix, 39, 149
Freud, Sigmund, 18

Gardner, Judge Sam, 62–3
Garfield, Judge (pseudonym), 139,
 155, 165
 interview with, 68–102
Georgia, 33
Goffman, Erving, 24
government employees, cases involving, 105–9

gradation
 of crimes and sentences, 191–2,
  230
 of sentences after confinement,
  124–6
Great Depression, sentencing pattern in, 29
Green, Edward, 30

Hamilton, Mary, case of, 33–4
Hitler
 on law and order, 66–7
 sentencing theories applied to,
  25–6
Hoffman, Walter E., 11
Hogarth, John, 31
homicidal crimes, *see* assaultive
 crimes
Huxley, Aldous, 20

Illinois, 65
indeterminate sentences, 124–6,
 143–4
 first offenders, 183
 loss of control by judge, 230
 parole supervision, 133
 power structure and, 61–2
 rehabilitation and, 193–4
Iowa, 9–10

Jehovah's Witnesses, as war resisters, 4, 36
Judicial Conference, 181
Judicial Sentencing Institute, 8
jury trials, 61, 156–7, 164
justice
 definition of, 5–6
 individualization of, and judicial
  discretion, 58–60, 88–97,
  122–3, 173, 183–90, 216–
  19, 226
 law as jurisdiction vs., 52–3
 responsibility, assignment, 207–8

Kansas, 12
Keeley, Judge Florence M., 206–7

Lanpher, Henry, 7–8
law(s)
 enforcement failure, 109–11

law(s) (*cont.*)
  federal, disparity correction and,
    11
  justice vs., 52–3
  psychology and, 20–4
  punishment limits, 16, 122–3
  purpose of, 5
  "law and order," 35, 60–2, 65–7,
    109 *passim*
length of sentence, 64–5, 82–4,
  105–8, 112–14, 141–2, 173–
  4, 187–94
  average, federal, 22–3
  gradation of crimes, 191–2, 230
  indeterminate (open-ended), 61–
    2, 124–6, 133, 143–4, 183,
    193–4, 230
  mandatory, 16, 60–3, 122–3,
    157–8, 178–9, 186, 217–18,
    231–2
  parole, 112, 133, 142–3, 191
  plea bargaining and, 74, 82
Levin, Judge Theodore, 11
liberalism, judicial, 68–102, 106,
  130–61
Lombard, Judge Edward, 8

mandatory sentences, 16, 122–3,
  157–8, 186, 217–18
  discretionary process, other than
    judicial, and, 220–1
  length, gradation downward,
    231–2
  plea bargaining and, 178–9
  power structure and, 60–3
marijuana, *see* narcotic offenses
Medina, Judge, 38–40
Menninger, Dr. Karl, 20
methadone, 213–14
Michigan, 44 *passim*
Mississippi, 6–7, 23
morality
  living standard stereotypes and,
    205–7
  punishment and, 117–18
  sexuality and, 36–7, 120, 151–3
murder, *see* assaultive crimes

Nagel, Stewart, 29
Narcotic Addiction Commission,
  167–8

Narcotic Control Commission
  (New York), 212–13
narcotic offenses, 12, 35, 100, 122–
  3, 183, 202, 205, 212–14
*Nature of Prejudice, The* (Allport),
  197–9
New York, 12, 191
New York City, 9, 208–9, 229
*New York Times, The,* 205–7
Nicholson, Judge (pseudonym),
  interview with, 130–61

ombudsman, sentencing by, 222
Oregon, 6

panel sentencing, 64, 223–4
parole, 112, 133, 142–3, 191, 225
Partington, Donald H., 29
plea bargaining, 71–9, 177–8
  calendar, considerations and, 73–
    6, 178–9
  conviction improbable on greater
    crime, and, 179–80
  opposition to, 73, 180–1
  precluded crimes, 77
  pre-pleading investigations, 71
  sentence length and, 74, 82
political bias, 29, 38–40, 106, 162
  assaultive crimes, 50–2, 55–7,
    109–10
  conservative, 103–29, 142, 149–
    50
  draft cases, 6–7
  liberal, 68–102, 106, 130–61
  racial bias and, 33, 405
  radical, 44–67
  religious bias and, 35–6
political pressure, resistance to,
  210
pornography, 36–7, 120, 152–3
pre-pleading investigation, 71–2
pre-sentence reports, 99–100, 103–4
prison(s) and imprisonment, 46,
  107
  alternatives to, 85, 87–91, 97–8,
    132–3
  rehabilitation and, 46–8, 115–17,
    167–71, 225
  sentencing to, discretion and, 84–
    9, 105–8

prison(s) and imprisonment (*cont.*)
  sentencing to (*cont.*)
    dependence of judges on, 13
    discharges from probation and,
      225
    probation officers, qualifica-
      tions of, 13, 133–4
    reports, interpretation of, 12–
      13
    reports, pre-sentence, 99–100
  probation, sentencing to
    homicide case, 202–3
    as punishment, 217
    rehabilitation and, 217–18
  property crimes, 29, 30, 51–2, 54,
    86, 60–4
  protection of society, sentencing
    and, 17–18, 176–7
  psychology
    of judges, 10, 38–42, 68–71, 88–
      97, 118–19, 121–2, 126–8,
      138–40, 144–52, 154–61,
      210–16
    of offenders, judicial discretion
      and, 58–60, 88–97, 173,
      183–90
    rehabilitative model, 20–4
    research into and knowledge of
      bias, 197–9
  punishment (retribution), 24–6,
    140–1, 171–6
    capital punishment, 65–6, 100–1,
      128–9
    evaluation of crime and, 6, 16
    limits, 16, 122–3, 157–8
    morality and, 117–18
    sentence length, *see* length of
      sentence
  purposes of sentencing, 17, 84–6
    deterrence, general, 18–19, 166,
      176
    deterrence, individual, 19–20,
      174
    protection of society, 17–18,
      176–7
    rehabilitation, 20–4, 166
    retribution (punishment), 24–7,
      166
    *see also specific purposes*

Quakers, as war resisters, 36

racial bias
  address forms, 33–4
  assaultive crimes, 30
  and black judges, 201–5, 214
  jury trials, 156–7
  property crimes, 29–30, 215
  sex crimes, 29
  war resisters, 4–5
radicalism
  bias against, 38–40
  crimes against wealthy, 51–2
  judges, 44–67
Radzinowicz, Leon, 24
Ravitz, Judge Justin C., 162–3,
    165, 199
  interview with, 44–67
recidivism, 18, 46
  discretion, judicial, and, 81–2, 86
reform, 11, 101–2, 194
rehabilitation
  as disparity defense, 12–13
  drug addicts and, 167–8, 213–14
  failure, individual, 116–17
  as goal, 117, 166–7, 172–3
  indeterminate sentences, 193–4
  nonincarcerative sentences, 85,
    87–91, 97–8, 132–4, 217–18
  prisons and, 46–8, 115–17, 167–
    70, 225
  probation sentence and, 217–18
  programs and facilities, 85, 97–8,
    132–4
  as sentencing model, 20–4
religious bias, 34–6, 93, 119, 120–1
  pornography, 120
researches and research methods,
    28–32
retribution, sentencing and, 24–6
  *see also* punishment
Robinson, Judge, 215–16
Rothman, David, 20
Rothwax, Harold J., 208–9
Rubin, Sol, 226–7

Sartre, Jean-Paul, 197
Scandinavia, 19, 84
selection of judges, 208–9

Selective Service violators, 4–5, 6–7, 35–6
sentencing reasons, proposed statement of, 226–7
sex
crimes, 29, 93, 151
pornography and sexuality, 36–7, 120, 152–3
Skinner, B. F., 219
Smith, Judge Talbot, 223
Sobeloff, Judge Simon E., 228
social climate, 13–14, 112–13
social organization
criminality and, 46–67
group prejudice and, 198–9
Stern, Leon, 29
Stone, Judge (pseudonym), 99–100, 165
interview with, 103–29

Texas, 6, 8, 12
*Time* magazine, 32

Tracy, Judge (pseudonym), 209–12
training for sentencing, 130–2, 135–8
tribunals, sentencing, 64, 223–4
Tyler, Judge Harold R. Jr., 13, 216

victimless crime, 152
Vietnam War resisters, 4–5, 6–7, 35–6

*Wall Street Journal*, 11–12
Walsh, Judge Lawrence E., 227
Warren Court, 127
Washington (state), 107–8
white collar crime, 105–9, 153–4, 174–6, 215

youth
correctional centers, 133–4
as scapegoats, 35

# A Note on the Type

The text of this book was set in Electra, a type face designed by William Addison Dwiggins for the Mergenthaler Linotype Company and first made available in 1935. Electra cannot be classified as either "modern" or "old-style." It is not based on any historical model, and hence does not echo any particular period or style of type design. It avoids the extreme contrast between thick and thin elements that marks most modern faces, and is without eccentricities that catch the eye and interfere with reading. In general, Electra is a simple, readable typeface that attempts to give a feeling of fluidity, power, and speed.

W. A. Dwiggins (1880–1956) began an association with the Mergenthaler Linotype Company in 1929 and over the next twenty-seven years designed a number of book types which include the Metro series, Electra, Caledonia, Eldorado, and Falcon.

Composed, printed and bound by American Book–Stratford Press, Inc., New York, New York. Typography and binding design by Virginia Tan.